WITHDRAWN

PUBLICATIONS OF THE
ROOSEVELT MEMORIAL ASSOCIATION

III. THE AMERICANISM OF THEODORE
ROOSEVELT

Theodore Roosevelt

At his desk in the Outlook office in 1915

THE AMERICANISM OF THEODORE ROOSEVELT

*Selections from his Writings
and Speeches*

COMPILED BY

HERMANN HAGEDORN

Author of "Roosevelt in the Bad Lands"

BOSTON AND NEW YORK

HOUGHTON MIFFLIN COMPANY

The Riverside Press Cambridge

The Riverside Press
CAMBRIDGE · MASSACHUSETTS
PRINTED IN THE U.S.A.

CONTENTS

CONTENTS

INTRODUCTION

THIS book is intended to serve a double purpose — to provide a selection of striking passages from Theodore Roosevelt's writings, and to serve as an interpretation of his mental processes, of his moral, social, and political philosophy and of the life in which that philosophy expressed itself. The book is a unit; and, unless the compiler is altogether deceiving himself, the reader will find in the material contained in it a logical progression from the first page to the last.

The selections, the reader will note, are divided into three major parts. In the first will be found stories from Mr. Roosevelt's historical writings which reveal in vivid flashes the background of his mind. To understand fully the significance of his doctrine, it is important to realize with what ardor Mr. Roosevelt dwelt on heroic actions. In his mind, the memory of the Nation's inspiring past hung like a glowing tapestry — the "back-drop" of the scene in which dream and thought and will fought out the tremendous drama of his life. No one can understand Roosevelt's approach to the problems of personal and national life who does not take into account how firmly his feet were planted on certain elementary conceptions of heroic virtue. It was not at all that he wished to turn back the hands of the clock, and, rejecting modern progress, return to the simpler customs of the fathers; but that, accepting the age of electricity, he wished to see it made sound and

fundamentally progressive by being based on the same
qualities which had made progress possible in the days
of the pioneer.

Roosevelt's doctrine may be regarded as a pyramid,
with the "pioneer virtues" as the base and the brotherhood of man as the apex. The selections from his writings have been arranged to make clear this unity and
coherence of his philosophy, and whereas the first
principal division of the book reveals the background
of his mind, the second emphasizes the simple, solid
structure of his thinking. All his moral, social, political
and economic ideas may be grouped about five fundamental conceptions, bound together into one compact
and aspiring whole:

I. The elemental virtues — the basis of good citi-
    zenship;
II. Good citizenship — the basis of just government;
III. Just government — the basis of national unity;
IV. National unity — the basis of national strength;
V. National strength — the basis of international
    peace.

The supreme test of a preacher is, and always will be,
the power of the gospel which he expounds to guide his
own actions. In other words, does he practice what he
preaches? There is, logically or illogically, justice in the
popular conviction that there is something the matter
with adjurations which notably fail to determine the
acts of the man who utters them. The third main division of the book is, therefore, devoted to autobiographi-
cal narratives and letters intended to reveal how Roosevelt himself practiced the strenuous, the virtuous, the
patriotic life in pursuit of "realizable ideals," which he

preached. "Be ye doers of the Word, and not hearers only," was his favorite text. He could afford to preach it boldly and without shame.

The editor is indebted to the executors of the Estate of Theodore Roosevelt and to the following publishers for permission to reprint excerpts from Colonel Roosevelt's writings and speeches: Messrs. Charles Scribner's Sons (*The Great Adventure, Autobiography, History as Literature, America and the World War, Outdoor Pastimes of an American Hunter, Theodore Roosevelt and His Time, African Game Trails*); Messrs. G. P. Putnam's Sons (*American Ideals, The Winning of the West, The Wilderness Hunter, Hunting Trips of a Ranchman*); the Outlook Company (*The New Nationalism* and *American Problems*); The Century Company (*Hero Tales from American History, The Strenuous Life*); the George H. Doran Company (*The Foes of Our Own Household, Fear God and Take Your Own Part*); the Harvard University Press (*Applied Ethics*); the Harr Wagner Company (*Realizable Ideals*); The Review of Reviews Company (*Presidential Addresses and State Papers*); Houghton Mifflin Company (*Roosevelt in the Bad Lands*).

The compiler is conscious of a special debt of gratitude to Dr. John A. Lester, who has prepared the school edition of this book, for the aid of his discriminating and practical mind in making the selections.

HERMANN HAGEDORN

THE NATION'S DEBT TO ITS HEROES

Every great nation owes to the men whose lives have formed part of its greatness not merely the material effect of what they did, not merely the laws they placed upon the statute books or the victories they won over armed foes, but also the immense but indefinable moral influence produced by their deeds and words themselves upon the national character. . . . It is not only the country which these men helped to make and helped to save that is ours by inheritance; we inherit also all that is best and highest in their characters and in their lives.

THEODORE ROOSEVELT

THE AMERICANISM
OF THEODORE ROOSEVELT

I

THE BACKGROUND

THE AMERICANISM
OF THEODORE ROOSEVELT
.. .

I. THE PIONEERS [1]

ALONG the western frontier of the colonies that were so
soon to be the United States, among the foothills of the
Alleghanies, on the slopes of the wooded mountains, and
in the long trough-like valleys that lay between the
ranges, dwelt a peculiar and characteristically American
people.

These frontier folk, the people of the up-country, or
back-country, who lived near and among the forest-clad
mountains, far away from the long-settled districts of
flat coast plain and sluggish tidal river, were known to
themselves and to others as backwoodsmen. They all
bore a strong likeness to one another in their habits of
thought and ways of living, and differed markedly from
the people of the older and more civilized communities
to the eastward. The western border of our country was
then formed by the great barrier-chains of the Alleghanies, which ran north and south from Pennsylvania
through Maryland, Virginia, and the Carolinas, the
trend of the valleys being parallel to the seacoast, and
the mountains rising highest to the southward. It was
difficult to cross the ranges from east to west, but it was

[1] From *The Winning of the West*, vol. I. Copyright, 1889. G. P. Putnam's Sons, New York and London, publishers.

both easy and natural to follow the valleys between. From Fort Pitt to the high hill-homes of the Cherokees this great tract of wooded and mountainous country possessed nearly the same features and characteristics, differing utterly in physical aspect from the alluvial plains bordering the ocean.

So, likewise, the backwoodsmen and mountaineers who dwelt near the great water-shed that separates the Atlantic streams from the springs of the Watauga, the Kanawha, and the Monongahela, were all cast in the same mould, and resembled each other much more than any of them did their immediate neighbors of the plains. The backwoodsmen of Pennsylvania had little in common with the peaceful population of Quakers and Germans who lived between the Delaware and the Susquehanna; and their near kinsmen of the Blue Ridge and the Great Smoky Mountains were separated by an equally wide gulf from the aristocratic planter communities that flourished in the tide-water regions of Virginia and the Carolinas. Near the coast the lines of division between the colonies corresponded fairly well with the differences between the populations; but after striking the foothills, though the political boundaries continued to go east and west, those both of ethnic and of physical significance began to run north and south.

The backwoodsmen were Americans by birth and parentage, and of mixed race; but the dominant strain in their blood was that of the Presbyterian Irish — the Scotch-Irish as they were often called. These Irish representatives of the Covenanters were in the west almost what the Puritans were in the northeast, and more than the Cavaliers were in the south. Mingled with the descendants of many other races, they nevertheless formed the kernel of the distinctively and intensely American stock who were the pioneers of our people in their march westward, the vanguard of the army of fighting settlers, who with axe and rifle won their way from the Alleghanies to the Rio Grande and the Pacific.

These Presbyterian Irish were, however, far from being the only settlers on the border, although more than any others they impressed the stamp of their peculiar character on the pioneer civilization of the west and southwest. Great numbers of immigrants of English descent came among them from the settled districts on the east; and though these later arrivals soon became indistinguishable from the people among whom they settled, yet they certainly sometimes added a tone of their own to backwoods society, giving it here and there a slight dash of what we are accustomed to consider the distinctively southern or cavalier spirit. There was likewise a large German admixture, not only from the Germans of Pennsylvania, but also from these of the Carolinas. A good many Huguenots likewise came, and a few Hollanders and even Swedes, from the banks of the Delaware, or perhaps from farther off still.

A single generation, passed under the hard conditions of life in the wilderness, was enough to weld together into one people the representatives of these numerous and widely different races; and the children of the next generation became indistinguishable from one another. Long before the first Continental Congress assembled, the backwoodsmen, whatever their blood, had become Americans, one in speech, thought, and character, clutching firmly the land in which their fathers and grandfathers had lived before them. They had lost all remembrance of Europe and all sympathy with things European; they had become as emphatically products native to the soil as were the tough and supple hickories out of which they fashioned the handles of their long, light axes. Their grim, harsh, narrow lives were yet strangely fascinating and full of adventurous toil and danger; none but natures as strong, as freedom-loving, and as full of bold defiance as theirs would have endured existence on the terms which these men found pleasurable. Their iron surroundings made a mould which turned out all alike in the same shape. They resembled one another, and they differed from the rest of the world — even the world of America, and infinitely more the world of Europe — in dress, in customs, and in mode of life.

Where their lands abutted on the more settled districts to the eastward, the population was of course thickest, and their peculiarities least. Here and there at such points they built small backwoods burgs or towns, rude, straggling, unkempt villages, with a store or two, a tavern — sometimes good, often a "scandalous hog-sty," where travelers were devoured by fleas, and every one slept and ate in one room — a small log school-house, and a little church, presided over by a hard-featured Presbyterian preacher, gloomy, earnest, and zealous, probably bigoted and narrow-minded, but nevertheless a great power for good in the community.

However, the backwoodsmen as a class neither built towns nor loved to dwell therein. They were to be seen at their best in the vast, interminable forests that formed their chosen home. They won and kept their lands by

force, and ever lived either at war or in dread of war.
Hence they settled always in groups of several families
each, all banded together for mutual protection. Their
red foes were strong and terrible, cunning in council,
dreadful in battle, merciless beyond belief in victory. The
men of the border did not overcome and dispossess cow-
ards and weaklings; they marched forth to spoil the
stout-hearted and to take for a prey the possessions of
the men of might. Every acre, every rood of ground
which they claimed had to be cleared by the axe and held
with the rifle. Not only was the chopping down of the
forests the first preliminary to cultivation, but it was also
the surest means of subduing the Indians, to whom the
unending stretches of choked woodland were an impene-
trable cover behind which to move unseen, a shield in
making assaults, and a strong tower of defense in repel-
ling counter-attacks. In the conquest of the west the
backwoods axe, shapely, well-poised, with long haft and
light head, was a servant hardly standing second even to
the rifle; the two were the national weapons of the American backwoodsman, and in their use he has never been
excelled.

When a group of families moved out into the wilderness they built themselves a station or stockade fort; a
square palisade of upright logs, loop-holed, with strong
blockhouses as bastions at the corners. One side at least
was generally formed by the backs of the cabins themselves, all standing in a row; and there was a great door
or gate, that could be strongly barred in case of need.
Often no iron whatever was employed in any of the
buildings. The square inside contained the provision
sheds and frequently a strong central blockhouse as well.

These forts, of course, could not stand against cannon, and they were always in danger when attacked with fire; but save for this risk of burning they were very effectual defenses against men without artillery, and were rarely taken, whether by whites or Indians, except by surprise. Few other buildings have played so important a part in our history as the rough stockade fort of the backwoods.

The families only lived in the fort when there was war with the Indians, and even then not in the winter. At other times they all separated out to their own farms, universally called clearings, as they were always made by first cutting off the timber. The stumps were left to dot the fields of grain and Indian corn. The corn in especial was the stand-by and invariable resource of the Western settler; it was the crop on which he relied to feed his family, and when hunting or on a war trail the parched grains were carried in his leather wallet to serve often as his only food. But he planted orchards and raised melons, potatoes, and many other fruits and vegetables as well; and he had usually a horse or two, cows, and perhaps hogs and sheep, if the wolves and bears did not interfere. If he was poor his cabin was made of unhewn logs, and held but a single room; if well-to-do, the logs were neatly hewed, and besides the large living and eating-room with its huge stone fireplace, there was also a small bedroom and a kitchen, while a ladder led to the loft above, in which the boys slept. The floor was made of puncheons, great slabs of wood hewed carefully out, and the roof of clapboards. Pegs of wood were thrust into the sides of the house, to serve instead of a wardrobe; and buck antlers, thrust into joists, held the ever-ready rifles. The table was a great clapboard set on four wooden legs; there were three-legged stools, and in the better sort of houses old-fashioned rocking-chairs. The couch or bed was warmly covered with blankets, bear-skins, and deer-hides.

These clearings lay far apart from one another in the wilderness. Up to the door-sills of the log-huts stretched the solemn and mysterious forest. There were no openings to break its continuity; nothing but endless leagues on leagues of shadowy, wolf-haunted woodland. The great trees towered aloft till their separate heads were lost in the mass of foliage above, and the rank underbrush choked the spaces between the trunks. On the higher peaks and ridge-crests of the mountains there were straggling birches and pines, hemlocks and balsam firs; elsewhere, oaks, chestnuts, hickories, maples, beeches, walnuts, and great tulip trees grew side by side with many other kinds. The sunlight could not penetrate the roofed archway of murmuring leaves; through the gray aisles of the forest men walked always in a kind of midday gloaming. Those who had lived in the open plains felt when they came to the backwoods as if their heads were hooded. Save on the border of a lake, from a cliff top, or on a bald knob — that is, a bare hill-shoulder — they could not anywhere look out for any distance.

Backwoods society was simple, and the duties and rights of each member of the family were plain and clear. The man was the armed protector and provider, the bread-winner; the woman was the housewife and child-bearer. They married young and their families were large, for they were strong and healthy, and their success in life depended on their own stout arms and willing hearts. There was everywhere great equality of conditions. Land was plenty and all else scarce; so courage, thrift, and industry were sure of their reward. All had small farms, with the few stock necessary to cultivate them; the farms being generally placed in the hollows, the division lines between them, if they were close together, being the tops of the ridges and the watercourses, especially the former. The buildings of each farm were usually at its lowest point, as if in the center of an amphitheater. Each was on an average of about 400 acres, but sometimes more. Tracts of low, swampy grounds, possibly some miles from the cabin, were cleared for meadows, the fodder being stacked, and hauled home in winter.

The first lesson the backwoodsmen learnt was the necessity of self-help; the next, that such a community could only thrive if all joined in helping one another. Log-rollings, house-raisings, house-warmings, corn-shuckings, quiltings, and the like were occasions when all the neighbors came together to do what the family itself could hardly accomplish alone. Every such meeting was the occasion of a frolic and dance for the young people, whiskey and rum being plentiful, and the host exerting his utmost power to spread the table with backwoods delicacies — bear-meat and venison, vegetables from the "truck patch," where squashes, melons, beans, and the like were grown, wild fruits, bowls of milk, and apple pies, which were the acknowledged standard of luxury. At the better houses there was metheglin or small beer, cider, cheese, and biscuits. Tea was so little known that many of the backwoods people were not aware it was a beverage and at first attempted to eat the leaves with salt or butter.

There was not much schooling, and few boys or girls learnt much more than reading, writing, and ciphering up to the rule of three. Where the schoolhouses existed they were only dark, mean log-huts, and if in the southern colonies, were generally placed in the so-called "old fields," or abandoned farms grown up with pines. The schoolmaster boarded about with the families; his learning was rarely great, nor was his discipline good, in spite of the frequency and severity of the canings. The price for such tuition was at the rate of twenty shillings a year, in Pennsylvania currency.

Each family did everything that could be done for itself. The father and sons worked with axe, hoe, and sickle. Almost every house contained a loom, and almost every woman was a weaver. Linsey-woolsey, made from flax grown near the cabin, and of wool from the backs of the few sheep, was the warmest and most substantial cloth; and when the flax crop failed and the flocks were destroyed by wolves, the children had but scanty covering to hide their nakedness. The man tanned the buckskin, the woman was tailor and shoemaker, and made the deer-skin sifters to be used instead of bolting-cloths. There were a few pewter spoons in use; but the table furniture consisted mainly of hand-made trenchers, platters, noggins, and bowls. The cradle was of peeled hickory bark. Ploughshares had to be imported, but harrows and sleds were made without difficulty; and the cooper work was well done. Chaff beds were thrown on the floor of the loft, if the house-owner was well off. Each cabin had a hand-mill and a hominy block; the last was borrowed from the Indians, and was only a large block of wood, with a hole burned in the top, as a mortar, where the pestle was worked. If there were any sugar maples accessible, they were tapped every year.

The life of the backwoodsmen was one long struggle. The forest had to be felled, droughts, deep snows, freshets, cloudbursts, forest fires, and all the other dangers of a wilderness life faced. Swarms of deer-flies, mosquitoes, and midges rendered life a torment in the weeks of hot weather. Rattlesnakes and copperheads were very plentiful, and, the former especially, constant sources of danger and death. Wolves and bears were incessant and inveterate foes of the live stock, and the cougar or panther occasionally attacked man as well. More terrible still, the wolves sometimes went mad, and the men who then encountered them were almost certain to be bitten and to die of hydrophobia.

Every true backwoodsman was a hunter. Wild turkeys were plentiful. The pigeons at times filled the woods with clouds that hid the sun and broke down the branches on their roosting grounds as if a whirlwind had passed. The black and gray squirrels swarmed, devastating the cornfields, and at times gathering in immense companies and migrating across mountain and river. The hunters' ordinary game was the deer, and after that the bear; the elk was already growing uncommon. No form of labor is harder than the chase, and none is so fascinating nor so excellent as a training-school for war. The successful still-hunter of necessity possessed skill in hiding and in creeping noiselessly upon the wary quarry, as well as in imitating the notes and calls of the different beasts and birds; skill in the use of the rifle and in throwing the tomahawk he already had; and he perforce acquired keenness of eye, thorough acquaintance with woodcraft, and the power of standing the severest strains of fatigue, hardship, and exposure. He lived out in the woods for many months with no food but meat, and no shelter whatever, unless he made a lean-to of brush or crawled into a hollow sycamore.

Such training stood the frontier folk in good stead when they were pitted against the Indians; without it they could not even have held their own, and the white advance would have been absolutely checked. Our frontiers were pushed westward by the warlike skill and adventurous personal prowess of the individual settlers; regular armies by themselves could have done little. For one square mile the regular armies added to our domain, the settlers added ten — a hundred would probably be nearer the truth. A race of peaceful unwarlike farmers would have been helpless before such foes as the red Indians, and no auxiliary military force would have protected them or enabled them to move westward. Colonists fresh from the old world, no matter how thrifty, steady-going, and industrious, could not hold their own on the frontier; they had to settle where they were protected from the Indians by a living barrier of bold and self-reliant American borderers. The West would never have been settled save for the fierce courage and the eager desire to brave danger so characteristic of the stalwart backwoodsmen.

These armed hunters, woodchoppers, and farmers were their own soldiers. They built and manned their own forts; they did their own fighting under their own commanders. There were no regiments of regular troops along the frontier. In the event of an Indian inroad each borderer had to defend himself until there was time for them all to gather together to repel or avenge it. Every man was accustomed to the use of arms from his childhood; when a boy was twelve years old he was given a rifle and made a fort-soldier, with a loophole where he was to stand if the station was attacked. The war was never-ending, for even the times of so-called peace were broken by forays and murders; a man might grow from babyhood to middle age on the border, and yet never remember a year in which some one of his neighbors did not fall a victim to the Indians.

There was everywhere a rude military organization, which included all the able-bodied men of the community. Every settlement had its colonels and captains; but these officers, both in the training and in the authority they exercised, corresponded much more nearly to Indian chiefs than to the regular army men whose titles they bore. They had no means whatever of enforcing their orders, and their tumultuous and disorderly levies of sinewy riflemen were hardly as well disciplined as the Indians themselves. The superior officer could advise, entreat, lead, and influence his men, but he could not command them, or, if he did, the men obeyed him only just as far as it suited them. If an officer planned a scout or campaign, those who thought proper accompanied him, and the others stayed at home, and even those who went out came back if the fit seized them, or perchance followed the lead of an insubordinate junior officer whom they liked better than they did his superior. There was no compulsion to perform military duties beyond dread of being disgraced in the eyes of the neighbors, and there was no pecuniary reward for performing them; nevertheless the moral sentiment of a backwoods community was too robust to tolerate habitual remissness in military affairs, and the coward and laggard were treated with utter scorn, and were generally in the end either laughed out, or "hated out," of the neighborhood, or else got rid of in a still more summary manner. Among a people naturally brave and reckless, this public opinion acted fairly effectively, and there was generally but little shrinking from military service.

The frontier, in spite of the outward uniformity of means and manners, is preëminently the place of sharp contrasts. The two extremes of society, the strongest, best, and most adventurous, and the weakest, most shiftless, and vicious, are those which seem naturally to drift to the border. Most of the men who came to the backwoods to hew out homes and rear families were stern, manly, and honest; but there was also a large influx of people drawn from the worst immigrants that perhaps ever were brought to America — the mass of convict servants, redemptioners, and the like, who formed such an excessively undesirable substratum to the otherwise excellent population of the tidewater regions in Virginia and the Carolinas.

In the backwoods the lawless led lives of abandoned wickedness; they hated good for good's sake, and did their utmost to destroy it. Where the bad element was large, gangs of horse thieves, highwaymen, and other criminals often united with the uncontrollable young men of vicious tastes who were given to gambling, fighting, and the like. They then formed half-secret organizations, often of great extent and with wide ramifications; and if they could control a community they established a reign of terror, driving out both ministers and magistrates, and killing without scruple those who interfered with them. The good men in such a case banded themselves together as regulators and put down the wicked with ruthless severity, by the exercise of lynch law, shooting and hanging the worst off-hand.

Jails were scarce in the wilderness, and often were entirely wanting in a district, which, indeed, was quite likely to lack legal officers also. If punishment was inflicted at all it was apt to be severe, and took the form of death or whipping. An impromptu jury of neighbors decided with a rough-and-ready sense of fair play and justice what punishment the crime demanded, and then saw to the execution of their own decree. Whipping was the usual reward of theft. Occasionally torture was resorted to, but not often; but to their honor be it said, the backwoodsmen were horrified at the treatment accorded both to black slaves and to white convict servants in the lowlands.

They were superstitious, of course, believing in witchcraft, and signs and omens; and it may be noted that their superstition showed a singular mixture of old-world survivals and of practices borrowed from the savages or evolved by the very force of their strange surroundings. At the bottom they were deeply religious in their tendencies; and although ministers and meeting-houses were rare, yet the backwoods cabins often contained Bibles, and the mothers used to instill into the minds of their children reverence for Sunday, while many even of the hunters refused to hunt on that day.

Those of them who knew the right honestly tried to live up to it, in spite of the manifold temptations to back-sliding offered by their lives of hard and fierce contention. But Calvinism, though more congenial to them than Episcopacy, and infinitely more so than Catholicism, was too cold for the fiery hearts of the borderers; they were not stirred to the depths of their natures till other creeds, and, above all, Methodism, worked their way to the wilderness.

Thus the backwoodsmen lived on the clearings they had hewed out of the everlasting forest; a grim, stern people, strong and simple, powerful for good and evil, swayed by gusts of stormy passion, the love of freedom rooted in their very hearts' core. Their lives were harsh and narrow; they gained their bread by their blood and sweat, in the unending struggle with the wild ruggedness of nature. They suffered terrible injuries at the hands of the red men, and on their foes they waged a terrible warfare in return. They were relentless, revengeful, suspicious, knowing neither ruth nor pity; they were also upright, resolute, and fearless, loyal to their friends, and devoted to their country. In spite of their many failings, they were of all men the best fitted to conquer the wilderness and hold it against all comers.

II. DANIEL BOONE AND THE FOUNDING OF KENTUCKY [1]

DANIEL BOONE will always occupy a unique place in our history as the archetype of the hunter and wilderness wanderer. He was a true pioneer, and stood at the head of that class of Indian-fighters, game-hunters. forest-fellers, and backwoods farmers who, generation after generation, pushed westward the border of civilization from the Alleghanies to the Pacific. As he himself said, he was "an instrument ordained of God to settle the wilderness." Born in Pennsylvania, he drifted south into western North Carolina, and settled on what was then the extreme frontier. There he married, built a log cabin, and hunted, chopped trees, and tilled the ground like any other frontiersman. The Alleghany Mountains still marked a boundary beyond which the settlers dared not go; for west of them lay immense reaches of frowning forest, uninhabited save by bands of warlike Indians. Occasionally some venturesome hunter or trapper penetrated this immense wilderness, and returned with strange stories of what he had seen and done.

In 1769 Boone, excited by these vague and wondrous tales, determined himself to cross the mountains and find out what manner of land it was that lay beyond. With a few chosen companions he set out, making his own trail through the gloomy forest. After weeks of wandering, he at last emerged into the beautiful and fertile

[1] From *Hero Tales from American History.* Copyright, 1895. The Century Company, publishers. Other narratives in this collection were written by Henry Cabot Lodge.

country of Kentucky, for which, in after years, the red men and the white strove with such obstinate fury that it grew to be called "the dark and bloody ground." But when Boone first saw it, it was a fair and smiling land of groves and glades and running waters, where the open forest grew tall and beautiful, and where innumerable herds of game grazed, roaming ceaselessly to and fro along the trails they had trodden during countless generations. Kentucky was not owned by any Indian tribe, and was visited only by wandering war-parties and hunting-parties who came from among the savage nations living north of the Ohio or south of the Tennessee.

A roving war-party stumbled upon one of Boone's companions and killed him, and the others then left Boone and journeyed home; but his brother came out to join him. and the two spent the winter together. Self-reliant, fearless, and possessed of great bodily strength and hardihood, they cared little for the loneliness. The teeming myriads of game furnished abundant food; the herds of shaggy-maned bison and noble-antlered elk, the bands of deer and the numerous black bear, were all ready for the rifle, and they were tame and easily slain. The wolf and the cougar, too, sometimes fell victims to the prowess of the two hunters.

At times they slept in hollow trees, or in some bush lean-to of their own making; at other times, when they feared Indians, they changed their resting place every night, and after making a fire would go off a mile or two to sleep. Surrounded by brute and human foes, they owed their lives to their sleepless vigilance, their keen senses, their eagle eyes, and their resolute hearts.

When the spring came, and the woods were white with

the dogwood blossoms, and crimsoned with the red-bud, Boone's brother left him, and Daniel remained for three months alone in the wilderness. The brother soon came back again with a party of hunters; and other parties likewise came in, to wander for months and years through the wilderness; and they wrought huge havoc among the vast herds of game.

In 1771 Boone returned to his home. Two years later he started to lead a party of settlers to the new country; but while passing through the frowning defiles of Cumberland Gap, they were attacked by Indians, and driven back — two of Boone's own sons being slain. In 1775, however, he made another attempt; and this attempt was successful. The Indians attacked the newcomers; but by this time the parties of would-be settlers were sufficiently numerous to hold their own. They beat back the Indians, and built rough little hamlets, surrounded by log stockades, at Boonesborough and Harrodsburg; and the permanent settlement of Kentucky had begun.

The next few years were passed by Boone amid unending Indian conflicts. He was a leader among the settlers, both in peace and in war. At one time he represented them in the House of Burgesses of Virginia; at another time he was a member of the first little Kentucky parliament itself; and he became a colonel of the frontier militia. He tilled the land, and he chopped the trees himself; he helped to build the cabins and stockades with his own hands, wielding the long-handled, light-headed frontier axe as skillfully as other frontiersmen. His main business was that of surveyor, for his knowledge of the country, and his ability to travel through it,

in spite of the danger from Indians, created much demand for his services among people who wished to lay
off tracts of wild land for their own future use. But
whatever he did, and wherever he went, he had to be
sleeplessly on the lookout for his Indian foes. When he
and his fellows tilled the stump-dotted fields of corn, one
or more of the party were always on guard, with weapon
at the ready, for fear of lurking savages. When he went
to the House of Burgesses he carried his long rifle, and
traversed roads not a mile of which was free from the
danger of Indian attack. The settlements in the early
years depended exclusively upon game for their meat,
and Boone was the mightiest of all the hunters, so that
upon him devolved the task of keeping his people sup-
plied. He killed many buffaloes, and pickled the buffalo
beef for use in winter. He killed great numbers of black
bear, and made bacon of them, precisely as if they had
been hogs. The common game were deer and elk. At
that time none of the hunters of Kentucky would waste
a shot on anything so small as a prairie-chicken or wild
duck, but they sometimes killed geese and swans when
they came south in winter and lit on the rivers. But
whenever Boone went into the woods after game, he had
perpetually to keep watch lest he himself might be
hunted in turn. He never lay in wait at a game-lick,
save with ears strained to hear the approach of some
crawling red foe. He never crept up to a turkey he heard
calling, without exercising the utmost care to see that it
was not an Indian; for one of the favorite devices of the
Indians was to imitate the turkey call, and thus allure
within range some inexperienced hunter.

Besides this warfare, which went on in the midst of his

usual vocations, Boone frequently took the field on set expeditions against the savages. Once when he and a party of other men were making salt at a lick, they were surprised and carried off by the Indians. The old hunter was a prisoner with them for some months, but finally made his escape and came home through the trackless woods as straight as the wild pigeon flies. He was ever on the watch to ward off the Indian inroads, and to follow the war-parties, and try to rescue the prisoners. Once his own daughter, and two other girls who were with her, were carried off by a band of Indians. Boone raised some friends and followed the trail steadily for two days and a night; then they came to where the Indians had killed a buffalo calf and were camped around it. Firing from a little distance, the whites shot two of the Indians, and, rushing in, rescued the girls. On another occasion, when Boone had gone to visit a salt-lick with his brother, the Indians ambushed them and shot the latter. Boone himself escaped, but the Indians followed him for three miles by the aid of a tracking dog, until Boone turned, shot the dog, and then eluded his pursuers. In company with Simon Kenton and many other noted hunters and wilderness warriors, he once and again took part in expeditions into the Indian country, where they killed the braves and drove off the horses. Twice bands of Indians, accompanied by French, Tory, and British partisans from Detroit, bearing the flag of Great Britain, attacked Boonesborough. In each case Boone and his fellow-settlers beat them off with loss. At the fatal battle of the Blue Licks, in which two hundred of the best riflemen of Kentucky were beaten with terrible slaughter by a great force of Indians from the lakes, Boone commanded the left wing. Leading his men, rifle in hand, he pushed back and overthrew the force against him; but meanwhile the Indians destroyed the right wing and center, and got round in his rear, so that there was nothing left for Boone's men except to flee with all possible speed.

As Kentucky became settled, Boone grew restless and ill at ease. He loved the wilderness; he loved the great forests and the great prairie-like glades, and the life in the little lonely cabin, where from the door he could see the deer come out into the clearing at nightfall. The neighborhood of his own kind made him feel cramped and ill at ease. So he moved ever westward with the frontier; and as Kentucky filled up he crossed the Mississippi and settled on the borders of the prairie country of Missouri, where the Spaniards, who ruled the territory, made him an alcalde, or judge. He lived to a great age, and died out on the border, a backwoods hunter to the last.

III. THE LEWIS AND CLARK EXPEDITION [1]

AFTER leaving the final straggling log cabins of the settled country, the explorers, with sails and paddles, made their way through what is now the State of Missouri. They lived well, for their hunters killed many deer and wild turkey and some black bear and beaver, and there was an abundance of breeding waterfowl. Here and there were Indian encampments, but not many, for the tribes had gone westward to the great plains of what is now Kansas to hunt the buffalo. Already buffalo and elk were scarce in Missouri, and the party did not begin to find them in any numbers until they reached the neighborhood of what is now southern Nebraska.

From there onwards the game was found in vast herds and the party began to come upon those characteristic animals of the Great Plains which were as yet unknown to white men of our race. The buffalo and the elk had once ranged eastward to the Alleghanies and were familiar to early wanderers through the wooded wilderness; but in no part of the east had their numbers ever remotely approached the astounding multitudes in which they were found on the Great Plains. The curious prong-buck or prong-horned antelope was unknown east of the Great Plains. So was the blacktail, or mule deer, which our adventurers began to find here and there as they gradually worked their way northwestward. So were the coyotes, whose uncanny wailing after nightfall

[1] From *The Winning of the West*, vol. IV. Copyright, 1896. G. P. Putnam's Sons, New York and London, publishers.

varied the sinister baying of the gray wolves; so were many of the smaller animals, notably the prairie dogs, whose populous villages awakened the lively curiosity of Lewis and Clark.

In their note-books the two captains faithfully described all these new animals and all the strange sights they saw. They were men with no pretensions to scientific learning, but they were singularly close and accurate observers and truthful narrators. Very rarely have any similar explorers described so faithfully not only the physical features but the animals and plants of a newly discovered land. Their narrative was not published until some years later, and then it was badly edited, notably the purely scientific portion; yet it remains the best example of what such a narrative should be. Few explorers who did and saw so much that was absolutely new have written of their deeds with such quiet absence of boastfulness, and have drawn their descriptions with such complete freedom from exaggeration.

Moreover, what was of even greater importance, the two young captains possessed in perfection the qualities necessary to pilot such an expedition through unknown lands and among savage tribes. They kept good discipline among the men; they never hesitated to punish severely any wrong-doer; but they were never over-severe; and as they did their full part of the work, and ran all the risks and suffered all the hardship exactly like the other members of the expedition, they were regarded by their followers with devoted affection, and were served with loyalty and cheerfulness. In dealing with the Indians they showed good humor and common sense mingled with ceaseless vigilance and unbending resolution. Only men who possessed their tact and daring could have piloted the party safely among the war-like tribes they encountered. Any sort of weakness or timidity on the one hand, or of harshness or cruelty on the other, would have been fatal to the expedition; but they were careful to treat the tribes well and to try to secure their good-will, while at the same time putting an immediate stop to any insolence or outrage. Several times they were in much jeopardy when they reached the land of the Dakotas and passed among the various ferocious tribes whom they knew, and whom we yet know, as the Sioux. The French traders frequently came up river to the country of the Sioux, who often maltreated and robbed them. In consequence Lewis and Clark found that the Sioux were inclined to regard the whites as people whom they could safely oppress. The resolute bearing of the newcomers soon taught them that they were in error, and after a little hesitation the various tribes in each case became friendly.

As the fall weather grew cold the party reached the Mandan village, where they halted and went into camp for the winter, building huts and a stout stockade, which they christened Fort Mandan. Traders from St. Louis and also British traders from the North reached these villages, and the inhabitants were accustomed to dealing with the whites. Throughout the winter the party was well treated by the Indians, and kept in good health and spirits; the journals frequently mention the fondness the men showed for dancing, although without partners of the opposite sex. Yet they suffered much from the extreme cold, and at times from hunger, for it was hard to hunt in the winter weather, and the game was thin and poor. Generally game could be killed in a day's hunt from the fort; but occasionally small parties of hunters went off for a trip of several days, and returned laden with meat; in one case they killed thirty-two deer, eleven elk, and a buffalo; in another forty deer, sixteen elk, and three buffalo; thirty-six deer and fourteen elk, etc., etc. The buffalo remaining in the neighborhood during the winter were mostly old bulls, too lean to eat; and as the snows came on most of the antelope left for the rugged country farther west, swimming the Missouri in great bands. Before the bitter weather began the explorers were much interested by the methods of the Indians in hunting, especially when they surrounded and slaughtered bands of buffalo on horseback; and by the curious pens, with huge V-shaped wings, into which they drove antelope.

In the spring of 1805, Lewis and Clark again started westward, first sending downstream ten of their companions, to carry home the notes of their trip so far, and a few valuable specimens. The party that started westward numbered thirty-two adults, all told; for one sergeant had died, and two or three persons had volunteered at the Mandan villages, including a rather worthless French "squawman," with an intelligent Indian wife, whose baby was but a few weeks old.

From this point onwards, when they began to travel west instead of north, the explorers were in a country where no white man had ever trod. It was not the first time the continent had been crossed. The Spaniards had crossed and recrossed it, for two centuries, farther south. In British America Mackenzie had already pen-

etrated to the Pacific, while Hearne had made a far more
noteworthy and difficult trip than Mackenzie, when he
wandered over the terrible desolation of the Barren
Grounds, which lie under the Arctic circle. But no man
had ever crossed or explored that part of the continent
which the United States had just acquired; a part far
better fitted to be the home of our stock than the regions
to the north or south. It was the explorations of Lewis
and Clark, and not those of Mackenzie on the north or
of the Spaniards in the south, which were to bear fruit,
because they pointed the way to the tens of thousands of
settlers who were to come after them, and who were to
build thriving commonwealths in the lonely wilderness
which they had traversed.

From the Little Missouri on to the head of the Missouri proper the explorers passed through a region where
they saw few traces of Indians. It literally swarmed
with game, for it was one of the finest hunting grounds
in all the world. There were great numbers of sage fowl,
sharp-tailed prairie fowl, and ducks of all kinds; and
swans, and tall white cranes; and geese, which nested in
the tops of the cottonwood trees. But the hunters paid
no heed to birds, when surrounded by such teeming myriads of big game. Buffalo, elk, and antelope, whitetail
and blacktail deer, and bighorn sheep swarmed in extraordinary abundance throughout the lands watered by
the upper Missouri and the Yellowstone; in their journals the explorers dwell continually on the innumerable
herds they encountered while on these plains, both when
traveling upstream and again the following year when
they were returning. The antelopes were sometimes
quite shy; so were the bighorn; though on occasions both

kinds seemed to lose their wariness, and in one instance the journal specifies the fact that, at the mouth of the Yellowstone, the deer were somewhat shy, while the antelope, like the elk and buffalo, paid no heed to the men whatever. Ordinarily all the kinds of game were very tame. Sometimes one of the many herds of elk that lay boldly, even at midday, on the sandbars, or on the brush-covered points, would wait until the explorers were within twenty yards of them before starting. The buffalo would scarcely move out of the path at all, and the bulls sometimes, even when unmolested, threatened to assail the hunters. Once, on the return voyage, when Clark was descending the Yellowstone River, a vast herd of buffalo, swimming and wading, ploughed its way across the stream where it was a mile broad, in a column so thick that the explorers had to draw up on shore and wait for an hour, until it passed by, before continuing their journey. Two or three times the expedition was thus brought to a halt; and as the buffalo were so plentiful, and so easy to kill, and as their flesh was very good, they were the mainstay for the explorers' table. Both going and returning this wonderful hunting country was a place of plenty. The party of course lived almost exclusively on meat, and they needed much; for, when they could get it, they consumed either a buffalo, or an elk and a deer, or four deer, every day.

In the plains country the life of the explorers was very pleasant save only for the mosquitoes and the incessant clouds of driving sand along the river bottoms. On their journey west through these true happy hunting grounds they did not meet with any Indians, and their encounters with the bears were only just sufficiently dangerous

to add excitement to their life. Once or twice they were
in peril from cloud-bursts, and they were lamed by the
cactus spines on the prairie, and by the stones and sand
of the river bed while dragging the boats against the current; but all these trials, labors, and risks were only
enough to give zest to their exploration of the unknown
land. At the Great Falls of the Missouri they halted,
and were enraptured with their beauty and majesty;
and here, as everywhere, they found the game so abundant that they lived in plenty. As they journeyed upstream through the bright summer weather, though they
worked hard, it was work of a kind which was but a long
holiday. At nightfall they camped by the boats on the
river bank. Each day some of the party spent in hunting, either along the river bottoms through the groves
of cottonwoods with shimmering, rustling leaves, or
away from the river where the sunny prairies stretched
into seas of brown grass, or where groups of rugged hills
stood, fantastic in color and outline, and with stunted
pines growing on the sides of their steep ravines. The
only real suffering was that which occasionally befell
some one who got lost, and was out for days at a time,
until he exhausted all his powder and lead before finding
the party.

Fall had nearly come when they reached the headwaters of the Missouri. The end of the holiday-time was
at hand, for they had before them the labor of crossing
the great mountains so as to strike the headwaters of
the Columbia. Their success at this point depended
somewhat upon the Indian wife of the Frenchman who
had joined them at Mandan. She had been captured
from one of the Rocky Mountains tribes and they relied

on her as interpreter. Partly through her aid, and partly by their own exertions, they were able to find, and make friends with, a band of wandering Shoshones, from whom they got horses. Having cached their boats and most of their goods they started westward through the forest-clad passes of the Rockies; before this they had wandered and explored in several directions through the mountains and the foothills. The open country had been left behind, and with it the time of plenty. In the mountain forests the game was far less abundant than on the plains and far harder to kill; though on the tops of the high peaks there was one new game animal, the white antelope-goat, which they did not see, though the Indians brought them hides. The work was hard, and the party suffered much from toil and hunger, living largely on their horses, before they struck one of the tributaries of the Snake sufficiently low down to enable them once more to go by boat.

They now met many Indians of various tribes, all of them very different from the Indians of the Western Plains. At this time the Indians, both east and west of the Rockies, already owned numbers of horses. Although they had a few guns, they relied mainly on the spears and tomahawks, and bows and arrows with which they had warred and hunted from time immemorial; for only the tribes on the outer edges had come in contact with the whites, whether with occasional French and English traders who brought them goods, or with the mixed bloods of the northern Spanish settloments, upon which they raided. Around the mouth of the Columbia, however, the Indians knew a good deal about the whites; the river had been discovered by Captain Gray of Bos-

ton thirteen years before, and ships came there continually, while some of the Indian tribes were occasionally
visited by traders from the British fur companies.

With one or two of these tribes the explorers had some
difficulty, and owed their safety to their unceasing vigilance, and to the prompt decision with which they gave
the Indians to understand that they would tolerate no
bad treatment; while yet themselves refraining carefully
from committing any wrong. By most of the tribes they
were well received, and obtained from them not only information of the route, but also a welcome supply of
food. At first they rather shrank from eating the dogs
which formed the favorite dish of the Indians; but after
a while they grew quite reconciled to dog's flesh; and in
their journals noted that they preferred it to lean elk and
deer meat, and were much more healthy while eating it.

They reached the rain-shrouded forests of the coast
before cold weather set in, and there they passed the
winter; suffering somewhat from the weather, and now
and then from hunger, though the hunters generally
killed plenty of elk, and deer of a new kind, the blacktail of the Columbia.

In March, 1806, they started eastward to retrace their
steps.

They had done a great deed, for they had opened the
door into the heart of the far West.

IV. THE FALL OF THE ALAMO [1]

DAVID CROCKETT journeyed south, by boat and horse, making his way steadily toward the distant plains where the Texans were waging their life-and-death fight. Texas was a wild place in those days and the old hunter had more than one hairbreadth escape from Indians, desperadoes, and savage beasts, ere he got to the neighborhood of San Antonio, and joined another adventurer, a bee-hunter, bent on the same errand as himself. The two had been in ignorance of exactly what the situation in Texas was; but they soon found that the Mexican army was marching toward San Antonio, whither they were going. Near the town was an old Spanish fort, the Alamo, in which the hundred and fifty American defenders of the place had gathered. Santa Anna had four thousand troops with him. The Alamo was a mere shell, utterly unable to withstand either a bombardment or a regular assault. It was evident, therefore, that those within it would be in the utmost jeopardy if the place were seriously assaulted but old Crockett and his companion never wavered. They were fearless and resolute, and masters of woodcraft, and they managed to slip through the Mexican lines and join the defenders within the walls. The bravest, the hardiest, the most reckless men of the border were there; among them were Colonel Travis, the commander of the fort, and Bowie, the inventor of the famous bowie-knife. They were a

[1] From *Hero Tales from American History*. Copyright, 1895. The Century Company, publishers.

wild and ill-disciplined band, little used to restraint or control, but they were men of iron courage and great bodily powers, skilled in the use of their weapons, and ready to meet with stern and uncomplaining indifference whatever doom fate might have in store for them.

Soon Santa Anna approached with his army, took possession of the town, and besieged the fort. The defenders knew there was scarcely a chance of rescue, and that it was hopeless to expect that one hundred and fifty men, behind defenses so weak, could beat off four thousand trained soldiers, well armed and provided with heavy artillery; but they had no idea of flinching, and made a desperate defense. The days went by, and no help came, while Santa Anna got ready his lines, and began a furious cannonade. His gunners were unskilled, however, and he had to serve the guns from a distance; for when they were pushed nearer, the American riflemen crept forward under cover, and picked off the artillerymen. Old Crockett thus killed five men at one gun. But, by degrees, the bombardment told. The walls of the Alamo were battered and riddled; and when they had been breached so as to afford no obstacle to the rush of his soldiers, Santa Anna commanded that they be stormed.

The storming took place on March 6, 1836. The Mexican troops came on well and steadily, breaking through the outer defenses at every point, for the lines were too long to be manned by the few Americans. The frontiersmen then retreated to the inner building, and a desperate hand-to-hand conflict followed, the Mexicans thronging in, shooting the Americans with their muskets, and thrusting at them with lance and bayonet, while the Americans, after firing their long rifles, clubbed them, and fought desperately, one against many; and they also used their bowie-knives and revolvers with deadly effect. The fight reeled to and fro between the shattered walls, each American the center of a group of foes; but, for all their strength and their wild fighting courage, the defenders were too few, and the struggle could have but one end. One by one the tall riflemen succumbed, after repeated thrusts with bayonet and lance, until but three or four were left. Colonel Travis, the commander, was among them; and so was Bowie, who was sick and weak from a wasting disease, but who rallied all his strength to die fighting, and who, in the final struggle, slew several Mexicans with his revolver, and with his big knife, of the kind to which he had given his name. Then these fell too, and the last man stood at bay. It was old Davy Crockett. Wounded in a dozen places, he faced his foes with his back to the wall, ringed around by the bodies of the men he had slain. So desperate was the fight he waged, that the Mexicans who thronged round about him were beaten back for the moment, and no one dared to run in upon him. Accordingly, while the lancers held him where he was, for, weakened by wounds and loss of blood, he could not break through them, the musketeers loaded their carbines and shot him down. Santa Anna declined to give him mercy. Some say that when Crockett fell from his wounds, he was taken alive, and was then shot by Santa Anna's order; but his fate cannot be told with certainty, for not a single American was left alive. At any rate, after Crockett fell the fight was over. Every one of the hardy men who had held the Alamo lay still in death. Yet they died well avenged, for four times their number fell at their hands in the battle.

Santa Anna had but a short while in which to exult over his bloody and hard-won victory. Already a rider from the rolling Texas plains, going north through the Indian Territory, had told Houston that the Texans were up and were striving for their liberty. At once in Houston's mind there kindled a longing to return to the men of his race at the time of their need. Mounting his horse, he rode south by night and day, and was hailed by the Texans as a heaven-sent leader. He took command of their forces, eleven hundred stark riflemen, and at the battle of San Jacinto, he and his men charged the Mexican hosts with the cry of "Remember the Alamo." Almost immediately, the Mexicans were overthrown with terrible slaughter; Santa Anna himself was captured, and the freedom of Texas was won at a blow.

V. THE DEATH OF STONEWALL JACKSON [1]

IT is often said that the Civil War was in one sense a repetition of the old struggle between the Puritan and the Cavalier; but Puritan and Cavalier types were common to the two armies. In dash and light-hearted daring, Custer and Kearny stood as conspicuous as Stuart and Morgan; and, on the other hand, no Northern general approached the Roundhead type — the type of the stern, religious warriors who fought under Cromwell — so closely as Stonewall Jackson. He was a man of intense religious conviction, who carried into every thought and deed of his daily life the precepts of the faith he cherished. He was a tender and loving husband and father, kind-hearted and gentle to all with whom he was brought in contact, yet in the times that tried men's souls, he proved not only a commander of genius, but a fighter of iron will and temper, who joyed in the battle, and always showed at his best when the danger was greatest. The vein of fanaticism that ran through his character helped to render him a terrible opponent. He knew no such word as falter, and when he had once put his hand to a piece of work, he did it thoroughly and with all his heart. It was quite in keeping with his character that this gentle, high-minded, and religious man should, early in the contest, have proposed to hoist the black flag, neither take nor give quarter, and make the war one of extermination. No such policy was practical in

[1] From *Hero Tales from American History*. Copyright, 1895. The Century Company, publishers.

the nineteenth century and in the American Republic; but it would have seemed quite natural and proper to Jackson's ancestors, the grim Scotch-Irish, who defended Londonderry against the forces of the Stuart king, or to their forefathers, the Covenanters of Scotland, and the Puritans who in England rejoiced at the beheading of King Charles I. In the first battle in which Jackson took part, the confused struggle at Bull Run, he gained his name of Stonewall from the firmness with which he kept his men to their work and repulsed the attack of the Union troops. From that time until his death, less than two years afterward, his career was one of brilliant and almost uninterrupted success; whether serving with an independent command in the Valley, or acting under Lee as his right arm in the pitched battles with McClellan, Pope, and Burnside. Few generals as great as Lee have ever had as great a lieutenant as Jackson. He was a master of strategy and tactics, fearless of responsibility, able to instill into his men his own intense ardor in battle, and so quick in his movements, so ready to march as well as fight, that his troops were known to the rest of the army as the "foot cavalry."

In the spring of 1863 Hooker had command of the Army of the Potomac. Like McClellan, he was able to perfect the discipline of his forces and to organize them, and as a division commander he was better than McClellan, but he failed even more signally when given a great independent command. He had under him 120,000 men when, toward the end of April, he prepared to attack Lee's army, which was but half as strong.

The Union army lay opposite Fredericksburg, looking at the fortified heights where they had received so bloody a repulse at the beginning of the winter. Hooker decided to distract the attention of the Confederates by letting a small portion of his force, under General Sedgwick, attack Fredericksburg, while he himself took the bulk of the army across the river to the right hand so as to crush Lee by an assault on his flank. All went well at the beginning, and on the first of May Hooker found himself at Chancellorsville, face to face with the bulk of Lee's forces; and Sedgwick, crossing the river and charging with the utmost determination, had driven out of Fredericksburg the Confederate division of Early; but when Hooker found himself in front of Lee he hesitated, faltered instead of pushing on, and allowed the consummate general to whom he was opposed to take the initiative.

Lee fully realized his danger, and saw that his only chance was, first to beat back Hooker, and then to turn and overwhelm Sedgwick, who was in his rear. He consulted with Jackson, and Jackson begged to be allowed to make one of his favorite flank attacks upon the Union army; attacks which could have been successfully delivered only by a skilled and resolute general, and by troops equally able to march and to fight. Lee consented, and Jackson at once made off. The country was thickly covered with a forest of rather small growth, for it was a wild region, in which there was still plenty of game. Shielded by the forest, Jackson marched his gray columns rapidly to the left along the narrow country roads until he was square on the flank of the Union right wing, which was held by the Eleventh Corps, under Howard. The Union scouts got track of the movement and reported it at headquarters, but the Union generals thought the Confederates were retreating; and when finally the scouts brought word to Howard that he was menaced by a flank attack he paid no heed to the information, and actually let his whole corps be surprised in broad daylight. Yet all the while the battle was going on elsewhere, and Berdan's sharpshooters had surrounded and captured a Georgia regiment, from which information was received showing definitely that Jackson was not retreating, and must be preparing to strike a heavy blow.

The Eleventh Corps had not the slightest idea that it was about to be assailed. The men were not even in line. Many of them had stacked their muskets and were lounging about, some playing cards, others cooking supper, intermingled with the pack-mules and beef cattle. While they were thus utterly unprepared, Jackson's gray-clad veterans pushed straight through the forest and rushed fiercely to the attack. The first notice the troops of the Eleventh Corps received did not come from the pickets, but from the deer, rabbits, and foxes which, fleeing from their coverts at the approach of the Confederates, suddenly came running over and into the Union lines. In another minute the frightened pickets came tumbling back, and right behind them came the long files of charging, yelling Confederates. With one fierce rush Jackson's men swept over the Union lines, and at a blow the Eleventh Corps became a horde of panic-struck fugitives. Some of the regiments resisted for a few moments, and then they too were carried away in the flight.

For a while it seemed as if the whole army would be swept off; but Hooker and his subordinates exerted every effort to restore order. It was imperative to gain time so that the untouched portions of the army could form across the line of the Confederate advance.

Keenan's regiment of Pennsylvania cavalry, but four hundred sabers strong, was accordingly sent full against the front of the ten thousand victorious Confederates.

Keenan himself fell, pierced by bayonets, and the charge was repulsed at once; but a few priceless moments had been saved, and Pleasonton had been given time to post twenty-two guns, loaded with double canister, where they would bear upon the enemy.

The Confederates advanced in a dense mass, yelling and cheering, and the discharge of the guns fairly blew them back across the works they had just taken. Again they charged, and again were driven back; and when the battle once more began the Union reinforcements had arrived.

It was about this time that Jackson himself was mortally wounded. He had been leading and urging on the advance of his men, cheering them with voice and gesture, his pale face flushed with joy and excitement, while from time to time as he sat on his horse he took off his hat and, looking upward, thanked heaven for the victory it had vouchsafed him. As darkness drew near he was in the front, where friend and foe were mingled in almost inextricable confusion. He and his staff were fired at, at close range, by the Union troops, and, as they turned, were fired at again, through a mistake, by the Confederates behind them. Jackson fell, struck in several places. He was put in a litter and carried back; but he never lost consciousness, and when one of his generals complained of the terrible effect of the Union cannonade he answered:

"You must hold your ground."

For several days he lingered, hearing how Lee beat Hooker, in detail, and forced him back across the river. Then the old Puritan died. At the end his mind wandered, and he thought he was again commanding in battle, and his last words were:

"Let us cross over the river and rest in the shade."

Thus perished Stonewall Jackson, one of the ablest of soldiers and one of the most upright of men, in the last of his many triumphs.

II
THE ROOSEVELT PHILOSOPHY

My countrymen, I believe in you with all my heart. I am proud that it has been granted to me to be a citizen in a nation of such glorious opportunities. We have no choice, we people of the United States, as to whether or not we shall play a great part in the world. That has been determined for us by fate, by the march of events. We have to play that part. All that we can decide is whether we shall play it well or ill. We are not, and cannot, and never will be one of those nations that can progress from century to century doing little and suffering little, standing aside from the great world currents. We must either succeed greatly or fail greatly. The citizen of a small nation may keep his self-respect if that nation plays but a small part in the world, because it is physically impossible for the nation to do otherwise; but the citizen of a great nation which plays a small part shall hang his head with shame.

I ask that this people rise level to the greatness of its opportunities.

THEODORE ROOSEVELT

THE ELEMENTAL VIRTUES—THE BASIS OF GOOD CITIZENSHIP

THE old pioneer days are gone, with their roughness and their hardship, their incredible toil and their wild, half-savage romance. But the need for the pioneer virtues remains the same as ever.

THEODORE ROOSEVELT

I. CHARACTER

I

THERE was scant room for the coward and the weakling in the ranks of the adventurous frontiersmen — the pioneer settlers who first broke up the wild prairie soil, who first hewed their way into the primeval forest, who guided their white-topped wagons across the endless leagues of Indian-haunted desolation, and explored every remote mountain-chain in the restless quest for metal wealth. Behind them came the men who completed the work they had roughly begun: who drove the great railroad system over plain and desert and mountain pass; who stocked the teeming ranches, and under irrigation saw the bright green of the alfalfa and the yellow of the golden stubble supplant the gray of the sage-brush desert; who have built great populous cities — cities in which every art and science of civilization are carried to the highest point — on tracts which, when the nineteenth century had passed its meridian, were still known only to the grim trappers and hunters and the red lords of the wilderness with whom they waged eternal war.

Such is the record of which we are so proud. It is a record of men who greatly dared and greatly did; a record of wanderings wider and more dangerous than those of the Vikings; a record of endless feats of arms, of victory after victory in the ceaseless strife waged against wild man and wild nature. The winning of the West was the great epic feat in the history of our race.

We have then a right to meet to-day in a spirit of just pride in the past. But when we pay homage to the hardy, grim, resolute men who, with incredible toil and risk, laid deep the foundations of the civilization that we inherit, let us steadily remember that the only homage that counts is the homage of deeds — not merely of words. It is well to gather here to show that we remember what has been done in the past by the Western pioneers of our people, and that we glory in the greatness for which they prepared the way. But lip-loyalty by itself avails very little, whether it is expressed concerning a nation or an ideal. It would be a sad and evil thing for this country if ever the day came when we considered the great deeds of our forefathers as an excuse for our resting slothfully satisfied with what has been already done. On the contrary, they should be an inspiration and appeal, summoning us to show that we too have courage and strength; that we too are ready to dare greatly if the need arises; and, above all, that we are firmly bent upon that steady performance of every-day duty which, in the long run, is of such incredible worth in the formation of national character.

The old iron days have gone, the days when the weakling died as the penalty of inability to hold his own in the rough warfare against his surroundings. We live in softer times. Let us see to it that, while we take advantage of every gentler and more humanizing tendency of the age, we yet preserve the iron quality which made our forefathers and predecessors fit to do the deeds they did. It will of necessity find a different expression now, but the quality itself remains just as necessary as ever. Surely you men of the West, you men who with stout heart, cool head, and ready hand have wrought out your own success and built up these great new commonwealths, surely you need no reminder of the fact that if either man or nation wishes to play a great part in the world there must be no dallying with the life of lazy ease. In the abounding energy and intensity of existence in our mighty democratic republic there is small space indeed for the idler, for the luxury-loving man who prizes ease more than hard, triumph-crowned effort.

We hold work not as a curse but as a blessing, and we regard the idler with scornful pity. It would be in the highest degree undesirable that we should all work in the same way or at the same things, and for the sake of the real greatness of the nation we should in the fullest and most cordial way recognize the fact that some of the most needed work must, from its very nature, be unremunerative in a material sense. Each man must choose so far as the conditions allow him the path to which he is bidden by his own peculiar powers and inclinations. But if he is a man he must in some way or shape do a man's work. If, after making all the effort that his strength of body and of mind permits, he yet honorably fails, why, he is still entitled to a certain share of respect because he has made the effort. But if he does not make the effort, or if he makes it half-heartedly and recoils from the labor, the risk, or the irksome monotony of his task, why, he has forfeited all right to our respect, and has shown himself a mere cumberer of the earth. It is not given to us all to succeed, but it is given to us all to strive manfully to deserve success.

We need, then, the iron qualities that must go with true manhood. We need the positive virtues of resolution, of courage, of indomitable will, of power to do without shrinking the rough work that must always be done, and to persevere through the long days of slow progress or of seeming failure which always come before any final triumph, no matter how brilliant. But we need more than these qualities. This country cannot afford to have its sons less than men; but neither can it afford to have them other than good men. If courage and strength and intellect are unaccompanied by the moral purpose, the moral sense, they become merely forms of expression for unscrupulous force and unscrupulous cunning. If the strong man has not in him the lift toward lofty things, his strength makes him only a curse to himself and to his neighbor. All this is true in private life, and it is no less true in public life. If Washington and Lincoln had not had in them the whipcord fiber of moral and mental strength, the soul that steels itself to endure disaster unshaken and with grim resolve to wrest victory from defeat, then the one could not have founded, nor the other preserved, our mighty federal Union. The least touch of flabbiness, of unhealthy softness, in either would have meant ruin for this nation, and therefore the downfall of the proudest hope of mankind. But no less is it true that had either been influenced by self-seeking ambition, by callous disregard of others, by contempt for the moral law, he would have dashed us down into the black gulf of failure. Woe to all of us if ever as a people we grow to condone evil because it is successful. We can no more afford to lose social and civic decency and honesty than we can afford to lose the qualities of courage and strength. It is the merest truism to say that the nation rests upon the individual, upon the family — upon individual manliness and womanliness, using the words in their widest and fullest meaning.

To be a good husband or good wife, a good neighbor and friend, to be hard-working and upright in business and social relations, to bring up many healthy children — to be and to do all this is to lay the foundations of good citizenship as they must be laid. But we cannot stop even with this. Each of us has not only his duty to himself, his family, and his neighbors, but his duty to the State and to the Nation. We are in honor bound each to strive according to his or her strength to bring ever nearer the day when justice and wisdom shall obtain in public life as in private life. We cannot retain the full measure of our self-respect if we cannot retain pride in our citizenship. For the sake not only of ourselves, but of our children and our children's children, we must see that this nation stands for strength and honesty both at home and abroad. In our internal policy we cannot afford to rest satisfied until all that the government can do has been done to secure fair dealing and equal justice as between man and man. In the great part which hereafter, whether we will or not, we must play in the world at large, let us see to it that we neither do wrong nor shrink from doing right because the right is difficult; that on the one hand we inflict no injury, and that on the other we have a due regard for the honor and the interest of our mighty nation; and that we keep unsullied the renown of the flag which beyond all others of the present time or of the ages of the past stands for confident faith in the future welfare and greatness of mankind.[1]

II

It is character that counts in a nation as in a man. It is a good thing to have a keen, fine intellectual development in a nation, to produce orators, artists, successful business men; but it is an infinitely greater thing to have those solid qualities which we group together under the name of character — sobriety, steadfastness, the sense of obligation toward one's neighbor and one's God, hard common sense, and, combined with it, the lift of generous enthusiasm toward whatever is right. These are the qualities which go to make up true national greatness.[2]

III

In the long run, in the great battle of life, no brilliancy of intellect, no perfection of bodily development, will count when weighed in the balance against that assemblage of virtues, active and passive, of moral qualities, which we group together under the name of character; and if between any two contestants, even in college sport or in college work, the difference in character on the right side is as great as the difference of

[1] Address at the Quarter-Centennial Celebration of Statehood in Colorado, at Colorado Springs, August 2, 1901. From *The Strenuous Life*. Second augmented edition. Copyright, 1901. The Century Company, publishers.

[2] From *The Strenuous Life*. Copyright, 1900.

intellect or strength the other way, it is the character side that will win.[1]

IV

I RECOLLECT saying to a young friend who was about to enter college, "My friend, I know that you feel that you ought to be a good man; now, be willing to fight for your principles whenever it is necessary; if you 're willing enough to fight, nobody will complain about your being too virtuous."

If you accept only the weak man, who cannot hold his own, as the type of virtuous man, you will inevitably create an atmosphere among ordinary, vigorous young men in which they will translate their contempt of weakness into contempt of virtue. My plea is that the virtuous man, the decent man, shall be a strong man, able to hold his own in any way, just because I wish him to be an agent in eradicating the misconception that being decent somehow means being weak; I want this to apply to every form of decency, public as well as private.

The worst development that we could see in civic life in this country would be a division of citizens into two camps, one camp containing nice, well-behaved, well-meaning little men, with receding chins and small feet, men who mean well and who if they are insulted feel shocked and want to go home; and the other camp containing robust and efficient creatures who do not mean well at all. I wish to see our side — the side of decency — include men who have not the slightest fear of the

[1] From *The Strenuous Life.* Copyright, 1900. The Century Company, publishers.

people on the other side. I wish to see the decent man in any relation of life, including politics, when hustled by the man who is not decent, able so to hold his own that the other gentleman shall feel no desire to hustle him again. My plea is for the virtue that shall be strong and that shall also have a good time. You recollect that Wesley said he wasn't going to leave all the good times to the Devil. In the same way we must not leave strength and efficiency to the Devil's agents. The decent man must realize that it is his duty to be strong just as much as to be decent. There are a good many types of men for whom I do not care; and among those types I would put in prominent place the timid good man — the good man who means well but is afraid. I wish to see it inculcated from the pulpit by every ethical teacher, and in the home, that just to be decent is not enough; that in addition to being a decent man it is the duty of the man to be a strong man. And also this; to let the fact that he is a decent man dawn on his neighbors by itself, and without his announcing it or emphasizing it.[1]

V

IT is a good thing that of these great landmarks of our history — Gettysburg and Valley Forge — one should commemorate a single tremendous effort and the other what we need, on the whole, much more commonly, and what I think is, on the whole, rather more difficult to do — long-sustained effort. Only men with a touch of the heroic in them could have lasted out that three days' struggle at Gettysburg. Only men fit to rank with the

[1] Permission to use this excerpt granted by The Harr Wagner Publishing Company, publishers of Theodore Roosevelt's *Realizable Ideals.*

great men of all time could have beaten back the mighty onslaught of that gallant and wonderful army of Northern Virginia, whose final supreme effort faded at the stone wall on Cemetery Ridge on that July day forty-one years ago.

But after all, hard though it is to rise to the supreme height of self-sacrifice and of effort at a time of crisis that is short, to rise to it for a single great effort — it is harder yet to rise to the level of a crisis when that crisis takes the form of needing constant, patient, steady work, month after month, year after year, when, too, it does not end after a terrible struggle in a glorious day — when it means months of gloom and effort steadfastly endured, and triumph wrested only at the very end.

Here at Valley Forge Washington and his Continentals warred not against the foreign soldiery, but against themselves, against all the appeals of our nature that are most difficult to resist — against discouragement, discontent, the mean envies and jealousies and heart-burnings sure to arise at any time in large bodies of men, but especially sure to arise when defeat and disaster have come to large bodies of men. Here the soldiers who carried our national flag had to suffer from cold, from privation, from hardship, knowing that their foes were well housed, knowing that time went easier for the others than it did for them. And they conquered, because they had in them the spirit that made them steadfast, not merely on an occasional great day, but day after day in the life of daily endeavor to do duty well.

When two lessons are both indispensable, it seems hardly worth while to dwell more on one than on the other. Yet I think that as a people we need more to learn the lesson of Valley Forge even than that of Gettysburg. I have not the slightest anxiety but that this people, if the need should come in the future, will be able to show the heroism, the supreme effort that was shown at Gettysburg, though it may well be that it would mean a similar two years of effort, checkered by disaster, to lead up to it. But the vital thing for this Nation to do is steadily to cultivate the quality which Washington and those under him so preëminently showed during the winter at Valley Forge — the quality of steady adherence to duty in the teeth of difficulty, in the teeth of discouragement, and even disaster, the quality that makes a man do what is straight, and decent, not one day when a great crisis comes, but every day, day in and day out, until success comes at the end.[1]

VI

REMEMBER always that the securing of a substantial education, whether by the individual or by a people, is attained only by a process, not by an act. You can no more make a man really educated by giving him a certain curriculum of studies than you can make a people fit for self-government by giving it a paper constitution. The training of an individual so as to fit him to do good work in the world is a matter of years; just as the training of a nation to fit it successfully to fulfill the duties of self-government is a matter, not of a decade or two, but of generations. There are foolish empiricists who believe that the granting of a paper constitution, prefaced by some high-sounding declaration, of itself confers the

[1] Remarks at the Washington Memorial Chapel, Valley Forge, Pennsylvania, June 19, 1904.

power of self-government upon a people. This is never so. Nobody can "give" a people "self-government," any more than it is possible to "give" an individual "self-help." You know that the Arab proverb runs, "God helps those who help themselves." In the long run, the only permanent way by which an individual can be helped is to help him to help himself, and this is one of the things your University should inculcate. But it must be his own slow growth in character that is the final and determining factor in the problem.

In this long and even tedious but absolutely essential process, I believe your University will take an important part. When I was recently in the Sudan I heard a vernacular proverb, based on a text in the Koran, which is so apt that, although not an Arabic scholar, I shall attempt to repeat it in Arabic: "Allah ma el saberin, izza sabaru" — God is with the patient, *if they know how to wait*.[1]

[1] Address before the National University in Cairo, Egypt, March 28, 1910. From *African and European Addresses*. Copyright, 1910. G. P. Putnam's Sons, New York and London, publishers.

II. THE STRENUOUS LIFE

I

I wish to preach, not the doctrine of ignoble ease, but the doctrine of the strenuous life, the life of toil and effort, of labor and strife; to preach that highest form of success which comes, not to the man who desires mere easy peace, but to the man who does not shrink from danger, from hardship, or from bitter toil, and who out of these wins the splendid ultimate triumph.

A life of slothful ease, a life of that peace which springs merely from lack either of desire or of power to strive after great things, is as little worthy of a nation as of an individual. I ask only that what every self-respecting American demands from himself and from his sons shall be demanded of the American Nation as a whole. Who among you would teach your boys that ease, that peace, is to be the first consideration in their eyes — to be the ultimate goal after which they strive? You men of Chicago have made this city great, you men of Illinois have done your share, and more than your share, in making America great, because you neither preach nor practice such a doctrine. You work yourselves, and you bring up your sons to work. If you are rich and are worth your salt, you will teach your sons that though they may have leisure, it is not to be spent in idleness; for wisely used leisure merely means that those who possess it, being free from the necessity of working for their livelihood, are all the more bound to carry on some kind of non-remunerative work in science, in letters, in art, in exploration, in historical research — work of the type we most need in this country, the successful carrying out of which reflects most honor upon the Nation. We do not admire the man of timid peace. We admire the man who embodies victorious effort; the man who never wrongs his neighbor, who is prompt to help a friend, but who has those virile qualities necessary to win in the stern strife of actual life. It is hard to fail, but it is worse never to have tried to succeed.

In the last analysis a healthy state can exist only when the men and women who make it up lead clean, vigorous, healthy lives; when the children are so trained that they shall endeavor, not to shirk difficulties, but to overcome them; not to seek ease, but to know how to wrest triumph from toil and risk. The man must be glad to do a man's work, to dare and endure and to labor; to keep himself, and to keep those dependent upon him. The woman must be the housewife, the helpmeet of the home-maker, the wise and fearless mother of many healthy children. In one of Daudet's powerful and melancholy books he speaks of "the fear of maternity, the haunting terror of the young wife of the present day." When such words can be truthfully written of a nation, that nation is rotten to the heart's core. When men fear work or fear righteous war, when women fear motherhood, they tremble on the brink of doom; and well it is that they should vanish from the earth, where they are fit subjects for the scorn of all men and women who are themselves strong and brave and high-minded.

As it is with the individual, so it is with the nation. It is a base untruth to say that happy is the nation that has no history. Thrice happy is the nation that has a glorious history. Far better it is to dare mighty things, to win glorious triumphs, even though checkered by failure, than to take rank with those poor spirits who neither enjoy much nor suffer much, because they live in the gray twilight that knows not victory nor defeat. If in 1861 the men who loved the Union had believed that peace was the end of all things, and war and strife the worst of all things, and had acted up to their belief, we would have saved hundreds of thousands of lives, we would have saved hundreds of millions of dollars. Moreover, besides saving all the blood and treasure we then lavished, we would have prevented the heartbreak of many women, the dissolution of many homes, and we would have spared the country those months of gloom and shame when it seemed as if our armies marched only to defeat. We could have avoided all this suffering simply by shrinking from strife. And if we had thus avoided it, we would have shown that we were weaklings, and that we were unfit to stand among the great nations of the earth. Thank God for the iron in the blood of our fathers, the men who upheld the wisdom of Lincoln, and bore sword or rifle in the armies of Grant! Let us, the children of the men who proved themselves equal to the mighty days, let us, the children of the men who carried the great Civil War to a triumphant conclusion, praise the God of our fathers that the ignoble counsels of peace were rejected; that the suffering and loss, the blackness of sorrow and despair, were unflinchingly faced, and the years of strife endured; for in the end the slave was freed, the Union restored, and the mighty American republic placed once more as a helmeted queen among nations.

I preach to you, then, my countrymen, that our
country calls not for the life of ease but for the life of
strenuous endeavor. The twentieth century looms before us big with the fate of many nations. If we stand
idly by, if we seek merely swollen, slothful ease and ignoble peace, if we shrink from the hard contests where
men must win at hazard of their lives and at the risk of
all they hold dear, then the bolder and stronger peoples
will pass us by, and will win for themselves the domina-
tion of the world. Let us therefore boldly face the life of
strife, resolute to do our duty well and manfully; resolute to uphold righteousness by deed and by word;
resolute to be both honest and brave, to serve high
ideals, yet to use practical methods. Above all, let us
shrink from no strife, moral or physical, within or
without the nation, provided we are certain that the
strife is justified, for it is only through strife, through
hard and dangerous endeavor, that we shall ultimately
win the goal of true national greatness.[1]

II

Your work is hard. Do you suppose I mention that because I pity you? No; not a bit. I don't pity any man
who does hard work worth doing. I admire him. I pity
the creature who does n't work, at whichever end of the
social scale he may regard himself as being. The law of
worthy work well done is the law of successful American
life. I believe in play, too — play, and play hard while you
play; but don't make the mistake of thinking that that

[1] Address before the Hamilton Club, Chicago, April 10, 1899. From
The Strenuous Life. Copyright, 1900. The Century Company, publishers.

is the main thing. The work is what counts, and if a man does his work well and it is worth doing, then it matters but little in which line that work is done; the man is a good American citizen. If he does his work in slipshod fashion, then no matter what kind of work it is, he is a poor American citizen.[1]

[1] Speech to the Brotherhood of Locomotive Firemen, Chattanooga, Tenn., September 8, 1902.

III. TENDERNESS AND STRENGTH

I

I want to see you game, boys; I want to see you brave and manly; and I also want to see you gentle and tender. In other words, you should make it your object to be the right kind of boys at home, so that your family will feel a genuine regret, instead of a sense of relief, when you stay away; and at the same time you must be able to hold your own in the outside world. You cannot do that if you have not manliness, courage in you. It does no good to have either of those two sets of qualities if you lack the other. I do not care how nice a little boy you are, how pleasant at home, if when you are out you are afraid of other little boys lest they be rude to you; for if so you will not be a very happy boy nor grow up a very useful man. When a boy grows up I want him to be of such a type that when somebody wrongs him he will feel a good, healthy desire to show the wrong-doers that he cannot be wronged with impunity. I like to have the man who is a citizen feel, when a wrong is done to the community by any one, when there is an exhibition of corruption or betrayal of trust, or demagogy or violence, or brutality, not that he is shocked and horrified and would like to go home; but I want to have him feel the determination to put the wrong-doer down, to make the man who does wrong aware that the decent man is not only his superior in decency, but his superior in strength; not necessarily physical strength, but strength of character, the kind of strength that makes a good and forceful citizen.

The place in which each of you should try to be most useful is his own home, and each of you should wish for and should practice in order to have courage and strength, so that they can be used in protecting the gentle, in protecting the weak, against those who would wrong weakness and gentleness. The boy who will maltreat either a smaller child, a little boy or a little girl, or a dumb animal, is just about the meanest boy that you can find anywhere in the world. You should be brave and able to hold your own just because you should be able to put down such a bully. It should be your pride to be the champion of the weak. You will find a certain number of boys who have strength and who pride themselves in it, and who misuse it. The boy who will torture something harmless, who will oppress the boy or girl who is weak, or do wrong to those who cannot resist, almost always proves to have a weak streak in him, and not to have the stuff in him that would make him stand up to an equal foe under punishment. That boy has not real courage, real strength; and much though I dislike seeing a boy who is timid, who is afraid, who cannot hold his own, I dislike infinitely more, I abhor, the boy who uses strength and courage to oppress those who cannot help themselves.[1]

II

[MANLINESS and courage] — these qualities are all-important, but they are not all-sufficient. It is necessary absolutely to have them. No nation can rise to greatness without them, but by them alone no nation will ever

[1] Address at the Graduating Exercises of Friends' School, Washington, May 24, 1907.

become great. Reading through the pages of history you come upon nation after nation in which there has been a high average of individual strength, bravery, and hardihood, and yet in which there has been nothing approaching to national greatness, because those qualities were not supplemented by others just as necessary. With the courage, with the hardihood, with the strength, must come the power of self-restraint, the power of self-mastery, the capacity to work for and with others as well as for one's self, the power of giving to others the love which each of us must bear for his neighbor, if we are to make our civilization really great.

The other day in a little Lutheran church at Sioux Falls I listened to a most interesting and most stimulating sermon, which struck me particularly because of the translation of a word which, I am ashamed to say, I myself had always before mistranslated. It was on the old text of faith, hope, and charity. The sermon was delivered in German, and the word that the preacher used for charity was not charity, but love; preaching that the greatness of all the forces with which we deal for betterment is love. Looking it up I found, of course, what I ought to have known, but did not, that the Greek word which we have translated into the word charity should be more properly translated love. That is, we use the word charity at present in a sense which does not make it correspond entirely to the word used in the original Greek. This Lutheran preacher developed in a very striking but very happy fashion the absolute need of love in the broadest sense of the word, in order to make mankind even approximately perfect.

We need then the two qualities — the quality of

which I first spoke to you, which has many shapes, the quality which rests upon courage, upon bodily and mental strength, upon will, upon daring, upon resolution, the quality which makes a man work; and then we need the quality of which the preacher spoke when he spoke of love as being the great factor, the ultimate factor, in bringing about the kind of human fellowship which will even approximately enable us to come up towards the standard after which I think all of us with many shortcomings strive. Work and love, using each in its broadest sense — work, the quality which makes a man ashamed not to be able to pull his own weight, not to be able to do for himself as well as for others without being beholden to any one for what he is doing. No man is happy if he does not work. Of all miserable creatures the idler, in whatever rank of society, is in the long run the most miserable. If a man is utterly selfish, if utterly disregardful of the rights of others, if he has no ideals, if he works simply for the sake of ministering to his own base passions, if he works simply to gratify himself, small is his good in the community. I think even then he is probably better off than if he is an idler, but he is of no real use unless together with the quality which enables him to work he has the quality which enables him to love his fellows, to work with them and for them for the common good of all.[1]

[1] Speech at Topeka, Kansas, May 1, 1903.

IV. THE FAMILY AND THE HOME

I

THE Nation is in a bad way if there is no real home, if the family is not of the right kind; if the man is not a good husband and father, if he is brutal or cowardly or selfish, if the woman has lost her sense of duty, if she is sunk in vapid self-indulgence or has let her nature be twisted so that she prefers sterile pseudo-intellectuality to that great and beautiful development of character which comes only to those whose lives know the fullness of duty done, or effort made and self-sacrifice undergone.

In the last analysis the welfare of the State depends absolutely upon whether or not the average family, the average man and woman and their children, represent the kind of citizenship fit for the foundation of a great nation; and if we fail to appreciate this we fail to appreciate the root morality upon which all healthy civilization is based.

There are certain old truths which will be true as long as this world endures, and which no amount of progress can alter. One of these is the truth that the primary duty of the husband is to be the homemaker, the breadwinner for his wife and children, and that the primary duty of the woman is to be the helpmeet, the housewife, and mother. The woman should have ample educational advantages; but save in exceptional cases the man must be, and she need not be, and generally ought not to be, trained for a lifelong career as the family breadwinner;

and, therefore, after a certain point the training of the two must normally be different because the duties of the two are normally different. This does not mean inequality of function, but it does mean that normally there must be dissimilarity of function. On the whole, I think the duty of the woman the more important, the more difficult, and the more honorable of the two; on the whole, I respect the woman who does her duty even more than I respect the man who does his.

No ordinary work done by a man is either as hard or as responsible as the work of a woman who is bringing up a family of small children; for upon her time and strength demands are made not only every hour of the day but often every hour of the night. She may have to get up night after night to take care of a sick child, and yet must by day continue to do all her household duties as well; and if the family means are scant she must usually enjoy even her rare holidays taking her whole brood of children with her. The birth pangs make all men the debtors of all women. Above all, our sympathy and regard are due to the struggling wives among those whom Abraham Lincoln called the plain people, and whom he so loved and trusted; for the lives of these women are often led on the lonely heights of quiet, self-sacrificing heroism.

Just as the happiest and most honorable and most useful task that can be set any man is to earn enough for the support of his wife and family, for the bringing up and starting in life of his children, so the most important, the most honorable and desirable task which can be set any woman is to be a good and wise mother in a home marked by self-respect and mutual forbearance, by willingness to perform duty, and by refusal to sink into self-indulgence or avoid that which entails effort and self-sacrifice. Of course, there are exceptional men and exceptional women who can do and ought to do much more than this, who can lead and ought to lead great careers of outside usefulness in addition to — not as substitute for — their home work; but I am not speaking of exceptions; I am speaking of the primary duties, I am speaking of the average citizens, the average men and women who make up the Nation.

Inasmuch as I am speaking to an assemblage of mothers I shall have nothing whatever to say in praise of any easy life. Yours is the work which is never ended. No mother has an easy time, and most mothers have very hard times; and yet what true mother would barter her experience of joy and sorrow in exchange for a life of cold selfishness, which insists upon perpetual amusement and the avoidance of care, and which often finds its fit dwelling-place in some flat designed to furnish with the least possible expenditure of effort the maximum of comfort and of luxury, but in which there is literally no place for children?

The woman who is a good wife, a good mother, is entitled to our respect as is no one else; but she is entitled to it only because, and so long as, she is worthy of it. Effort and self-sacrifice are the law of worthy life for the man as for the woman; though neither the effort nor the self-sacrifice may be the same for the one as for the other. I do not in the least believe in the patient Griselda type of woman, in the woman who submits to gross and long-continued ill-treatment, any more than I believe in a man who tamely submits to wrongful aggression. No wrong doing is so abhorrent as wrong doing by a man toward the wife and the children who should arouse every tender feeling in his nature. Selfishness toward them, lack of tenderness toward them, lack of consideration for them, above all brutality in any form toward them, should arouse the heartiest scorn and indignation in every upright soul.

I believe in the woman's keeping her self-respect just as I believe in the man's doing so. I believe in her rights just as much as I believe in the man's, and indeed a little more; and I regard marriage as a partnership in which each partner is in honor bound to think of the rights of the other as well as of his or her own. But I think that the duties are even more important than the rights; and in the long run I think that the reward is ampler and greater for duty well done than for the insistence upon individual rights, necessary though this, too, must often be. Your duty is hard, your responsibility great; but greatest of all is your reward. I do not pity you in the least. On the contrary, I feel respect and admiration for you. . . .

The woman's task is not easy — no task worth doing is easy — but in doing it, and when she has done it, there shall come to her the highest and holiest joy known to mankind; and having done it, she shall have the reward prophesied in Scripture; for her husband and her children, yes, and all people who realize that her work lies at the foundation of all national happiness and greatness, shall rise up and call her blessed.[1]

[1] Address before the National Congress of Mothers, Washington, D.C., March 13, 1905.

II

To all who have known really happy family lives, that
is to all who have known or have witnessed the greatest
happiness which there can be on this earth, it is hardly
necessary to say that the highest ideal of the family is
attainable only where the father and mother stand to
each other as lovers and friends, with equal rights. In
these homes the children are bound to father and mother
by ties of love, respect, and obedience, which are simply
strengthened by the fact that they are treated as reasonable beings with rights of their own, and that the rule
of the household is changed to suit the changing years,
as childhood passes into manhood and womanhood. In
such a home the family is not weakened; it is strengthened. This is no unattainable ideal. Every one knows
hundreds of homes where it is more or less perfectly realized, and it is an ideal incomparably higher than the
ideal of the beneficent autocrat which it has so largely
supplanted.[1]

III

We all of us know the type of man, frequently found at
crossroad groceries, who in his abundant leisure is able
to explain precisely how humanity should be benefited
and the nation run, while he himself exists at all only
because his wife takes in washing. We also know the
man who in public life is filled with the loftiest aspira-
tions; but whose family unite in breathing a sigh of relief whenever he is absent from the house.

[1] From *American Ideals*. Copyright, 1897. G. P. Putnam's Sons,
New York and London, publishers.

Of course there is now and then a man who in some given crisis plays the hero although on other occasions he plays the brute — there are such cases; but it is a mighty unsafe thing to proceed upon the assumption that because a man is ordinarily a brute he will therefore be a hero in a crisis. Disregarding the exceptions, and speaking normally, no man can be of any service to the State, no man can amount to anything from the standpoint of usefulness to the community at large, unless first and foremost he is a decent man in the close relations of life. No community can afford to think for one moment that great public service, that great material achievement, that ability shown in no matter how many different directions, will atone for the lack of a sound family life.

Multiplication of divorces means that there is something rotten in the community, that there is some principle of evil at work which must be counteracted and overcome or widespread disaster will follow. In the same way, if the man preaches and practices a different code of morality for himself than that which he demands that his wife shall practice, then no profession on his part of devotion to civic ideals will in the least avail to alter the fact that he is fundamentally a bad citizen. I do not believe in weakness. I believe in a man's being a man; and for that very reason I abhor the creature who uses the expression that "a man must be a man" in order to excuse his being a vile and vicious man.[1]

[1] Permission to use this excerpt granted by The Harr Wagner Publishing Company, publishers of Theodore Roosevelt's *Realizable Ideals*.

V. SUCCESS

I

IF you leave Groton, and the college to which you afterward go, if you go to any — if you leave simply with the feeling that you have had ten delightful years; that you have just barely got through your examinations; that you have graduated; that you are not positively disgraced; that you have met decent people, and that life has been easy and it won't be your fault if it does not continue as easy — if that is the feeling with which you have left school and college, then you are poor creatures, and there is small good that will ever come out of you.

Of course, the worst of all lives is the vicious life; the life of a man who becomes a positive addition to the forces of evil in a community. Next to that — and when I am speaking to people who, by birth and training and standing, ought to amount to a great deal, I have a right to say only second to it in criminality — comes the life of mere vapid ease. Of all the miserable people that I know I should put high in the top rank those who reach middle age having steadfastly striven only to amuse themselves as they went through life. If there ever was a pursuit which stultified itself by its very conditions, it is the pursuit of pleasure as the all-sufficing end of life. Happiness cannot come to any man capable of enjoying true happiness unless it comes as the sequel to duty well and honestly done. To do that duty you need to have more than one trait. You will meet plenty of well-meaning people who speak to you as if one trait were enough. That is not so. You might just as well in any rough sport in any game, think that a man could win by mere strength if he was clumsy; or by mere agility and precision of movement without strength; or by strength and agility if he had no heart. You need a great many qualities to make a successful man on a nine or an eleven; and just so you need a great many different qualities to make a good citizen. In the first place, of course, it is almost tautological to say that to make a good citizen the prime need is to be decent in thought, clean in mind, clean in action; to have an ideal and not to keep that ideal purely for the study — to have an ideal which you will in good faith strive to live up to when you are out in life. If you have an ideal only good while you sit at home, an ideal that nobody can live up to in outside life, then I advise you strongly to take that ideal, examine it closely, and then cast it away. It is not a good one. The ideal that it is impossible for a man to strive after in practical life is not the type of ideal that you wish to hold up and follow. Be practical as well as generous in your ideals. Keep your eyes on the stars, but remember to keep your feet on the ground.

Be truthful; a lie implies fear, vanity or malevolence; and be frank; furtiveness and insincerity are faults incompatible with true manliness. Be honest, and remember that honesty counts for nothing unless back of it lie courage and efficiency. If in this country we ever have to face a state of things in which on one side stand the men of high ideals who are honest, good, well-meaning, pleasant people, utterly unable to put those ideals into shape in the rough field of practical life, while on the other side are grouped the strong, powerful, efficient men with no ideals, then the end of the Republic will be near. The salvation of the Republic depends — the salvation of our whole social system depends — upon the production year by year of a sufficient number of citizens who possess high ideals combined with the practical power to realize them in actual life.

You often hear people speaking as if life was like striving upward toward a mountain peak. That is not so. Life is as if you were traveling a ridge crest. You have the gulf of inefficiency on one side and the gulf of wickedness on the other, and it helps not to have avoided one gulf if you fall into the other. It shall profit us nothing if our people are decent and ineffective. It shall profit us nothing if they are efficient and wicked. In every walk of life, in business, politics; if the need comes, in war; in literature, science, art, in everything, what we need is a sufficient number of men who can work well and who will work with a high ideal. The work can be done in a thousand different ways. Our public life depends primarily not upon the men who occupy public positions for the moment, because they are but an infinitesimal fraction of the whole. Our public life depends upon men who take an active interest in that public life; who are bound to see public affairs honestly and competently managed; but who have the good sense to know what honesty and competency actually mean. And any such man, if he is both sane and high-minded, can be a greater help and strength to any one in public life than you can easily imagine without having had yourselves the experience. It is an immense strength to a public man to know a certain number of people to whom he can appeal for advice and for backing; whose character is so high that baseness would shrink ashamed before them; and who have such good sense that any decent public servant is entirely willing to lay before them every detail of his actions, asking only that they know the facts before they pass final judgment.

Success does not lie entirely in the hands of any one of us. From the day the tower of Siloam fell, misfortune has fallen sometimes upon the just as well as the unjust. We sometimes see the good man, the honest man, the strong man, broken down by forces over which he had no control. If the hand of the Lord is heavy upon us the strength and wisdom of man shall avail nothing. But as a rule in the long run each of us comes pretty near to getting what he deserves. Each of us can, as a rule — there are, of course, exceptions — finally achieve the success best worth having, the success of having played his part honestly and manfully; of having lived so as to feel at the end he has done his duty; of having been a good husband, a good father; of having tried to make the world a little better off rather than worse off because he has lived; of having been a doer of the word and not a hearer only — still less a mere critic of the doers. Every man has it in him, unless fate is indeed hard upon him, to win out that measure of success if he will honestly try.[1]

II

THE first thing I want to say to you here, is that the only efficient way in which, in after life, you can show your gratitude to the school, is by the kind of reputation you

[1] Speech at the Prize Day Exercises at Groton School, Groton, Mass., May 24, 1904.

win in the great world. Your return must be in the way of adding to the school's good name, adding to the sum of reputation which will come, and can only come, from the part played by the graduates in the life of the nation after they have graduated.

You must be efficient. You must be able to hold your own in the world of politics, the world of business; able to keep your head above water, to make your work satisfactory, to make it pay. If you do not, you cannot do good to others. You must never forget for a moment that so far from the doctrine of efficiency being a base doctrine, it is a doctrine vital to good in this country. If the elders as well as the boys would keep that in mind, they would appreciate better what I regard as one of the cardinal political doctrines that should be preached ever in this country, the doctrine that we should never penalize efficiency; that the line we should draw in business is on conduct and not on size, and what we should discriminate against is misconduct in any phase, and not efficiency.

So with politics. One of the hardest things to do is make men understand that efficiency in politics does not atone for public morality, and that morality, good intentions, decent conduct, all together do not atone for inefficiency. You must have both traits. I am always tempted to illustrate what I mean, by referring, simply because it is so easy to understand and so clear, to army experiences. Take my own brief military experience — merely an experience of four months; but it gave me in part an understanding of all the problems that come in connection with soldiery, with the problems that were confronted on a gigantic scale in the case of your fathers in the days of the Civil War. I could gain nothing with any man in the regiment unless he had the right purpose in him. I did not want him unless he had the right purpose in him; but even if he had the right purpose, even if he was boiling with patriotic enthusiasm, he was not of the least use to me if he could not shoot and walk and ride. And I could not accept any amount of patriotic fervor as offsetting a slight tendency to run away. You will amount to nothing unless you have the ideals, and you will amount to nothing unless in good faith you strive to realize them.[1]

III

If there is one thing which I should like to eradicate from the character of every American, it is the dreadful practice of paying a certain mean admiration and homage to the man who, whether in business or politics, achieves success at the cost of sacrificing all those principles for the lack of which, in the eye of any righteous man, no possible achievement of success can in any way compensate. That applies just as much to the smart politician, who by bribery and chicanery and sharp practice, who by misuse of public office, by mendacity, by cleverness in hoodwinking the people, rises to high station, as it applies to the unscrupulous man of affairs who makes a fortune, not legitimately, but illegitimately in some form of gambling, which is not merely gambling, but gambling with loaded dice, and who can count upon having, from no inconsiderable section of our people, the same admiring homage that would be gained by

[1] Address delivered at the Hill School, Pottstown, Pennsylvania, June 10, 1913.

the most respected business man whose success has been even more beneficial to the community than to himself.[1]

IV

MR. PRESIDENT, and gentlemen, it is a very great pleasure for me to be here to-day and to address you and to wear what the Secretary has called the gilded trappings which show that I am one of the youngest living graduates of Cambridge. Something in the nature of a tract was handed to me before I came up here. It was an issue of the *Gownsman* (*holding up, amid laughter, a copy of an undergraduate publication*) with a poem portraying the poet's natural anxiety lest I should preach at him. Allow me to interpose an anecdote taken from your own hunting field. A one-time Master of Foxhounds strongly objected to the presence of a rather near-sighted and very hard-riding friend who at times insisted on riding in the middle of the pack; and on one occasion he earnestly addressed him as follows: "Mr. So and So, would you mind looking at those two dogs, Ploughboy and Melody. They are very valuable, and I really wish you would not jump on them." To which his friend replied, with great courtesy: "My dear sir, I should be delighted to oblige you, but unfortunately I have left my glasses at home, and I am afraid they must take their chance." I will promise to preach as little as I can, but you must take your chance, for it is impossible to break the bad habit of a lifetime at the bidding of a comparative stranger. I was deeply touched by the allusion to the lion and the coat-of-

[1] Speech at the Independent Club, Buffalo, N.Y., May 15, 1899.

arms. Before I reached London I was given to understand that it was expected that when I walked through Trafalgar Square, I should look the other way as I passed the lions. . . .

Now I am going to disregard your poet and preach to you for just one moment, but I will make it as little obnoxious as possible. The Secretary spoke of me as if I were an athlete. I am not, and never have been one, although I have always been very fond of outdoor amusement and exercise. . . . I have always led an outdoor life, and have accomplished something in it, simply because my theory is that almost any man can do a great deal, if he will, by getting the utmost possible service out of the qualities that he actually possesses.

There are two kinds of success. One is the very rare kind that comes to the man who has the power to do what no one else has the power to do. That is genius. I am not discussing what form that genius takes; whether it is the genius of a man who can write a poem that no one else can write, *The Ode on a Grecian Urn,* for example, or *Helen, thy beauty is to me;* or of a man who can do a hundred yards in nine and three-fifths seconds. Such a man does what no one else can do. Only a very limited amount of the success of life comes to persons possessing genius. The average man who is successful — the average statesman, the average public servant, the average soldier, who wins what we call great success — is not a genius. He is a man who has merely the ordinary qualities that he shares with his fellows, but who has developed those ordinary qualities to a more than ordinary degree.

Take such a thing as hunting or any form of vigorous

bodily exercise. Most men can ride hard if they choose. Almost any man can kill a lion if he will exercise a little resolution in training the qualities that will enable him to do it.

(*Taking a tumbler from the table, Mr. Roosevelt held it up.*)

Now it is a pretty easy thing to aim straight at an object about that size. Almost any one, if he practices with the rifle at all, can learn to hit that tumbler; and he can hit the lion all right if he learns to shoot as straight at its brain or heart as at the tumbler. He does not have to possess any extraordinary capacity, not a bit — all he has to do is to develop certain rather ordinary qualities, but develop them to such a degree that he will not get flustered, so that he will press the trigger steadily instead of jerking it — and then he will shoot at the lion as well as he will at that tumbler. It is a perfectly simple quality to develop. You don't need any remarkable skill; all you need is to possess ordinary qualities, but to develop them to a more than ordinary degree.

It is just the same with the soldier. What is needed is that the man as soldier should develop certain qualities that have been known for thousands of years, but develop them to such a point that in an emergency he does, as a matter of course, what a great multitude of men can do but what a very large proportion of them don't do. And in making the appeal to the soldier, if you want to get out of him the stuff that is in him, you will have to use phrases which the intellectual gentlemen who do not fight will say are platitudes.

It is just so in public life. It is not genius, it is not extraordinary subtlety, or acuteness of intellect, that is important. The things that are important are the rather commonplace, the rather humdrum, virtues that in their sum are designated as character. If you have in public life men of good ability, not geniuses, but men of good abilities, with character — and, gentlemen, you must include as one of the most important elements of character common sense — if you possess such men, the Government will go on very well.

I have spoken only of the great successes; but what I have said applies just as much to the success that is within the reach of almost every one of us. I think that any man who has had what is regarded in the world as a great success must realize that the element of chance has played a great part in it. Of course a man has to take advantage of his opportunities; but the opportunities have to come. If there is not the war, you don't get the great general; if there is not a great occasion you don't get the great statesman; if Lincoln had lived in times of peace no one would have known his name now. The great crisis must come, or no man has the chance to develop great qualities.

There are exceptional cases, of course, where there is a man who can do just one thing, such as a man who can play a dozen games of chess or juggle with four rows of figures at once — and as a rule he can do nothing else. A man of this type can do nothing unless in the one crisis for which his powers fit him. But normally the man who makes the great success when the emergency arises is the man who would have made a fair success in any event. I believe that the man who is really happy in a great position — in what we call a career — is the man who would also be happy and regard his life as successful if he had never been thrown into that position. If a man lives a decent life and does his work fairly and squarely so that those dependent on him and attached to him are better for his having lived, then he is a success, and he deserves to feel that he has done his duty and he deserves to be treated by those who have had greater success as nevertheless having shown the fundamental qualities that entitle him to respect. We have in the United States an organization composed of the men who forty-five years ago fought to a finish the great Civil War. One thing that has always appealed to me in that organization is that all of the men admitted are on a perfect equality provided the records show that their duty was well done. Whether a man served as a lieutenant-general or an eighteen-year-old recruit, so long as he was able to serve for six months and did his duty in his appointed place, then he is called Comrade and stands on an exact equality with the other men. The same principle should shape our associations in ordinary civil life.

I am not speaking cant to you. I remember once sitting at a table with six or eight other public officials, and each was explaining how he regarded being in public life, how only the sternest sense of duty prevented him from resigning his office, and how the strain of working for a thankless constituency was telling upon him, and nothing but the fact that he felt he ought to sacrifice his comfort to the welfare of his country kept him in the arduous life of statesmanship. It went round the table until it came to my turn. This was during my first term of office as President of the United States. I said: "Now, gentlemen, I do not wish there to be any misunderstanding. I like my job, and I want to keep it for four years longer."

I don't think any President ever enjoyed himself more than I did. Moreover, I don't think any ex-President ever enjoyed himself more. I have enjoyed my life and my work because I thoroughly believe that success — the real success — does not depend upon the position you hold, but upon how you carry yourself in that position. There is no man here to-day who has not the chance so to shape his life after he leaves this university that he shall have the right to feel, when his life ends, that he has made a real success of it; and his making a success of it does not in the least depend upon the prominence of the position he holds. Gentlemen, I thank you, and I am glad I have violated the poet's hope and have preached to you.[1]

[1] Address at Cambridge Union, Cambridge, England, May 26, 1910. From *African and European Addresses*. Copyright, 1910. G. P. Putnam's Sons, New York and London, publishers.

VI. SERVICE

I

UNLESS democracy is based on the principle of service by everybody who claims the enjoyment of any right, it is not true democracy at all. The man who refuses to render, or is ashamed to render, the necessary service is not fit to live in a democracy. And the man who demands from another a service which he himself would esteem it dishonorable or unbecoming to render is to that extent not a true democrat. No man has a right to demand a service which he does not regard as honorable to render; nor has he a right to demand it unless he pays for it in some way, *the payment to include respect for the man who renders it.* Democracy must mean mutuality of service rendered, and of respect for the service rendered.

A leading Russian revolutionist (who is, of course, like every true friend of freedom, an opponent of the Bolsheviki) recently came to this country from Vladivostock. He traversed the Siberian railway. The porter on his train refused to get him hot water or to black his boots; stating with true Bolshevistic logic that democracy meant that nobody must do anything for any one else and that anyhow his union would turn him out if he rendered such service.

Now, this Bolsheviki porter was foolish with a folly that can only be induced by prolonged and excessive indulgence in Bolshevism or some American analogue. But the root trouble in producing his folly was the fact that under the old system the men whose boots the porter blacked looked down on him for blacking them. Are we entirely free from this attitude in America? Until we are we may as well make up our minds that to just that extent we are providing for the growth of Bolshevism here. No man has a right to ask or accept any service unless under changed conditions he would feel that he could keep his entire self-respect while rendering it. Service which carries with it the slightest implication of social abasement should not be rendered.

For a number of years I lived on a ranch in the old-time cattle country; and I also visited at the house of a backwoods lumberjack friend. In both places we lived under old-style American conditions. We all of us worked, and our social distinctions were essentially based on individual worth. We accepted as a matter of course that the difference in degree of service rendered ought at least roughly to correspond to the difference in reward. Each did most of the purely personal things for himself. But nobody thought of any necessary work as degrading.

I remember that once, when there was a lull in outdoor work, I endeavored to be useful in and around the house. I fed the pigs; and on an idle morning I blacked all the boots. Ordinarily our boots did not need blacking — most of them were not that kind. On this occasion I started, with an enthusiasm that outran my judgment, to black the dress boots of every one, of both sexes. I coated them with a thick, dull paste; only a few knobs became shiny; and the paste came off freely on what it touched. As a result I temporarily lost not merely the respect but even the affection of all the other inmates of the house. However, I did not lose caste because I had blacked the boots, I lost caste because I had blacked them badly. But I was allowed to continue feeding the pigs. The pigs were not so particular as the humans.

Now, there is no more reason for refusing to bring hot water or black boots or serve a dinner or make up a bed or cook or wash clothes (I have cooked and washed clothes often — but neither wisely nor well) than for refusing to shoe a horse, run a motor, brake a train, sell carpets, manage a bank, or run a farm. A few centuries back men of good lineage felt that they lost caste if they were in trade or finance — in some countries they feel so to this day. In most civilized lands, however, the feeling has disappeared, and it never occurs to any one to look down on any one else because he sells things. Just the same feeling should obtain, and as we grow more civilized will obtain, about all other kinds of service. This applies to domestic service. It is as entirely right to employ housemaids, cooks, and gardeners as to employ lawyers, bankers, and business men or cashiers, factory-hands, and stenographers. But only on condition that we show the same respect to the individuals in one case as in the other cases!

Ultimately I hope that this respect will show itself in the forms of address, in the courtesy titles used, as well as the consideration shown, and the personal liberty expected and accorded. I am not demanding an instant change — I believe in evolution rather than revolution. But I am sure the change is possible and desirable; and even although it would be foolish and undesirable to set up the entirely new standard immediately, I hope we can work toward it. One of the most charming gentle-women I know, the wife of a man of rare cultivation, ability, and public achievement, lives on the top floor of a tenement-house in a Western city. The rooms are comfortably and daintily furnished — with an abundance of books. In this household the maid was introduced to me as Miss So-and-So; and this is the ideal. Of course it cannot be realized until there has been much education *on both sides*. But it should be the ideal. All relations between employer and employee should be based on mutuality of respect and consideration; arrogance met by insolence, or an alternation of arrogance and insolence, offers but a poor substitute.[1]

II

ISAIAH, the seer, the man of the vision, condemned ritual and formalism, and exalted conduct, when he thundered: "Hear the word of the Lord; to what purpose is the multitude of your sacrifices unto me? I delight not in the blood of bullocks. Your appointed feasts my soul hateth. Cease to do evil; learn to do well; seek judgment, relieve the oppressed, judge the fatherless, plead for the widow."

Amos — no son of a prophet, but a laboring man, a herdsman and a gatherer of sycamore fruit — said: "Hear ye the Word; I despise your feast days; I will not accept your burnt offerings. But let judgment run down as waters, and righteousness as a mighty stream; hate the evil, and love the good, and establish judgment in the gate." What is this but insistence on the great

[1] From *The Great Adventure*. Copyright, 1918. Charles Scribner's Sons, publishers.

law of service? In peace and in war we must spend and be spent, in the endless battle for right against wrong; deeds, not words, alone shall save us.

"By their fruits ye shall know them," is a teaching of the Sermon on the Mount; and James, spurning the unctuous professions of righteousness by those who do not make good what they preach, by those who profess a faith which is dead — which was never alive — because it bears no fruit in works, sums up the matter by insisting that we must be doers and not hearers only, because "Pure religion and undefiled before God and the Father is this, to visit the fatherless and widows in their affliction, and to keep oneself unspotted from the world."

I know not how philosophers may ultimately define religion; but from Micah to James it has been defined as service to one's fellow men rendered by following the great rule of justice and mercy, of wisdom and righteousness.[1]

III

To my fellow Americans I preach the sword of the Lord and of Gideon. In this great war for righteousness, we Americans have a tremendous task ahead of us. I believe the American people are entirely willing to make any sacrifice, and to render any service, and I believe that they should be explicitly shown how great the service is they are called upon to render, how great the need is that they should unflinchingly face any sacrifice that is to be made. I ask of you, and I ask of those

[1] From *The Foes of Our Own Household.* Copyright, 1917. George H. Doran Company, publishers.

who govern you — who govern this great mass of people — that we may be given direct practical lines of effort. With all my heart I believe that our people have in them the same patriotism, the same nobility of soul to which Washington and Lincoln were able to appeal. I ask that the appeal be made, the appeal for effort, and with it the guarantee by actual governmental performance that the effort shall not be wasted.

Let us give every man in this country his rights without regard to creed or birthplace, or national origin, or color. Let us in return exact from every man the fullest performance of duty, the fullest loyalty to our flag, and the most resolute effort to serve it.

The test of our worth now is the service we render. Sacrifice? Yes, as an incident of service; but let us think only of the service, not of the sacrifice. There never yet was a service worth rendering that did not entail sacrifice; and no man renders the highest service if he thinks overmuch of the sacrifice.

Let us pay with our bodies for our souls' desire! [1]

IV

ONLY those are fit to live who do not fear to die; and none are fit to die who have shrunk from the joy of life and the duty of life. Both life and death are parts of the same Great Adventure. Never yet was worthy adventure worthily carried through by the man who put his personal safety first. Never yet was a country worth living in unless its sons and daughters were of that stern stuff which bade them die for it at need; and never yet

[1] From *The Foes of Our Own Household*. Copyright, 1916. George H. Doran Company, publishers.

was a country worth dying for unless its sons and daughters thought of life not as something concerned only with the selfish evanescence of the individual, but as a link in the great chain of creation and causation, so that each person is seen in his true relations as an essential part of the whole, whose life must be made to serve the larger and continuing life of the whole. Therefore it is that the man who is not willing to die, and the woman who is not willing to send her man to die, in a war for a great cause, are not worthy to live. Therefore it is that the man and woman who in peace-time fear or ignore the primary and vital duties and the high happiness of family life, who dare not beget and bear and rear the life that is to last when they are in their graves, have broken the chain of creation, and have shown that they are unfit for companionship with the souls ready for the Great Adventure.

The wife of a fighting soldier at the front recently wrote as follows to the mother of a gallant boy, who at the front had fought in high air like an eagle, and, like an eagle, fighting had died:

I write these few lines — not of condolence for who would dare to pity you? — but of deepest sympathy to you and yours as you stand in the shadow which is the earthly side of those clouds of glory in which your son's life has just passed. Many will envy you that when the call to sacrifice came you were not found among the paupers to whom no gift of life worth offering had been entrusted. They are the ones to be pitied, not we whose dearest are jeoparding their lives unto the death in the high places of the field. I hope my two sons will live as worthily and die as greatly as yours.

There spoke one dauntless soul to another! America is safe while her daughters are of this kind; for their lovers and their sons cannot fail, as long as beside the hearthstones stand such wives and mothers. And we have many, many such women; and their men are like unto them.

No nation can be great unless its sons and daughters have in them the quality to rise level to the needs of heroic days; and yet such spirit will in the long run avail nothing unless in the years of peace the average man and average woman of the duty-performing type realize that the highest of all duties, the one essential duty, is the duty of perpetuating the family life, based on the mutual love and respect of the one man and the one woman, and on their purpose to rear the healthy and fine-souled children whose coming into life means that the family, and therefore the nation, shall continue in life and shall not end in a sterile death.

Woe to those who invite a sterile death; a death not for them only, but for the race; the death which is insured by a life of sterile selfishness.

But honor, highest honor, to those who fearlessly face death for a good cause; no life is so honorable or so fruitful as such a death. Unless men are willing to fight and die for great ideals, including love of country, ideals will vanish, and the world will become one huge sty of materialism. And unless the women of ideals bring forth the men who are ready thus to live and die, the world of the future will be filled by the spawn of the unfit. Alone of human beings the good and wise mother stands on a plane of equal honor with the bravest soldier; for she has gladly gone down to the brink of the chasm of darkness to bring back the children in whose hands rests the future of the years. But the mother, and far more the father, who flinch from the vital task earn the scorn visited on the soldier who flinches in battle. And the nation should by action mark its attitude alike toward the fighter in war and toward the child-bearer in peace and war. The vital need of the nation is that its men and women of the future shall be the sons and daughters of the soldiers of the present. Excuse no man from going to war because he is married; but put all unmarried men above a fixed age at the hardest and most dangerous tasks; and provide amply for the children of soldiers, so as to give their wives the assurance of material safety.

In such a matter one can only speak in general terms. At this moment there are hundreds of thousands of gallant men eating out their hearts because the privilege of facing death in battle is denied them. So there are innumerable women and men whose undeserved misfortune it is that they have no children or but one child. These soldiers denied the perilous honor they seek, these men and women heart-hungry for the children of their longing dreams, are as worthy of honor as the men who are warriors in fact, as the women whose children are of flesh and blood. If the only son who is killed at the front has no brother because his parents coldly dreaded to play their part in the Great Adventure of Life, then our sorrow is not for them, but solely for the son who himself dared the Great Adventure of Death. If, however, he is the only son because the Unseen Powers denied others to the love of his father and mother, then we mourn doubly with them because their darling went up to the sword of Azrael, because he drank the dark drink proffered by the Death Angel.

In America to-day all our people are summoned to service and sacrifice. Pride is the portion only of those who know bitter sorrow or the foreboding of bitter sorrow. But all of us who give service, and stand ready for sacrifice, are the torch-bearers. We run with the torches until we fall, content if we can then pass them to the hands of other runners. The torches whose flame is brightest are borne by the gallant men at the front, and by the gallant women whose husbands and lovers, whose sons and brothers are at the front. These men are high of soul, as they face their fate on the shell-shattered earth, or in the skies above or in the waters beneath; and no less high of soul are the women with torn hearts and shining eyes; the girls whose boy lovers have been struck down in their golden morning, and the mothers and wives to whom word has been brought that henceforth they must walk in the shadow.

These are the torch-bearers; these are they who have dared the Great Adventure.[1]

[1] From *The Great Adventure*. Copyright, 1918. Charles Scribner's Sons, publishers.

II

GOOD CITIZENSHIP — THE BASIS OF JUST GOVERNMENT

I. THE DUTY OF THE INDIVIDUAL

I

MEN can never escape being governed. Either they must govern themselves or they must submit to being governed by others. If from lawlessness or fickleness, from folly or self-indulgence, they refuse to govern themselves, then most assuredly in the end they will have to be governed from the outside. They can prevent the need of government from without only by showing that they possess the power of government from within. A sovereign cannot make excuses for his failures; a sovereign must accept the responsibility for the exercise of the power that inheres in him; and where, as is true in our Republic, the people are sovereign, then the people must show a sober understanding and a sane and steadfast purpose if they are to preserve that orderly liberty upon which as a foundation every republic must rest.[1]

II

THERE used to be in the army an old proverb that there were no bad regiments, but plenty of bad colonels. So in private life I have grown to believe that if you always

[1] Speech at the Opening of the Jamestown Exposition, April 26, 1907.

find bad servants in a household you want to look out for the mistress. I wonder if you grasp just what I mean by that? If you always find bad public servants, look out for the public! We here — you my hearers and I — live in a government where we are the people and in consequence where we are not to be excused if the government goes wrong. There are many countries where the government can be very wrong indeed and where nevertheless it can be said that the people are fundamentally right, for they don't choose their public servants, they don't choose their government. On the contrary we do choose our government, not temporarily but permanently, and in the long run our public servants must necessarily be what we choose to have them. They represent us; they must represent our self-restraint and sense of decency and common sense, or else our folly, our wickedness, or at least our supine indifference in letting others do the work of government for us. Not only should we have the right type of public servants, but we should remember that the wrong type discredits not only the man himself but each of us whose servant he is. Sometimes I hear our countrymen inveigh against politicians; I hear our countrymen abroad saying, "Oh, you must n't judge us by our politicians." I always want to interrupt and answer, "You must judge us by our politicians." We pretend to be the masters — we, the people — and if we permit ourselves to be ill served, to be served by corrupt and incompetent and inefficient men, then on our own heads must the blame rest.[1]

[1] Permission to use this excerpt granted by The Harr Wagner Publishing Company, publishers of Theodore Roosevelt's *Realizable Ideals*.

III

IN a democracy like ours we cannot expect the stream to rise higher than its source. If the average man and the average woman are not of the right type, your public men will not be of the right type. The average man must be a decent man in his own home, he must pull his own weight, he must be a decent neighbor, and a man with whom you like to deal, or he cannot be a good citizen. That is good as a beginning; but it is not enough. He must show in his relations with his fellows and in his dealing with the State the essentials of good citizenship. Genius is not necessary. Genius is a fine thing; but fortunately character is not only more common, but better. What he needs to show is character, and there are three essential qualities going to make up character.

In the first place, there is honesty. The bolder a man is the worse he is, if he has n't honesty. Don't be misled by that unfortunate trait sometimes shown by our people — the trait of deifying mere smartness, meaning thereby mental subtlety and ability unencumbered by any sense of responsibility.

But honesty is not enough. I don't care how honest a man is, if he is timid he is no good. I don't want to see a division of our citizenship into good men who are afraid and bad men who are not at all afraid. The honest man who is afraid is of just as little use in civic life as in war.

You need honesty and then you need courage; but both of them together are not enough. I don't care how honest a man is and how brave he is, if he is a natural-born fool you can do nothing with him; and perhaps this applies particularly to people in the profession of politics. Of course, the bolder a politician is, if he is dishonest, the worse he is; hunt him out of public life; and a feeble, well-meaning, timid politician, like the other good, timid people, is of no use; but the bold, incorruptible politician who stupidly goes wrong may be just as useless to a community in the long run as if he were hired by some dishonest man to do his work. So there is a third quality; that is, you must possess the saving grace of common sense.

When you get into your average citizen honesty — militant, not merely passive, honesty — courage, and common sense, you will find that your representatives in public life will soon show the same traits; and when they do, we shall have gone a long way toward solving the questions which must be solved and must be solved aright, if this nation is to be, as it shall and will be, not merely the greatest republic upon which the sun has ever shone, but the nation which holds out the lamp of hope to all the other nations throughout the world.[1]

IV

As soon as I left college I wanted to take an interest in political life; I wanted to find out how the work of governing was really done. Quite a number of nice people in New York, along Fifth Avenue, solemnly advised me not to join any of the regular political organizations, because I would find that they were composed only of "muckers," not of "gentlemen." The answer was easy: "Then they are the ones that govern; if it is the muckers that govern, I want to see if I cannot hold my own with

[1] Speech at the Milwaukee Auditorium, September 7, 1910.

them. I will join with them in governing you if you are too weak to govern yourself." I intended to be one of the class that governs, not one of the class that is governed. So I joined the political club in my district. I joined it just as I joined the National Guard. If there came a time of civic disturbance in the community, or if we were invaded or were at war with any country, I did not intend to have to hire somebody else to do my shooting for me. I intended to do it myself; and in the same way I intended to do the governing myself, to do my part of it.

I want to see you feel the same way. Education is of good chiefly according to the use you put it to. If it teaches you to be so puffed with pride as to make you misestimate the relative values of things, it becomes a harm and not a benefit. There are few things less desirable than the arid cultivation, the learning and refinement which lead merely to that intellectual conceit which makes a man in a democratic community like ours hold himself aloof from his fellows and pride himself upon the weakness which he mistakes for supercilious strength. Small is the use of those educated men who in after life meet no one but themselves, and gather in parlors to discuss wrong conditions which they do not understand and to advocate remedies which have the prime defect of being unworkable. I remember ex-Speaker Reed speaking to me of how easy it was to get an absolutely perfect theory to meet any condition as long as you kept that theory in the study, and how difficult it was to get even moderately good results out of any theory when you tried to apply it to the hard facts of actual life. The judgment on practical affairs, political and social, of the men who keep aloof from conditions of practical life, is apt to be valueless to those other men who do wage effective war against the forces of baseness and of evil.

From the political standpoint an education that leads you into the ranks of the educated ineffectives is a harm, not a good. It is a harm to all of you here if it serves you as an excuse for refusing to mingle with your fellows, for standing aloof from the broad sweep of our national life in a curiously impotent spirit of fancied superiority. If you go into politics, if you go into a ward caucus and try to carry it you lose the feeling of superiority very quickly. The political wrong-headedness of such men is quite as great as that of wholly uneducated men; and no people could be less trustworthy as critics and advisers. The educated man who seeks to console himself for his own lack of the robust qualities necessary to bring success in American politics by moaning over the degeneracy of the times instead of trying to better them, by railing at the men who do the actual work of political life instead of trying himself to do the work, is a poor creature, and, so far as his feeble powers avail, is a damage and not a help to the country.

You may come far short of this disagreeable standard and still be a rather useless member of society. Your education, your cultivation, will not help you if you make the mistake of thinking that it is a substitute for instead of an addition to those qualities which in the struggle of life bring success to the ordinary man without your advantages. Your college training confers no privilege upon you save as tested by the use you make of it. It puts upon you the obligation to show yourselves better able to do certain things than your fellows who have not had your advantages. If it has served merely to make you believe that you are to be excused from effort in after life, that you are to be excused from contact with the actual world of men and events, then it will prove a curse and not a blessing. If on the other hand you treat your education as a weapon the more in your hands, a weapon to fit you to do better in the hard struggle of effort, and not as excusing you in any way from taking part in practical fashion in that struggle, then it will be a benefit to you.

Let each of you college men remember in after life that in the fundamentals he is very much like his fellows who have not been to college, and that if he is to achieve results, instead of confining himself exclusively to disparagement of other men who have achieved them, he must manage to come to some kind of working agreement with these fellows of his. There are times, of course, when it may be the highest duty of a citizen to stand alone, or practically alone. But if this is a man's normal attitude — if normally he is unable to work in combination with a considerable body of his fellows — it is safe to set him down as unfit for useful service in a democracy. In popular government results worth having can only be achieved by men who combine worthy ideals with practical good sense; who are resolute to accomplish good purposes, but who can accommodate themselves to the give and take necessary where work has to be done, as almost all important work has to be done, by combination. Moreover, remember that normally the prime object of political life should be to achieve results and not merely to issue manifestoes — save, of course, where the issuance of such manifestoes helps to achieve the results. It is a very bad thing to be morally callous, for moral callousness is disease. But inflammation of the conscience may be just as unhealthy so far as the public is concerned; and if a man's conscience is always telling him to do something foolish he will do well to mistrust its workings. The religious man who is most useful is not he whose sole care is to save his own soul, but the man whose religion bids him strive to advance decency and clean living and to make the world a better place for his fellows to live in; and all this is just as true of the ordinary citizen in the performance of the ordinary duties of political life. . . .

The last ten years have been years of great achievement for this Nation. During that period we have dealt and are dealing with many different matters of great moment. In all these matters there have been some men in public life and some men in private life whose action has been at every point one of barren criticism or fruitless obstruction. These men have had no part or lot in the great record of achievement and success; the record of good work worthily done. Some of these men have been college graduates; but all of them have been poor servants of the people, useless where they were not harmful. All the credit for the good thus accomplished in the public life of this decade belongs to those who have done affirmative work in such matters as those I have enumerated above, and not to those who, with more or less futility, have sought to hamper and obstruct the work that has thus been done.

In short, you college men, be doers rather than critics of the deeds that others do. Stand stoutly for your ideals; but keep in mind that they can only be realized, even partially, by practical methods of achievement. Remember always that this Republic of ours is a very real democracy, and that you can only win success by showing that you have the right stuff in you. The college man, the men of intellect and training, should take the lead in every fight for civic and social righteousness. He can take that lead only if in a spirit of thorough-going democracy he takes his place among his fellows, not standing aloof from them, but mixing with them, so that he may know, may feel, may sympathize with their hopes, their ambitions, their principles — and even their prejudices — as an American among Americans, as a man among men.[1]

[1] Address at the Harvard Union, February 23, 1907.

II. PRACTICAL POLITICS

I

THE political associations of the various districts are not organized merely at the approach of election day; on the contrary, they exist throughout the year, and for the greater part of the time are to a great extent merely social clubs. To a large number of the men who belong to them they are the chief social rallying-point. These men congregate in the association building in the evening to smoke, drink beer, and play cards, precisely as the wealthier men gather in the clubs whose purpose is avowedly social and not political — such as the Union, University, and Knickerbocker. Politics thus becomes a pleasure and relaxation as well as a serious pursuit. The different members of the same club or association become closely allied with one another, and able to act together on occasions with unison and esprit de corps; and they will stand by one of their own number for reasons precisely homologous to those which make a member of one of the upper clubs support a fellow-member if the latter happens to run for office. "He is a gentleman, and shall have my vote," says the swell club man. "He's one of the boys, and I'm for him," replies the heeler from the district party association. In each case the feeling is social rather than political, but where the club man influences one vote the heeler controls ten. A rich merchant and a small tradesman alike find it merely a bore to attend the meetings of the local political club; it is to them an irksome duty which is shirked whenever possible. But to the small politicians and to the various workers and hangers-on, these meetings have a distinct social attraction, and the attendance is a matter of preference. They are in congenial society and in the place where by choice they spend their evenings, and where they bring their friends and associates; and naturally all the men so brought together gradually blend their social and political ties, and work with an effectiveness impossible to the outside citizens whose social instincts interfere, instead of coinciding with their political duties. If an ordinary citizen wishes to have a game of cards or a talk with some of his companions, he must keep away from the local headquarters of his party; whereas under similar circumstances, the professional politician must go there. The man who is fond of his home naturally prefers to stay there in the evenings, rather than go among the noisy club frequenters, whose pleasure it is to see each other at least weekly, and who spend their evenings discussing neither sport, business, nor scandal, as do other sections of the community, but the equally monotonous subject of ward politics.

The strength of our political organizations arises from their development as social bodies; many of the hardest workers in their ranks are neither office-holders nor yet paid henchmen, but merely members who have gradually learned to identify their fortunes with the party whose hall they have come to regard as the headquarters in which to spend the most agreeable of their leisure moments. Under the American system it is impossible for a man to accomplish anything by himself; he must associate himself with others, and they must throw their weight together. This is just what the social functions of the political clubs enable their members to do. The great and rich society clubs are composed of men who are not apt to take much interest in politics anyhow, and never act as a body. The great effect produced by a social organization for political purposes is shown by the career of the Union League Club; and equally striking proof can be seen by every man who attends a ward meeting. There is thus, however much to be regretted it may be, a constant tendency towards the concentration of political power in the hands of those men who by taste and education are fitted to enjoy the social side of the various political organizations.[1]

II

THE terms machine and machine politician are now undoubtedly used ordinarily in a reproachful sense; but it does not at all follow that this sense is always the right one. On the contrary, the machine is often a very powerful instrument for good; and a machine politician really desirous of doing honest work on behalf of the community is fifty times as useful an ally as is the average philanthropic outsider. Indeed, it is of course true, that any political organization (and absolutely no good work can be done in politics without an organization) is a machine; and any man who perfects and uses this organization is himself, to a certain extent, a machine politician. In the rough, however, the feeling against machine politics and politicians is tolerably well justified by the facts, although this statement really reflects most severely upon the educated and honest people who largely

[1] From *American Ideals*. Copyright, 1897. G. P. Putnam's Sons, New York and London, publishers.

hold themselves aloof from public life, and show a curious incapacity for fulfilling their public duties.

The organizations that are commonly and distinctively known as machines are those belonging to the two great recognized parties, or to their factional subdivisions; and the reason why the word machine has come to be used, to a certain extent, as a term of opprobrium is to be found in the fact that these organizations are now run by the leaders very largely as business concerns to benefit themselves and their followers, with little regard to the community at large. This is natural enough. The men having control and doing all the work have gradually come to have the same feeling about politics that other men have about the business of a merchant or manufacturer; it was too much to expect that if left entirely to themselves they would continue disinterestedly to work for the benefit of others. Many a machine politician who is to-day a most unwholesome influence in our politics is in private life quite as respectable as any one else; only he has forgotten that his business affects the State at large, and, regarding it as merely his own private concern, he has carried into it the same selfish spirit that actuates in business matters the majority of the average mercantile community.[1]

III

ONE of the reasons why the boss so often keeps his hold, especially in municipal matters, is, or at least has been in the past, because so many of the men who claim to be reformers have been blind to the need of working in hu-

---

[1] From *American Ideals.* Copyright, 1897. G. P. Putnam's Sons, New York and London, publishers.

man fashion for social and industrial betterment. Such words as "boss" and "machine" now imply evil, but both the implication the words carry and the definition of the words themselves are somewhat vague. A leader is necessary; but his opponents always call him a boss. An organization is necessary; but the men in opposition always call it a machine. Nevertheless, there is a real and deep distinction between the leader and the boss, between organizations and machines. A political leader who fights openly for principles, and who keeps his position of leadership by stirring the consciences and convincing the intellects of his followers, so that they have confidence in him and will follow him because they can achieve greater results under him than under any one else, is doing work which is indispensable in a democracy. The boss, on the other hand, is a man who does not gain his power by open means, but by secret means, and usually by corrupt means. Some of the worst and most powerful bosses in our political history either held no public office or else some unimportant public office. They made no appeal either to intellect or conscience. Their work was done behind closed doors, and consisted chiefly in the use of that greed which gives in order that in return it may get. A boss of this kind can pull wires in conventions, can manipulate members of the Legislature, can control the giving or withholding of office, and serves as the intermediary for bringing together the powers of corrupt politics and corrupt business. If he is at one end of the social scale, he may through his agents traffic in the most brutal forms of vice and give protection to the purveyors of shame and sin in return for money bribes. If at the other end of the scale, he may

be the means of securing favors from high public officials, legislative or executive, to great industrial interests; the transaction being sometimes a naked matter of
bargain and sale, and sometimes being carried on in such
manner that both parties thereto can more or less successfully disguise it to their consciences as in the public
interest. The machine is simply another name for the
kind of organization which is certain to grow up in a
party or section of a party controlled by such bosses
as these and by their henchmen, whereas, of course, an
effective organization of decent men is essential in order
to secure decent politics.

If these bosses were responsible for nothing but pure
wickedness, they would probably last but a short time in
any community. And, in any event, if the men who are
horrified by their wickedness were themselves as practical and as thoroughly in touch with human nature, the
bosses would have a short shrift. The trouble is that
the boss does understand human nature, and that he fills
a place which the reformer cannot fill unless he likewise
understands human nature. Sometimes the boss is a man
who cares for political power purely for its own sake, as
he might care for any other hobby; more often he has
in view some definitely selfish object such as political or
financial advancement. He can rarely accomplish much
unless he has another side to him. A successful boss is
very apt to be a man who, in addition to committing
wickedness in his own interest, also does look after the
interests of others, even if not from good motives. There
are some communities so fortunate that there are very
few men who have private interests to be served, and in
these the power of the boss is at a minimum. There are

many country communities of this type. But in communities where there is poverty and ignorance, the conditions are ripe for the growth of a boss. Moreover, wherever big business interests are liable either to be improperly favored or improperly discriminated against and blackmailed by public officials — and the result is just as vicious in one case as in the other — the boss is almost certain to develop. The best way of getting at this type of boss is by keeping the public conscience aroused and alert, so that it will tolerate neither improper attack upon, nor improper favoritism towards, these corporations, and will quickly punish any public servant guilty of either.

There is often much good in the type of boss, especially common in big cities, who fulfills towards the people of his district in rough and ready fashion the position of friend and protector. He uses his influence to get jobs for young men who need them. He goes into court for a wild young fellow who has gotten into trouble. He helps out with cash or credit the widow who is in straits, or the breadwinner who is crippled or for some other cause temporarily out of work. He organizes clambakes and chowder parties and picnics, and is consulted by the local labor leaders when a cut in wages is threatened. For some of his constituents he does proper favors, and for others wholly improper favors; but he preserves human relations with all. He may be a very bad and very corrupt man, a man whose action in blackmailing and protecting vice is of far-reaching damage to his constituents. But these constituents are for the most part men and women who struggle hard against poverty and with whom the problem of living is very real and very close. They would prefer clean and honest government, if this clean and honest government is accompanied by human sympathy, human understanding. But an appeal made to them for virtue in the abstract, an appeal made by good men who do not really understand their needs, will often pass quite unheeded, if on the other side stands the boss, the friend and benefactor, who may have been guilty of much wrong doing in things that they are hardly aware concern them, but who appeals to them, not only for the sake of favors to come, but in the name of gratitude and loyalty, and above all of understanding and fellow-feeling. They have a feeling of clan-loyalty to him; his and their relations may be substantially those which are right and proper among primitive people still in the clan stage of moral development. The successful fight against this type of vicious boss, and the type of vicious politics which produces it, can be made only by men who have a genuine fellow-feeling for and understanding of the people for and with whom they are to work, and who in practical fashion seek their social and industrial benefit.[1]

IV

IN the better wards the difficulty comes in drilling a little sense and energy into decent people: they either do not care to combine or else refuse to learn how. In one district we did at one time and for a considerable period get control of affairs and elect a set of almost ideal delegates and candidates to the various nominating and legislative bodies, and in the end took an absolutely com-

[1] From *Autobiography of Theodore Roosevelt*. Copyright, 1913. Charles Scribner's Sons, publishers.

manding although temporary position in State and even in national politics.

This was done by the efforts of some twenty or thirty young fellows who devoted a large part of their time to thoroughly organizing and getting out the respectable vote. The moving spirits were all active, energetic men, with common sense, whose motives were perfectly disinterested. Some went in from principle; others, doubtless, from good-fellowship or sheer love of the excitement always attendant upon a political struggle. Our success was due to our absolute freedom from caste spirit. Among our chief workers were a Columbia College professor, a crack oarsman from the same institution, an Irish quarryman, a master carpenter, a rich young merchant, the owner of a small cigar store, the editor of a little German newspaper, and a couple of employees from the post office and custom house, who worked directly against their own seeming interests. One of our important committees was composed of a prominent member of a Jewish synagogue, of the son of a noted Presbyterian clergyman, and of a young Catholic lawyer. We won some quite remarkable triumphs, for the first time in New York politics carrying primaries against the machine, and as the result of our most successful struggle completely revolutionizing the State Convention held to send delegates to the National Republican Convention of 1884, and returning to that body, for the first and only time it was ever done, a solid delegation of independent Republicans. This was done, however, by sheer hard work on the part of a score or so of men; the mass of our good citizens, even after the victories which they had assisted in winning, understood nothing about how they were won. Many of them actually objected to organizing, apparently having a confused idea that we could always win by what one of their number called a "spontaneous uprising," to which a quiet young fellow in our camp grimly responded that he had done a good deal of political work in his day, but that he never in his life had worked so hard and so long as he did to get up the "spontaneous" movement in which we were then engaged.[1]

V

Now, gentlemen, don't be content with mere effervescent denunciation of one thing or another. Evil can't be done away with through one spasm of virtue.[2]

---

[1] From *American Ideals*. Copyright, 1897. G. P. Putnam's Sons, New York and London, publishers.

[2] Speech at the City Club, New York City, May 9, 1899.

III. POLITICAL MORALITY

I

THERE are two chief sources of danger to the American people: lawless violence and corruption; lawless violence, which we most often have to face from among the people who have least of the world's goods; and corruption, which we most often have to face from among the people that have most of the world's goods.

The last time I was in Chicago you were engaged in a struggle with the first evil. It was at the time of the great teamsters' strike, that you remember here, and there was some question of the city authorities not being able to deal with it. You were then face to face with an assault by lawless violence upon the foundation of the American government.

I was coming back from the Rocky Mountains at the time, and I had good friends who earnestly advised me to go around Chicago. I decided to go through it, and stopped here. A deputation of the labor men called upon me, and to them I said what I subsequently said at a dinner at which the then Mayor and the then Governor were present, that, vitally interested though I was in all real reforms for the betterment of our people, and eagerly though I desired to help uplift those who were down, and so far as was possible do away with the inequalities of fortune that come from the inequalities of opportunity, yet when there was disorder, when there was lawless violence, all questions of reform had to be postponed until the orderly process of the law was resumed; and that, while I hoped and believed that the municipal authorities themselves would be able to deal with the disorder, yet, if they found it impossible, back of the city stood the State, and back of the State the Nation.

I did not hesitate to speak directly then, and just as little shall I hesitate to speak directly now.

In the program to-night you have done me the honor to print certain quotations from speeches I have made, mostly before the Hamilton Club; and the final quotation is: "We must see that there is civic honesty, civic cleanliness, civic good sense, in our whole administration of the city, State, and Nation."

My friends, the value of a sentence like that consists exclusively in the way in which we try to live up to it. The worth of what I have to say to you, and whether or not it is worth your while to listen to me, depends upon the way in which we translate words into deeds. It is all right to applaud a sentence like that in favor of civic honesty, stating that civic honesty is essential to the welfare of a nation. It is well enough to applaud it, but woe to you if you applaud the sentence in the abstract and fail to act up to it in the concrete.

It has been well said that the progress, the true progress, of a people can best be gauged by their standard of moral conduct, by their judgment as to what conduct is moral and what conduct is immoral, and by the effectiveness with which they make their approbation of the moral and their disapprobation of the immoral felt. No republic can last if corruption is allowed to eat into its public life. No republic can last if the private citizens sit supinely by and either encourage or tolerate corruption among their representatives.

Each state of the nation, each important city of the Union, has from time to time to face this question. More than once we have been brought face to face with it in the State of New York. You are face to face with it now in the State of Illinois.

I have been reading the reports of the investigations by the two state's attorneys, which resulted in the indictment of four members of the legislature, and together with that I have read the reports of the confession of four other members of the legislature. I was advised to-day by a very worthy friend not to talk on this matter, because it was a "delicate" subject, and he added that no one had been convicted. Now, I feel most strongly that we make the question of public honesty a sham if we limit the use of the word "honesty" to mere law-honesty.

There are big business men whom I have counted as among the most insidious enemies of the real welfare of this republic, although they have been so advised that it would be impossible to convict them, and there have been in the United States, including the State of New York, many public men whose careers have been a scandal throughout the country, although they keep clear of the courts.

Read the confessions of the four men. Read what was developed by the two state's attorneys, one belonging to the one party and one belonging to the other, about the four men against whom they secured indictments, and about other men also. Read that, and I defy any honest man of intelligence not to come to the conclusion that the legislature whose doings have been exposed was guilty of the foulest and basest corruption, and, therefore, of the most infamous treason to American institutions.

Now, I am a good party man, but I am an American first. When we come to questions affecting the vital principles of American life, I know no party. When such a question as corruption is involved, we cannot afford to divide on party lines.

I take just this much account of party in such a case. While I will do my best to get hold of the thief of the opposite party, I will try, if possible, a little harder to get hold of the thief of my own party.

When I was President I endeavored to act so that there should be no need of raising the cry among my opponents of "Turn the rascals out," because I turned them out myself just as fast as I could get at them.

Now, mind you, take my words as worth less than nothing, unless, in looking back, you can see that they were justified by my deeds.

Examine what went on in the Post Office Department, or anywhere else, when corruption was alleged with anything like an offer of proof.

Now, in making these investigations I struck two different sets of cases. There was one set of cases where prosecutions would lie. In those cases I turned the matter over to the Department of Justice. In addition, there was the larger class of cases where there was not sufficient ground for prosecution, but where it was evident that the man was an unfit and an improper public servant; and there I turned him out; and when now and then the man back of him, occasionally belonging to a coördinate branch of the government, would come up and say: "Oh, there is no conviction against him," I said, "No, I dare say that he has practiced law-honesty, but he is a crook, and out he goes."

Now, I could do that with the appointive officers, who held office under me; with the elective officers there is but one body that can do that, and that is the people.

If the people of America are content to send to represent them in the State or the National legislature men who they know in their heart of hearts have not obtained their offices honestly, but have obtained their offices dishonestly and by corruption, who they know have practiced corruption in public life, they may make up their minds that they will get the government to which they are entitled, and a bad government it will be.

Now, my friends, I do not suppose that if we decline to be honest and to insist on honesty in public life for our own sakes, we can be expected to do so for the sake of others; and yet, in addition to making the appeal for honesty to you and to the citizens of Illinois, for the sake of Illinois, and for the sake of America, I make the appeal also for the sake of the world.

Last spring, in Europe, there were two things that struck me especially as I talked with the average man. The first was that the man looked toward America as the land of golden hope, as the land of a partially realized ideal, as a land where it was really being shown that the people could govern themselves justly and righteously and in their own interest.

And the second thing was that that faith in America was continually being shaken by stories that reached them of corruption in American business and in American public life. Every act of corruption here, every gross scandal, every bit of flagrant dishonesty in big business or in politics, or in connection with the complex web that weaves together strands of big business and strands of politics — every such instance, when carried abroad, brings sneering satisfaction to the heart of every reactionary, who is glad to say: "Yes, that is what comes of democracy. That is what you get when the people try to govern themselves. It shows that they cannot govern themselves." And every such instance dims the hope of the poor and the oppressed who strive to believe and haltingly do believe that here, somehow or other, we have arranged a condition of things in which the injustices of the world elsewhere are at least partially remedied.

My friends, I ask you men of Illinois that you purify your politics, that you hold accountable the scoundrel, great or small, who has been guilty of corruption, that you insist on cleanliness in your public life; and I ask it in your name and for your sakes; I ask it for the sake of the American people; and I ask it for the sake of all the nations of the world, that their hope may not be made dim, and that they may continue to cherish the ideal of the possibility of having a government of, by, and for the people, that shall mean also a government of justice and a government of honesty.[1]

II

IF I were asked to name the three influences which I thought were most dangerous to the perpetuity of American institutions, I should name corruption, in business

[1] Speech before the Hamilton Club, Chicago, September 8, 1910. From *The New Nationalism*. Copyright, 1910. The Outlook Company, publishers.

and politics alike, lawless violence, and mendacity, especially when used in connection with slander.

Corruption: You cannot afford to tolerate in your ranks the corrupt man, and the first duty of a constituency should be to see that its representative is not merely honest in the sense that he cannot be legally shown to be dishonest, but that he is a dead straight man whom no one can think of as crooked. I do not want it to be praise to a man that he is honest; I want it to be an impossible supposition for a representative to be thought of as anything else; but you cannot get that honesty unless you insist upon it among yourselves in your own relations of life. If you train up your children to hear a shady scoundrel spoken of with a certain half admiration as, "Well, he is smart"; if you let your children hear a man's crookedness excused on the ground that he is clever, that he is a cheat, but that he cheats mighty well, you have yourselves to blame if your legislatures betray you. More than that, distrust anything in the nature of class privilege; distrust the labor leader who will inveigh against corruption only when it is shown by the rich man; and distrust equally the rich man who will subscribe heavily to put down law-breaking among small politicians, and who is shocked at corruption among labor leaders, but who leaves you instantly as soon as you try to bring the big corporation to book. If you elect a man because you think he will be honest towards your class — capitalists, farmers, laborers — and if you are indifferent as to whether he is honest towards other people, you can make up your minds absolutely that he will betray you if he gets the chance. You cannot afford not to have a man honest all the way through, because if he is not, you do not know quite where the breaking down will come.

Lawless violence: Here again remember that in time of mob violence all reform has to wait until order is restored. As a people it is gravely to our discredit that there should be so much unpunished murder, so many deeds of lawlessness and mob violence. Let the friend of the people who is severe upon the corruption of wealth make up his mind that he is a mighty poor public servant if he does not set his face against disorder when it takes the form of violence, just as much as against corruption. The man who can only see evil in the corruption of the rich, and the man who can only see evil in the lawless violence of the poor, stand on the same plane of bad citizenship. Keep order. War both against corruption and against lawless violence. That is what you and public officials need to keep in mind.

Now as to critics: I don't like the thief, but I like the liar just as little. The very fact that we need to have corruption in every phase unflinchingly exposed, the very fact that we need to have every man shown up who has acted improperly, because it is not merely a disgrace but a vital injury to us to permit corruption in public life or corruption in business life, that very fact emphasizes the wrong done by the man who without warrant accuses another of corruption. He has committed one of the cardinal sins against the body politic. It is not merely an injury to the man accused, it is an injury of the deepest type to the body politic, because after awhile, when accusations are continually and sweepingly made against all men, good and bad, the public as a whole grow to believe in each accusation a little and in no accusation entirely, so that they grow to believe that there is a little something bad about the decent man and that there is not much bad about the crook. No greater harm can be done to the body politic than by those men who, through reckless and indiscriminate accusation of good men and bad man, honest men and dishonest men alike, finally so hopelessly puzzle the public that they do not believe that any man in public life is entirely straight; while, on the other hand, they lose all indignation against the man who really is crooked. Greatly though I scorn and despise the corrupt public servant, greatly though I wish to see him punished with the utmost severity of the law, my scorn and contempt for him are no greater than for the man who by mendacity and through slander attacks the character of honest men just as he attacks the character of dishonest men, and thereby does his best, be that best great or small, to tear down the pillar of the temple and bury us all under the ruins. I speak of the man who writes in the daily press. (*Loud applause.*)

I trust that it is not because this is a legislative assembly that you have applauded this more than what I said about public officials! Now, I will go with you to the last point in condemning the man who in the public press writes an untruth, if you will go with me to the last point in condemning equally actively the legislator who acts corruptly. Now, I will resume my sentence where I left off. I speak of the man who writes in the public press. I speak of the man who writes in the magazines. I speak of the politician on the stump.

(*A pause: Silence.*)

Applaud! (*Loud applause.*)

I knew I would get it when I pointed out the need of it! Judge men not by the class to which they belong, but by their conduct as individuals. The only man who I think is a little more useful than the wise and honest public official is the wise and honest man in the press, and the only man who I think is a little more noxious than the dishonest public official is the untruthful man in the public press. I will make myself perfectly clear. I ask you to stand by the official who is honest; I ask you to stand by the newspaper man and magazine writer who truthfully exposes corruption; and I ask you to stand against the official scoundrel who is dishonest and his equally base brother in the press who falsely accuses an honest man of dishonesty.

I thank you for the patience with which you have listened to me, and I am very glad I finally got all the applause I wanted at the points I wanted it.[1]

III

In Bunyan's *Pilgrim's Progress* you may recall the description of the Man with the Muck-rake, the man who could look no way but downward, with the muck-rake in his hand; who was offered a celestial crown for his muck-rake, but who would neither look up nor regard the crown he was offered, but continued to rake to himself the filth of the floor.

In *Pilgrim's Progress* the Man with the Muck-rake is set forth as the example of him whose vision is fixed on carnal instead of on spiritual things. Yet he also typifies the man who in this life consistently refuses to see aught

[1] Speech before the Colorado Legislature, Denver, August 29, 1910. From *The New Nationalism*. Copyright, 1910. The Outlook Company, publishers.

that is lofty, and fixes his eyes with solemn intentness only on that which is vile and debasing. Now, it is very necessary that we should not flinch from seeing what is vile and debasing. There is filth on the floor, and it must be scraped up with the muck-rake; and there are times and places where this service is the most needed of all the services that can be performed. But the man who never does anything else, who never thinks or speaks or writes, save of his feats with the muck-rake, speedily becomes, not a help to society, not an incitement to good, but one of the most potent forces for evil.

There are, in the body politic, economic and social, many and grave evils, and there is urgent necessity for the sternest war upon them. There should be relentless exposure of and attack upon every evil man whether politician or business man, every evil practice, whether in politics, in business, or in social life. I hail as a benefactor every writer or speaker, every man who, on the platform, or in book, magazine, or newspaper, with merciless severity makes such attack, provided always that he in his turn remembers that the attack is of use only if it is absolutely truthful. The liar is no whit better than the thief, and if his mendacity takes the form of slander, he may be worse than most thieves. It puts a premium upon knavery untruthfully to attack an honest man, or even with hysterical exaggeration to assail a bad man with untruth. An epidemic of indiscriminate assault upon character does no good, but very great harm. The soul of every scoundrel is gladdened whenever an honest man is assailed, or even when a scoundrel is untruthfully assailed.

Now, it is easy to twist out of shape what I have just

said, easy to affect to misunderstand it, and, if it is slurred over in repetition, not difficult really to misunderstand it. Some persons are sincerely incapable of understanding that to denounce mud slinging does not mean the endorsement of whitewashing; and both the interested individuals who need whitewashing, and those others who practice mud slinging, like to encourage such confusion of ideas. One of the chief counts against those who make indiscriminate assault upon men in business or men in public life, is that they invite a reaction which is sure to tell powerfully in favor of the unscrupulous scoundrel who really ought to be attacked, who ought to be exposed, who ought, if possible, to be put in the penitentiary. If Aristides is praised overmuch as just, people get tired of hearing it; and overcensure of the unjust finally and from similar reasons results in their favor. . . .

The men with the muck-rakes are often indispensable to the well-being of society; but only if they know when to stop raking the muck, and to look upward to the celestial crown above them, to the crown of worthy endeavor. There are beautiful things above and round about them; and if they gradually grow to feel that the whole world is nothing but muck, their power of usefulness is gone. If the whole picture is painted black there remains no hue whereby to single out the rascals for distinction from their fellows. Such painting finally induces a kind of moral color-blindness; and people affected by it come to the conclusion that no man is really black, and no man really white, but they are all gray. In other words, they neither believe in the truth of the attack, nor in the honesty of the man who is attacked; they grow as suspicious of the accusation as of the offense; it becomes well-nigh hopeless to stir them either to wrath against wrong doing or to enthusiasm for what is right; and such a mental attitude in the public gives hope to every knave, and is the despair of honest men.

To assail the great and admitted evils of our political and industrial life with such crude and sweeping generalizations as to include decent men in the general condemnation means the searing of the public conscience. There results a general attitude either of cynical belief in and indifference to public corruption or else of a distrustful inability to discriminate between the good and the bad. Either attitude is fraught with untold damage to the country as a whole. The fool who has not sense to discriminate between what is good and what is bad is well-nigh as dangerous as the man who does discriminate and yet chooses the bad. There is nothing more distressing to every good patriot, to every good American, than the hard, scoffing spirit which treats the allegation of dishonesty in a public man as a cause for laughter. Such laughter is worse than the crackling of thorns under a pot, for it denotes not merely the vacant mind, but the heart in which high emotions have been choked before they could grow to fruition.

There is any amount of good in the world, and there never was a time when loftier and more disinterested work for the betterment of mankind was being done than now. The forces that tend for evil are great and terrible, but the forces of truth and love and courage and honesty and generosity and sympathy are also stronger than ever before. It is a foolish and timid, no less than a wicked, thing to blink the fact that the forces of evil are strong, but it is even worse to fail to take into account the strength of the forces that tell for good. Hysterical sensationalism is the very poorest weapon wherewith to fight for lasting righteousness. The men who with stern sobriety and truth assail the many evils of our time, whether in the public press, or in magazines, or in books, are the leaders and allies of all engaged in the work for social and political betterment. But if they give good reason for distrust of what they say, if they chill the ardor of those who demand truth as a primary virtue, they thereby betray the good cause, and play into the hands of the very men against whom they are nominally at war.[1]

IV

IT is absolutely essential, if we are to have the proper standard of public life, that promise shall be square with performance. A lie is no more to be excused in politics than out of politics.

A promise is as binding on the stump as off the stump, and there are two facets to that crystal. In the first place, the man who makes a promise which he does not intend to keep, and does not try to keep, should rightly be adjudged to have forfeited in some degree what should be every man's most precious possession — his honor. On the other hand, the public that exacts a promise which ought not to be kept, or which cannot be kept, is by just so much forfeiting its rights to self-government. There is no surer way of destroying the capacity for self-government in a people than to

[1] Address at the Laying of the Corner-stone of the Office Building of the House of Representatives, Saturday, April 14, 1906.

accustom that people to demanding the impossible or the improper from its public men. No man fit to be a public man will promise either the impossible or the improper; and if the demand is made that he shall do so, it means putting a premium upon the unfit in public life.

There is the same sound reason for distrusting the man who promises too much in public that there is for distrusting the man who promises too much in private business. If you meet a doctor who asserts that he has a specific remedy that will cure all the ills to which human flesh is heir, distrust him. He has n't got it. If you meet the business man who vociferates that he is always selling everything to you at a loss, and you continue to deal with him, I am glad if you suffer for it. Any man who promises, as a result of legislation or administration, the millennium is making a promise which he will find difficulty in keeping. Any man who asserts that by any law it will be possible, out of hand, to make all humanity good and wise, is again promising what he cannot perform. It is indispensable that we should have good laws and upright and honest and fearless administration of the laws; and we are not to be excused if we fail to hold our public men to a rigid accountability if they fail, in their turn, to see that we have proper legislation and proper administration. No public man worth his salt will be other than glad to be held accountable in that fashion.[1]

[1] Address at the Union League Club of San Francisco, California, May 14, 1903.

IV. REALIZABLE IDEALS

I

ONE of the besetting sins of many of our public servants (and of not a few of our professional moralists, lay and clerical) is to cloak weakness or baseness of action behind insincere oratory on behalf of impractical ideals. The true servant of the people is the man who preaches realizable ideals; and who then practices what he has preached.[1]

II

I REGARD the study of ethics pursued merely as an intellectual recreation as being about as worthless as any form of mental amusement can be. In the course of my life I have had to deliver a good many lay sermons — my enemies being divided as to whether the sentiments that I utter are incitements to revolution or platitudes, and usually compromising by saying that they are both — I have had to deliver a good many sermons, and the more often I have had either to speak, or to listen to others speak, the more clearly and deeply I realize that it is not only no good to preach, or to listen to, a sermon which is not put into practical effect, but that it is a positive damage. The man who utters moral sentiments to which he does not try to live up, and the other man who listens and applauds the utterance of those sentiments and yet himself does not try to live up to

[1] From *Fear God and Take Your Own Part.* Copyright, 1916. George H. Doran Company, publishers.

them — both those men not only gain no good from what they have said and listened to, but have done themselves positive harm, because they have weakened just a little the spring of conscience within them.

I believe, to the last degree, in the duty of the man who preaches to preach realizable ideals. Of course, when I say realizable, I do not mean that we can completely realize any ideal. When in battle you spur your men on to perform some deed of valor and prowess, it is impossible that all of them shall live up to what your words call them to do. But what you have said in battle to your men is absolutely worthless, no matter how high and exalted the sentiment, unless it does make a reasonable proportion of the soldiers to whom it is addressed move forward into the battle and do their duty reasonably well. The word of command is useless in the fight unless a reasonable number of those to whom it is uttered not only listen to it but act upon it; and the man who utters it will not find that the other men to whom he utters it will pay much heed to it unless they know he is prepared himself to show them the way.

Now, friends, that is rather elementary. The word of command, you understand, is a "platitude." Every adjuration to men in a great crisis to bear themselves well is such a "platitude"; but it is a mighty useful platitude to translate into action. It is rather elementary, but after all it gives the exact analogue to what I mean should be our attitude in civil life. The preacher, whether he is in the pulpit or whether he is a lay preacher, whether he is a professor, an adviser, or a lecturer — the preacher is really trying to give the word of command, the word of direction and encouragement, to the men whom he is addressing; and if he gives that word simply to get himself a sense of intellectual satisfaction at having given it, and if his hearers listen to it only as they would to any other form of entertainment, then it is not worth while for him to have spoken and it is not worth while for them to have listened. The only value in a speech comes from there being the effort made with measurable success to translate the words into deeds. Of course, the man who preaches decency and straight dealing occupies a peculiarly contemptible position if he does not try himself to practice what he preaches; and, on the other hand, the men who listen to him — you here — should realize that if they treat listening to a lecture about their duties as a substitute for performing their duties they would better have stayed at home. The value of what is said arises solely from the effort measurably to realize it in action.[1]

III

IT is a misfortune for any people when the paths of the practical and the theoretical politicians diverge so widely that they have no common standing-ground. When the Greek thinkers began to devote their attention to purely visionary politics of the kind found in Plato's Republic, while the Greek practical politicians simply exploited the quarrelsome little commonwealths in their own interests, then the end of Greek liberty was at hand. No government that cannot command the respectful support of the best thinkers is in an entirely sound condition; but it is well to keep in mind the re-

[1] From *Applied Ethics*. Copyright, 1911. Harvard University Press, publishers.

mark of Frederick the Great, that if he wished to punish a province, he would allow it to be governed by the philosophers. It is a great misfortune for the country when the practical politician and the doctrinaire have no point in common, but the misfortune is, if anything, greatest for the doctrinaire.[1]

IV

"COMPROMISE" is so often used in a bad sense that it is difficult to remember that properly it merely describes the process of reaching an agreement. Naturally there are certain subjects on which no man can compromise. For instance, there must be no compromise under any circumstances with official corruption, and of course no man should hesitate to say as much. Again, an honest politician is entirely justified in promising on the stump that he will make no compromise on any question of right and wrong. This promise he can and ought to make good. But when questions of policy arise — and most questions, from the tariff to municipal ownership of public utilities and the franchise tax, are primarily questions of policy — he will have to come to some kind of working agreement with his fellows, and if he says that he will not, he either deliberately utters what he knows to be false, or else he insures for himself the humiliation of being forced to break his word. No decent politician need compromise in any way save as Washington and Lincoln did. He need not go nearly as far as Hamilton, Jefferson, and Jackson went; but some dis-

[1] From *American Ideals*. Copyright, 1897. G. P. Putnam's Sons, New York and London, publishers.

tance he must go if he expects to accomplish any-thing.[1]

V

ONLY peoples capable, not merely of mastering others, but of mastering themselves, can achieve real liberty, can achieve real self-government.[2]

[1] From *The Strenuous Life*. Copyright, 1900. The Century Company, publishers.
[2] Remarks at the Dinner of the Periodical Publishers' Association of America, Washington, D.C., April 7, 1904.

III

JUST GOVERNMENT — THE BASIS OF NATIONAL UNITY

I. GOVERNMENT AND BUSINESS

I

NOTHING needs closer attention, nothing deserves to be treated with more courage, caution, and sanity, than the relations of the State to corporate wealth, and indeed to vast individual wealth. For almost every gain there is a penalty, and the great strides in the industrial up-building of the country, which have on the whole been attended with marked benefit, have also been attended by no little evil. Great fortunes are usually made under very complex conditions both of effort and of surroundings, and the mere fact of the complexity makes it difficult to deal with the new conditions thus created. The contrast offered in a highly specialized industrial community between the very rich and the very poor is exceedingly distressing, and while under normal conditions the acquirement of wealth by an individual is necessarily of great incidental benefit to the community as a whole, yet this is by no means always the case. In our great cities there is plainly in evidence much wealth contrasted with much poverty, and some of the wealth has been acquired, or is used, in a manner for which there is no moral justification.

A profound political and social thinker has recently

written: "Wealth which is expended in multiplying and elaborating real comforts, or even in pleasures which produce enjoyment at all proportionate to their cost, will never excite serious indignation. It is the colossal waste of the means of human happiness in the most selfish and most vulgar forms of social advertisement and competition that gives a force to passions which menace the whole future of our civilization." But in continuance this writer points out that the only effectual check lies in the law of public opinion. Any attempt to interfere by statute in moral questions of this kind, by fettering the freedom of individual action, would be injurious to a degree far greater than is the evil aimed at. Probably the large majority of the fortunes that now exist in this country have been amassed, not by injuring mankind, but as an incident to the conferring of great benefits on the community — whatever the conscious purpose of those amassing them may have been. The occasional wrongs committed or injuries endured are on the whole far outweighed by the mass of good which has resulted. The true questions to be asked are: Has any given individual been injured by the acquisition of wealth by any man? Were the rights of that individual, if they have been violated, insufficiently protected by law? If so, these rights, and all similar rights, ought to be guaranteed by additional legislation. The point to be aimed at is the protection of the individual against wrong, not the attempt to limit and hamper the acquisition and output of wealth.

It is almost equally dangerous either to blink evils and refuse to acknowledge their existence, or to strike at them in a spirit of ignorant revenge, thereby doing far more harm than is remedied. The need can be met only by careful study of conditions, and by action which while taken boldly and without hesitation is neither heedless nor reckless. It is well to remember on the one hand that the adoption of what is reasonable in the demands of reformers is the surest way to prevent the adoption of what is unreasonable; and on the other hand that many of the worst and most dangerous laws which have been put upon statute books have been put there by zealous reformers with excellent intentions.

This problem has a hundred phases. The relation of the capitalist and the wage-worker makes one; the proper attitude of the State toward extreme poverty another; the proper attitude of the State toward the questions of the ownership and running of so-called "public utilities," a third. But among all these phases, the one which at this time has the greatest prominence, is the question of what are commonly termed "trusts," meaning by the name those vast combinations of capital, usually flourishing by virtue of some monopolistic element, which have become so startlingly common a feature in the industrial revolution which has progressed so rapidly during recent years.

The machinery of modern business is so vast and complicated that great caution must be exercised in introducing radical changes for fear the unforeseen effects may take the shape of widespread disaster. Moreover, much that is complained about is not really the abuse so much as the inevitable development of our modern industrial life. We have moved far away from the old simple days when each community transacted almost all its work for itself and relied upon outsiders for but a fraction of the necessaries, and for not a very large portion even of the luxuries, of life. Very many of the anti-trust laws which have made their appearance on the statute books of recent years have been almost or absolutely ineffective because they have blinked the all-important fact that much of what they thought to do away with was incidental to modern industrial conditions, and could not be eliminated unless we were willing to turn back the wheels of modern progress by also eliminating the forces which had brought about these industrial conditions. Not only trusts, but the immense importance of machinery, the congestion of city life, the capacity to make large fortunes by speculative enterprises, and many other features of modern existence could be thoroughly changed by doing away with steam and electricity; but the most ardent denouncer of trusts would hesitate to advocate so drastic a remedy. What remains for us to do, as practical men, is to look the conditions squarely in the face and not to permit the emotional side of the question, which has its proper place, to blind us to the fact that there are other sides. We must set about finding out what the real abuses are, with their causes, and to what extent remedies can be applied.

That abuses exist, and that they are of a very grave character, it is worse than idle to deny. Just so long as in the business world unscrupulous cunning is allowed the free rein which, thanks to the growth of humanity during the past centuries, we now deny to unscrupulous physical force, then just so long there will be a field for the best effort of every honest social and civic reformer who is capable of feeling an impulse of generous indignation and who is far-sighted enough to appreciate where the real danger to the country lies. The effects are bad enough when the unscrupulous individual works by himself. They are much worse when he works in conjunction with his fellows through a giant corporation or trust. Law is largely crystallized custom, largely a mass of remedies which have been slowly evolved to meet the wrongs with which humanity has become thoroughly familiar. In a simple society only simple forms of wrong can be committed. There is neither the ability nor the opportunity to inflict others. A primitive people provides for the punishment of theft, assault, and murder, because the conditions of the existing society allow the development of thieves and murderers and the commission of deeds of violence; but it does not provide for the punishment of forgery because there is nothing to forge, and, therefore, no forgers. The gradual growth of humanitarian sentiment, often unconscious or but semi-conscious, combined with other causes, step by step emancipated the serf from bodily subjection to his over-lord; he was then protected in his freedom by statute; but when he became a factory hand the conditions were new and there were no laws which prevented the use of unguarded machinery in the factories, or the abuses of child labor, forced upon the conscientious employers by the unscrupulous, until legislation put them on an equality. When new evils appear there is always at first difficulty in finding the proper remedy; and as the evils grow more complex, the remedies become increasingly difficult of application. There is no use whatever in seeking to apply a remedy blindly; yet this is just what has been done in reference to trusts.

Much of the legislation not only proposed but enacted

against trusts is not one whit more intelligent than the mediæval bull against the comet, and has not been one particle more effective. Yet there can and must be courageous and effective remedial legislation.

To say that the present system, of haphazard license and lack of supervision and regulation, is the best possible, is absurd. The men who endeavor to prevent the remedying of real abuses, not only show callous disregard for the suffering of others, but also weaken those who are anxious to prevent the adoption of indiscriminate would-be remedies which would subvert our whole industrial fabric. The chicanery and the dishonest, even though not technically illegal, methods through which some great fortunes have been made, are scandals to our civilization. The man who by swindling or wrongdoing acquires great wealth for himself at the expense of his fellow, stands as low morally as any predatory mediæval nobleman and is a more dangerous member of society. Any law, and any method of construing the law which will enable the community to punish him, either by taking away his wealth or by imprisonment, should be welcomed. Of course, such laws are even more needed in dealing with great corporations or trusts than with individuals. They are needed quite as much for the sake of honest corporations as for the sake of the public. The corporation that manages its affairs honestly has a right to demand protection against the dishonest corporation. We do not wish to put any burden on honest corporations. Neither do we wish to put an unnecessary burden of responsibility on enterprising men for acts which are immaterial; they should be relieved from such burdens, but held to a rigid financial accountability for acts that mislead the upright investor or stockholder, or defraud the public.

The first essential is knowledge of the facts, publicity. Much can be done at once by amendment of the corporation laws so as to provide for such publicity as will not work injustice as between business rivals.

The chief abuses alleged to arise from trusts are probably the following: Misrepresentation or concealment regarding material facts connected with the organization of an enterprise; the evils connected with unscrupulous promotion; overcapitalization; unfair competition, resulting in the crushing out of competitors who themselves do not act improperly; raising of prices above fair competitive rates; the wielding of increased power over the wage-earners. Of course none of these abuses may exist in a particular trust, but in many trusts, as well as in many corporations not ordinarily called trusts, one or more of them is evident. Some of these evils could be partially remedied by a modification of our corporation laws; here we can safely go along the lines of the more conservative New England States, and probably not a little farther. Such laws will themselves provide the needed publicity, and the needed circumstantiality of statement. We should know authoritatively whether stock represents actual value of plants, or whether it represents brands or good-will; or if not, what it does represent, if anything. It is desirable to know how much was actually bought, how much was issued free; and to whom; and, if possible, for what reason. In the first place, this would be invaluable in preventing harm being done as among the stockholders, for many of the grossest wrongs that are perpetrated are those of promoters and organizers at the expense of the general public who are invited to take shares in business organizations. In the next place, this would enable us to see just what the public have a right to expect in the way of service and taxation. There is no reason whatever for refusing to tax a corporation because by its own acts it has created a burden of charges under which it staggers. The extravagant man who builds a needlessly large house nevertheless pays taxes on the house; and the corporation which has to pay great sums of interest owing to juggling transactions in the issue of stocks and bonds has just as little right to consideration. But very great hardship may result to innocent purchasers; and publicity by lessening the possibility of this would also serve the purpose of the State.

Where a trust becomes a monopoly the State has an immediate right to interfere. Care should be taken not to stifle enterprise or disclose any facts of a business that are essentially private; but the State for the protection of the public should exercise the right to inspect, to examine thoroughly all the workings of great corporations just as is now done with banks; and wherever the interests of the public demand it, it should publish the results of its examination. Then, if there are inordinate profits, competition or public sentiment will give the public the benefit in lowered prices; and if not, the power of taxation remains. It is therefore evident that publicity is the one sure and adequate remedy which we can now invoke. There may be other remedies, but what these others are we can only find out by publicity, as the result of investigation. The first requisite is knowledge, full and complete.[1]

[1] Annual message as Governor of New York State (1900).

II

I AM going to speak, as you would have the right to expect me to speak, of what affects us at the present moment here in this State, of one of those problems with which we, who are for the time being your servants and representatives in public life, are trying to deal — the question of the taxation of franchises.

On the one hand we have the perfectly simple savage who believes that you should tax franchises to the extent of confiscating them, and that it is the duty of all railroad corporations to carry everybody free and give him a chromo.

On the other, we have the scarcely less primitive mortal who believes that there is something sacred in a franchise and that there is no reason why it should pay its share of the public burdens at all.

Now, gentlemen, remember that the man who occupies the last position inevitably tends to produce the man who occupies the first position, and that the worst enemy of property is the man who, whether from unscrupulousness or from mere heedlessness and thoughtlessness, takes the ground that there is something sacrosanct about all property, that the owners of it are to occupy a different position in the community from all others and are to have their burdens not increased, but diminished, because of their wealth. Oh, if I could only impress upon you, if I only had the eloquence and the power of enforcing conviction upon you to make you understand the two sides of the question — not understand it; you may do that in theory now — but to make you realize it, the two sides, that the rich man who buys a privilege from a board of aldermen for a railway which he represents, the rich man who gets a privilege through the Legislature by bribery and corruption, for any corporation, is committing an offense against the community, which it is possible may some day have to be condoned in blood and destruction, not by him, not by his sons, but by you and your sons. If I could only make you understand that, on one side, and make you, the mass of our people, the mass of our voters understand, on the other, that the worst thing they can do is to choose a representative who shall say, "I am against corporations; I am against capital," and not a man who shall say, "I stand by the Ten Commandments; I stand by doing equal justice to the man of means and the man without means; I stand by saying that no man shall be stolen from and that no man shall steal from any one else; I stand by saying that the corporation shall not be blackmailed, on the one side, and that the corporations shall not acquire any improper power by corruption, on the other; that the corporation shall pay its full share of the public burdens, and that when it does so it shall be protected in its rights exactly as any one else is protected." In other words, if I could only make our people realize that their one hope and one safety in dealing with this problem is to send into our public bodies men who shall be honest, who shall realize their obligations to rich and poor alike, and who shall draw the line, not between the rich man and the poor man, but between the honest man and the dishonest man.

Now, gentlemen, . . . I have not any new doctrine to declare to you. The doctrine that I preach, the doctrine that all men who wish their country well must preach, is a doctrine that was old when the children of Israel came out of Egypt; a doctrine as old as our civilization; as old as the civilizations that died thousands of years before ours was born; the doctrine that teaches us that men shall prosper as long as they do their duty to themselves and their neighbors alike; the doctrine that we shall thrive as long as we believe in those archaic rules of conduct which were set down in the Sermon on the Mount.[1]

III

WE are passing through a period of great commercial prosperity, and such a period is as sure as adversity itself to bring mutterings of discontent. At a time when most men prosper somewhat some men always prosper greatly; and it is as true now as when the tower of Siloam fell upon all alike, that good fortune does not come solely to the just, nor bad fortune solely to the unjust. When the weather is good for crops it is good for weeds. Moreover, not only do the wicked flourish when the times are such that most men flourish, but, what is worse, the spirit of envy and jealousy springs up in the breasts of those who, though they may be doing fairly well themselves, see others no more deserving, who do better.

Wise laws and fearless and upright administration of the laws can give the opportunity for such prosperity as we see about us. But that is all that they can do. When the conditions have been created which make prosperity possible, then each individual man must achieve it for himself, by his own energy and thrift and business intelligence. If when people wax fat they kick, as they have

[1] Address at the Independent Club, Buffalo, New York, May 15, 1899.

kicked since the days of Jeshurun, they will speedily destroy their own prosperity. If they go into wild specula-
tion and lose their heads, they have lost that which no
laws can supply. If in a spirit of sullen envy they insist
upon pulling down those who have profited most in the
years of fatness, they will bury themselves in the crash
of the common disaster. It is difficult to make our material condition better by the best laws, but it is easy
enough to ruin it by bad laws.

The upshot of all this is that it is peculiarly incumbent
upon us in a time of such material well-being, both collectively as a nation and individually as citizens, to
show, each on his own account, that we possess the
qualities of prudence, self-knowledge, and self-restraint.
In our Government we need above all things stability,
fixity of economic policy, while remembering that this
fixity must not be fossilization, that there must not be
inability to shift our laws so as to meet our shifting national needs. There are real and great evils in our social
and economic life, and these evils stand out in all their
ugly baldness in time of prosperity; for the wicked who
prosper are never a pleasant sight. There is every need
of striving in all possible ways, individually and collectively, by combinations among ourselves and through
the recognized governmental agencies, to cut out those
evils. All I ask is to be sure that we do not use the knife
with an ignorant zeal which would make it more dangerous to the patient than to the disease. . . .

We meet a peculiar difficulty under our system of
government, because of the division of governmental
power between the Nation and the States. When the
industrial conditions were simple, very little control was

needed, and the difficulties of exercising such control under our Constitution were not evident. Now the conditions are complicated and we find it hard to frame national legislation which shall be adequate; while as a matter of practical experience it has been shown that the States either cannot or will not exercise a sufficient control to meet the needs of the case. Some of our States have excellent laws — laws which it would be well indeed to have enacted by the national legislature. But the widespread differences in these laws, even between adjacent States, and the uncertainty of the power of enforcement, result practically in altogether insufficient control. I believe that the Nation must assume this power of control by legislation; if necessary, by constitutional amendment. The immediate necessity in dealing with trusts is to place them under the real, not the nominal, control of some sovereign to which, as its creatures, the trusts shall owe allegiance, and in whose courts the sovereign's orders may be enforced.

In my judgment this sovereign must be the National Government. When it has been given full power, then this full power can be used to control any evil influence, exactly as the Government is now using the power conferred upon it by the Sherman anti-trust law.

Even when the power has been granted, it would be most unwise to exercise it too much, to begin by too stringent legislation. The mechanism of modern business is as delicate and complicated as it is vast, and nothing would be more productive of evil to all of us, and especially to those least well off in this world's goods, than ignorant meddling with this mechanism — above all, meddling in a spirit of class legislation or hatred or rancor. It is eminently necessary that the power should be had, but it is just as necessary that it should be exercised with wisdom and self-restraint. The first exercise of that power should be the securing of publicity among all great corporations doing an interstate business. The publicity, though non-inquisitorial, should be real and thorough as to all important facts with which the public has concern. Daylight is a powerful discourager of evil. Such publicity would by itself tend to cure the evils of which there is just complaint; it would show us if evils existed, and where the evils are imaginary, and it would show us what next ought to be done.

Above all, let us remember that our success in accomplishing anything depends very much upon our not trying to accomplish everything. Distrust whoever pretends to offer you a patent cure-all for every ill of the body politic, just as you would a man who offers a medicine which would cure every evil of your individual body. A medicine that is recommended to cure both asthma and a broken leg is not good for either. Mankind has moved slowly upward through the ages, sometimes a little faster, sometimes a little slower, but rarely, indeed, by leaps and bounds. At times a great crisis comes in which a great people, perchance led by a great man, can at white heat strike some mighty blow for the right — make a long stride in advance along the path of justice and of orderly liberty. But normally we must be content if each of us can do something — not all that we wish, but something — for the advancement of those principles of righteousness which underlie all real national greatness, all true civilization and freedom. I see no promise of any immediate and complete solution of all the problems we group together when we speak of the trust question. But we can make a beginning in solving these problems, and a good beginning, if only we approach the subject with a sufficiency of resolution, of honesty, and of that hard common sense which is one of the most valuable, and not always one of the most common, assets in any nation's greatness. The existing laws will be fully enforced as they stand on the statute books without regard to persons, and I think good has already come from their enforcement. I think furthermore that additional legislation should be had and can be had, which will enable us to accomplish much more along the same lines. No man can promise a perfect solution, at least in the immediate future. But something has already been done, and much more can be done if our people temperately and determinedly will that it shall be done.[1]

IV

THE "business" which is hurt by the movement for honesty is the kind of business which, in the long run, it pays the country to have hurt. It is the kind of business which has tended to make the very name "high finance" a term of scandal to which all honest American men of business should join in putting an end. The special pleaders for business dishonesty, in denouncing the present Administration for enforcing the law against the huge and corrupt corporations which have defied the law, also denounce it for endeavoring to secure sadly needed labor legislation, such as a far-reaching law mak-

[1] Address at Providence, Rhode Island, August 23, 1902.

ing employers liable for injuries to their employees. It
is meet and fit that the apologists for corrupt wealth
should oppose every effort to relieve weak and helpless
people from crushing misfortune brought upon them by
injury in the business from which they gain a bare livelihood. The burden should be distributed. It is hypocrit-
ical baseness to speak of a girl who works in a factory
where the dangerous machinery is unprotected as having
the "right" freely to contract to expose herself to dangers to life and limb. She has no alternative but to suffer want or else to expose herself to such dangers, and
when she loses a hand or is otherwise maimed or disfig-
ured for life, it is a moral wrong that the whole burden
of the risk necessarily incidental to the business should
be placed with crushing weight upon her weak shoulders,
and all who profit by her work escape scot-free. This is
what opponents of a just employers' liability law advocate; and it is consistent that they should usually also
advocate immunity for those most dangerous members
of the criminal class — the criminals of great wealth.

The opponents of the measures we champion single
out now one and now another measure for especial attack, and speak as if the movement in which we are engaged was purely economic. It has a large economic side,
but it is fundamentally an ethical movement. We are
trying to secure equality of opportunity for all; and the
struggle for honesty is the same whether it is made on
behalf of one set of men or of another. In the interest of
the small settlers and landowners, and against the em-
bittered opposition of wealthy owners of huge wandering flocks of sheep, or of corporations desiring to rob the
people of coal and timber, we strive to put an end to the

theft of public land in the West. When we do this, and protest against the action of all men, whether in public life or in private life, who either take part in or refuse to try to stop such theft, we are really engaged in the same policy as when we endeavor to put a stop to rebates or to prevent the upgrowth of uncontrolled monopolies. Our effort is simply to enforce the principles of common honesty and common sense. It would indeed be ill for the country should there be any halt in our work.[1]

V

LINCOLN was a great radical. He was of course a wise and cautious radical — otherwise he could have done nothing for the forward movement. But he was the efficient leader of this forward movement. To-day many well-meaning men who have permitted themselves to fossilize, to become mere ultraconservative reactionaries, to reject and oppose all progress, but who still pay a conventional and perfunctory homage to Lincoln's memory, will do well to remember exactly what it was for which this great conservative leader of radicalism actually stood.

Much of what he said applies, with only a change of names, to the conditions of our own time.

In October, 1854, when it was objected that the course he advocated included some action demanded by the Northern abolitionists, and other action demanded by the Southern disunionists, to both of whom he had been opposed, he answered: "Stand with anybody that stands right. Stand with him while he is right and part

[1] Message communicated to the two Houses of Congress, January 31, 1908.

with him when he goes wrong. Stand with the aboli-
tionist in restoring the Missouri Compromise and stand
against him in attempting to repeal the Fugitive Slave
Law. In the latter case you stand with the Southern
disunionist. What of that? You are still right. In both
cases you are right. In both cases you oppose the dangerous extremes. In both you stand on middle ground
and hold the ship steady and level. In both you are national and nothing less than national. To desert such
ground because of any company is to be less than a man
— less than an American." And he remarked of those
who took the opposite view that he must be allowed "to
tell them, good-humoredly," that their course was "very
silly."

In precisely similar fashion to-day we find conservatives objecting to some piece of wise legislation because
it is demanded by the socialists, and radicals objecting
to some piece of wise legislation of another kind, because
it is looked upon favorably by Wall Street. In Lincoln's
words we must be allowed good-humoredly to say that
both attitudes are very silly — equally so whether we always oppose the Socialists or always oppose Wall Street.
In one case we uphold what the Socialists demand, in
the other case what Wall Street favors. In Lincoln's
words: "What of it? We are still right. In both cases
we are right."

In 1859 Lincoln announced as the true doctrine that
"the rights of property" are secondary to the "personal
rights of men," and that he was "for both the man and
the dollar, but in case of conflict, the man before the dollar"; and he added the pregnant sentence: "He who
would be no slave must consent to have no slave. Those

who deny freedom to others deserve it not for them-selves." This applied to black slavery then. It applies now to any wealthy corporation which fails to respect and preserve and encourage all the manhood rights of its workers and to treat them as partners; and it no less applies to any powerful labor union which shows brutality or insolent disregard for equity in dealing with the rights of any of our citizens. . . .

Lincoln's belief in the superiority of the rights of labor to those of capital was expressed again and again, but Lincoln also stood for the rights of capital; and here again we should follow his policy. If the laboring man permits himself to put improper burdens on capital, he will bring everything down with a crash; and even if the man higher up is smashed, this will be small comfort to the man lower down if he, too, is under the ruins. Lincoln explicitly disclaimed any hostility to a man because he was wealthy. He explicitly asserted that the accumulation of individual property was "right, and for the general good." He held up as the proper ideal, not burning down the house of another, but building up a house for one's self — a corollary to which is that it is better for the owner of a small house that another man should have a big house, rather than that neither should have any house. In other words, he believed in a constructive system which, while guarding the rights of capital, should see that the benefits were as widely diffused as possible and that all artificial obstacles to a fair start in the world, and to industrial democracy, were done away with. Finally, it is evident that, although he neither used modern terminology nor was familiar with modern industry, his ideal was a coöperative system in which each man labored and each man was to some extent an owner of the capital necessary for the work. . . .

In Lincoln's day, as in our day, there were wise men and foolish men, good men and evil men, both among those who called themselves conservatives and among those who called themselves radicals; and sometimes emphasis had to be placed on the need of daring, and sometimes on the need of caution. It was the radicals who were most interested in the destruction of slavery; and in this the radicals were right; and although Lincoln held them back, and steadied them and waited until the fullness of time, yet in the end he led them to victory. But on the whole the radicals put the destruction of slavery above the preservation of the Union, and herein they were wrong; and the conservatives took the reverse view, and herein they were right, and Lincoln sided with them; and in the end they followed him when he saw that it was best to make one cause both of freeing the slave and of saving the nation. From all his record it is safe to say that if Lincoln had lived to deal with our complicated social and industrial problems he would have furnished a wisely conservative leadership; but he would have led in the radical direction.[1]

VI

I BELIEVE in a steady effort, or perhaps it would be more accurate to say in steady efforts in many different directions, to bring about a condition of affairs under which the men who work with hand or with brain, the laborers, the superintendents, the men who produce for the market

[1] From *The Foes of Our Own Household*. Copyright, 1917. George H. Doran Company, publishers.

and the men who find a market for the articles produced, shall own a far greater share than at present of the wealth they produce, and be enabled to invest it in the tools and instruments by which all work is carried on. As far as possible I hope to see a frank recognition of the advantages conferred by machinery, organization, and division of labor, accompanied by an effort to bring about a larger share in the ownership by wage-workers of railway, mill, and factory. In farming, this simply means that we wish to see the farmer own his own land; we do not wish to see the farms so large that they become the property of absentee landlords who farm them by tenants, nor yet so small that the farmer becomes like a European peasant. Again, the depositors in our savings banks now number over one-tenth of our entire population. These are all capitalists, who through the savings banks loan their money to the workers — that is, in many cases to themselves — to carry on their various industries. The more we increase their number, the more we introduce the principles of coöperation into our industry. Every increase in the number of small stockholders in corporations is a good thing, for the same reasons; and where the employees are the stockholders the result is particularly good. Very much of this movement must be outside of anything that can be accomplished by legislation; but legislation can do a good deal. Postal savings banks will make it easy for the poorest to keep their savings in absolute safety. The regulation of the National highways must be such that they shall serve all people and with equal justice. Corporate finances must be supervised so as to make it far safer than at present for the man of small means to invest his money in

stocks. There must be prohibition of child labor, diminution of woman labor, shortening of hours of all me-
chanical labor; stock watering should be prohibited, and
stock gambling so far as is possible discouraged. There
should be a progressive inheritance tax on large fortunes.
Industrial education should be encouraged. As far as
possible we should lighten the burden of taxation on the
small man. We should put a premium upon thrift, hard
work, and business energy; but these qualities cease to
be the main factors in accumulating a fortune long before that fortune reaches a point where it would be seriously affected by any inheritance tax such as I propose.
It is eminently right that the Nation should fix the
terms upon which the great fortunes are inherited. They
rarely do good and they often do harm to those who inherit them in their entirety.

The above is the merest sketch, hardly even a sketch
in outline, of the reforms for which we should work.[1]

[1] Message communicated to the two Houses of Congress, December 8, 1908.

II. LABOR UNIONS

WAGES and other most important conditions of employment must remain largely outside of government control; must be left for adjustment by free contract between employers and wage-earners, subject — and I call your attention to the proviso — to legislation which will prevent conditions which compel men or women to accept wages representing less than will insure decent living. But to attempt to leave the question of contract between employer and employee merely to individual action means the absolute destruction of individualism; for where the individual is so weak that he, perforce, has to accept whatever a strongly organized body chooses to give him, his individual liberty becomes a mere sham and mockery. It is indispensably necessary, in order to preserve to the largest degree our system of individualism, that there should be effective and organized collective action. The wage-earners must act jointly, through the process of collective bargaining, in great industrial enterprises. Only thus can they be put upon a plane of economic equality with their corporate employers. Only thus is freedom of contract made a real thing and not a mere legal fiction. There are occasional occupations where this is not necessary; but, speaking broadly, it is necessary throughout the great world of organized industry. I believe this practice of collective bargaining, effective only through such organizations as the trades unions, to have been one of the most potent forces in the past century in promoting the progress of the wage-earners and in securing larger social progress for humanity. Wherever there is organized capital on a considerable scale I believe in the principle of organized labor and in the practice of collective bargaining, not merely as a desirable thing for the wage-earners, but as something which has been demonstrated to be essential in the long run to their permanent progress. Where capital is organized, as it must be organized under modern industrial conditions, the only way to secure proper freedom — proper treatment — for the individual laborer is to have labor organize also.

This does not mean that I unequivocally endorse any or all practices that labor organizations may happen to adopt, or any or all principles that they may choose to enunciate. Labor organizations have the weaknesses and defects common to all forms of human organizations. When any man tells you that the laboring man never goes wrong, make up your minds that he is telling you what he knows to be an untruth, and distrust him accordingly; for it is a good old principle to act upon in the long run, that the most uncomfortable truth is a safer traveling companion that the pleasantest falsehood. Sometimes labor organizations act very well, and sometimes, like the rest of mankind, they act very badly; and I am for them when they act well, and I am against them when they act badly. I believe that their existence is a necessity; I believe that their aims and purposes are generally good; and I believe that all of them have occasionally made mistakes, and that some of them have been guilty of wrongdoing. Just in so far as they are strong and effective they tempt designing men who seek to control them for their own interests, and stimulate the desires of ambitious leaders who may be clever, crooked men, or who may be honest but visionary and foolish. In other words, in treating of labor unions, as in treating of corporations, or of humanity generally, we shall do well to remember Abraham Lincoln's saying that "there is a deal of human nature in mankind."

I think that the next quarter of a century will be important politically in many ways (I do not use the word "politically" in the way of party politics; but I am speaking of the social development of our people); and in none more so than in the labor movement. Not only are the benefits of labor organizations more clearly understood than before, but any shortcoming or vice displayed in connection therewith is also more clearly understood and more quickly resented. Just as it is with corporations, just so it is with railroads. Forty years ago the railroads could do with absolute impunity, and without any criticism, things which would cause well nigh a revolution if they attempted them now. The public is growing more and more to understand that, in a contest between employer and employee — a corporation and a trades union — not only the interests of the contestants, but the interests of the third party — the public — must be considered. Anything like levity in provoking a strike, on the one hand or on the other, is certain more and more to be resented by the public. Strikes are sometimes necessary and proper; sometimes they represent the only way in which, after all other methods have been exhausted, it is possible for the laboring man to stand up for his rights; but it must be clearly understood that a strike is a matter of last resort, and, of course, violence, lawlessness, and mob rule must be promptly and sternly dealt with, no matter what the cause may be that excites them. Our social organization is too complex for us to fail quickly to condemn those who, with levity or in a spirit of wanton brutality, bring about far-reaching and disastrous interference with normal processes. More and more we are growing to understand that corruption and lawless disorder are twin foes of the body politic, and that neither can be tolerated.[1]

[1] Speech at Fargo, North Dakota, September 5, 1910. From *The New Nationalism*. Copyright, 1910. The Outlook Company, publishers.

III. THE JUDICIARY

THE rapid changes in our social and industrial life have made it necessary that, in applying to concrete cases the great rule of right laid down in our Constitution, there should be a full understanding and appreciation of the new conditions to which the rules are to be applied. What would have been an infringement upon liberty half a century ago may be the necessary safeguard of liberty to-day. What would have been an injury to property then may be necessary to the employment of property now. Every judicial decision involves two terms — one, an interpretation of the law; the other, the understanding of the facts to which it is to be applied. The great mass of our judicial officers are, I believe, alive to these changes of conditions which so materially affect the performance of their judicial duties. Our judicial system is sound and effective at core, and it remains, and must ever be maintained, as the safeguard of those principles of liberty and justice which stand at the foundation of American institutions; for, as Burke finely said, when liberty and justice are separated, neither is safe.

There are, however, some members of the judicial body who have lagged behind in their understanding of these great and vital changes in the body politic, whose minds have never been opened to the new applications of the old principles made necessary by the new conditions. Judges of this stamp do lasting harm by their decisions, because they convince poor men in need of pro-

tection that the courts of the land are profoundly ignorant of and out of sympathy with their needs, and profoundly indifferent or hostile to any proposed remedy.
To such men it seems a cruel mockery to have any court
decide against them on the ground that it desires to preserve "liberty" in a purely technical form, by withholding liberty in any real and constructive sense.

There are certain decisions by various courts which
have been exceedingly detrimental to the rights of wage-
workers. This is true of all the decisions that decide that
men and women are, by the Constitution, "guaranteed
their liberty" to contract to enter a dangerous occupation or to work an undesirable or improper number of
hours, or to work in unhealthy surroundings; and therefore cannot recover damages when maimed in that occupation, and cannot be forbidden to work what the legislature decides is an excessive number of hours, or to
carry on the work under conditions which the legislature
decides to be unhealthy. The most dangerous occupations are often the poorest paid and those where the
hours of work are longest; and in many cases those who
go into them are driven by necessity so great that they
have practically no alternative. Decisions such as those
alluded to above nullify the legislative effort to protect
the wage-workers who most need protection from those
employers who take advantage of their grinding need.
They halt or hamper the movement for securing better
and more equitable conditions of labor. The talk about
preserving to the misery-hunted beings who make con-
tracts for such service their "liberty" to make them, is
either to speak in a spirit of heartless irony or else to
show an utter lack of knowledge of the conditions of life

among the great masses of our fellow-countrymen, a lack which unfits a judge to do good service just as it would unfit any executive or legislative officer.

The decisions of the courts on economic and social questions depend upon their economic and social philosophy; and for the peaceful progress of our people during the twentieth century we shall owe most to those judges who hold to a twentieth century economic and social philosophy and not to a long outgrown philosophy, which was itself the product of primitive economic conditions. Of course a judge's views on progressive social philosophy are entirely second in importance to his possession of a high and fine character; which means the possession of such elementary virtues as honesty, courage, and fairmindedness. The judge who owes his election to pandering to demagogic sentiments or class hatreds and prejudices, and the judge who owes either his election or his appointment to the money or the favor of a great corporation, are alike unworthy to sit on the bench, are alike traitors to the people; and no profundity of legal learning, or correctness of abstract conviction on questions of public policy, can serve as an offset to such shortcomings. But it is also true that judges, like executives and legislators, should hold sound views on the questions of public policy which are of vital interest to the people.

Inasmuch as judges are chosen to serve the interests of the whole people, they should strive to find out what those interests are, and, so far as they conscientiously can, should strive to give effect to popular conviction when deliberately and duly expressed by the law-making body. The courts are to be highly commended and stanchly upheld when they set their faces against wrongdoing or tyranny by a majority; but they are to be blamed when they fail to recognize under a government like ours the deliberate judgment of the majority as to a matter of legitimate policy, when duly expressed by the legislature. Such lawfully expressed and deliberate judgment should be given effect by the courts, save in the extreme and exceptional cases where there has been a clear violation of a constitutional provision. Anything like frivolity or wantonness in upsetting such clearly taken governmental action is a grave offense against the Republic. To protest against tyranny, to protect minorities from oppression, to nullify an act committed in a spasm of popular fury, is to render a service to the Republic. But for the courts to arrogate to themselves functions which properly belong to the legislative bodies is all wrong, and in the end works mischief. The people should not be permitted to pardon evil and slipshod legislation on the theory that the court will set it right; they should be taught that the right way to get rid of a bad law is to have the legislature repeal it, and not have the courts by ingenious hair-splitting nullify it. A law may be unwise and improper; but it should not for these reasons be declared unconstitutional by a strained interpretation, for the result of such action is to take away from the people at large their sense of responsibility and ultimately to destroy their capacity for orderly self-restraint and self-government.

For many of the shortcomings of justice in our country our people as a whole are themselves to blame, and the judges and juries merely bear their share together with the public as a whole. It is discreditable to us as a

people that there should be difficulty in convicting murderers, or in bringing to justice men who as public servants have been guilty of corruption, or who have profited by the corruption of public servants. The result is
equally unfortunate, whether due to hair-splitting tech-
nicalities in the interpretation of law by judges, to sentimentality and class consciousness on the part of juries,
or to hysteria and sensationalism in the daily press.

The courts hold a place of peculiar and deserved sanctity under our form of government. Respect for the law
is essential to the permanence of our institutions; and respect for the law is largely conditioned upon respect for
the courts. But we must face the fact that there are
wise and unwise judges, just as there are wise and unwise executives and legislators. When a president or a
governor behaves improperly or unwisely, the remedy is
easy, for his term is short; the same is true with the legislator, although not to the same degree, for he is one of
many who belong to some given legislative body, and it
is therefore less easy to fix personal responsibility and
hold him accountable therefor. With a judge, who, being human, is also likely to err, but whose tenure is for
life, there is no similar way of holding him to responsibility. Under ordinary conditions the only forms of pressure to which he is in any way amenable are, public opinion, and the action of his fellow judges. It is the last
which is most immediately effective, and to which we
should look for the reform of abuses. Any remedy applied from without is fraught with risk. It is far better,
from every standpoint, that the remedy should come
from within. In no other nation in the world do the
courts wield such vast and far-reaching power as in the

United States. All that is necessary is that the courts as a whole should exercise this power with the far-sighted wisdom already shown by those judges who scan the future while they act in the present. Let them exercise this great power not only honestly and bravely, but with wise insight into the needs and fixed purposes of the people, so that they may do justice, and work equity, so that they may protect all persons in their rights, and yet break down the barriers of privilege, which is the foe of right.[1]

[1] Message communicated to the two Houses of Congress, December 8, 1908.

IV. CONSERVATION

THE policy of conservation is perhaps the most typical example of the general policies which this Government has made peculiarly its own during the opening years of the present century. The function of our Government is to insure to all its citizens, now and hereafter, their rights to life, liberty, and the pursuit of happiness. If we of this generation destroy the resources from which our children would otherwise derive their livelihood, we reduce the capacity of our land to support a population, and so either degrade the standard of living or deprive the coming generations of their right to life on this continent. If we allow great industrial organizations to exercise unregulated control of the means of production and the necessaries of life, we deprive the Americans of to-day and of the future of industrial liberty, a right no less precious and vital than political freedom. Industrial liberty was a fruit of political liberty, and in turn has become one of its chief supports, and exactly as we stand for political democracy so we must stand for industrial democracy.

The rights to life and liberty are fundamental, and like other fundamental necessities, when once acquired, they are little dwelt upon. The right to the pursuit of happiness is the right whose presence or absence is most likely to be felt in daily life. In whatever it has accomplished, or failed to accomplish, the administration which is just drawing to a close has at least seen clearly the fundamental need of freedom of opportunity for every citizen. We have realized that the right of every man to live his own life, provide for his family, and endeavor, according to his abilities, to secure for himself and for them a fair share of the good things of existence, should be subject to one limitation and to no other. The freedom of the individual should be limited only by the present and future rights, interests, and needs of the other individuals who make up the community. We should do all in our power to develop and protect individual liberty, individual initiative, but subject always to the need of preserving and promoting the general good. When necessary, the private right must yield, under due process of law and with proper compensation, to the welfare of the commonwealth. The man who serves the community greatly should be greatly rewarded by the community; as there is great inequality of service so there must be great inequality of reward; but no man and no set of men should be allowed to play the game of competition with loaded dice.

All this is simply good common sense. The underlying principle of conservation has been described as the application of common sense to common problems for the common good. Our aim is so far as possible to provide such conditions that there shall be equality of opportunity where there is equality of energy, fidelity, and intelligence; when there is a reasonable equality of opportunity the distribution of rewards will take care of itself.

The unchecked existence of monopoly is incompatible with equality of opportunity. The reason for the exercise of government control over great monopolies is to equalize opportunity. We are fighting against privilege.

It was made unlawful for corporations to contribute money for election expenses in order to abridge the power of special privilege at the polls. Railroad-rate control is an attempt to secure an equality of opportunity for all men affected by rail transportation; and that means all of us. The great anthracite coal strike was settled, and the pressing danger of a coal famine averted, because we recognized that the control of a public necessity involves a duty to the people, and that public intervention in the affairs of a public-service corporation is neither to be resented as usurpation nor permitted as a privilege by the corporations, but on the contrary to be accepted as a duty and exercised as a right by the Government in the interest of all the people. The efficiency of the army and the navy has been increased so that our people may follow in peace the great work of making this country a better place for Americans to live in, and our navy was sent round the world for the same ultimate purpose. All the acts taken by the Government during the last seven years, and all the policies now being pursued by the Government, fit in as parts of a consistent whole.

Our public-land policy has for its aim the use of the public land so that it will promote local development by the settlement of home makers; the policy we champion is to serve all the people legitimately and openly, instead of permitting the lands to be converted, illegitimately and under cover, to the private benefit of a few. Our forest policy was established so that we might use the public forests for the permanent public good, instead of merely for temporary private gain. The reclamation act, under which the desert parts of the public domain are converted to higher uses for the general benefit, was passed so that more Americans might have homes on the land.

These policies were enacted into law and have justified their enactment. Others have failed, so far, to reach the point of action. Among such is the attempt to secure public control of the open range and thus to convert its benefits to the use of the small man, who is the home maker, instead of allowing it to be controlled by a few great cattle and sheep owners.

The enactment of a pure food law was a recognition of the fact that the public welfare outweighs the right to private gain, and that no man may poison the people for his private profit. The employers' liability bill recognized the controlling fact that while the employer usually has at stake no more than his profit, the stake of the employee is a living for himself and his family.

We are building the Panama Canal; and this means that we are engaged in the giant engineering feat of all time. We are striving to add in all ways to the habitability and beauty of our country. We are striving to hold in the public hands the remaining supply of unappropriated coal, for the protection and benefit of all the people. We have taken the first steps toward the conservation of our natural resources, and the betterment of country life, and the improvement of our waterways. We stand for the right of every child to a childhood free from grinding toil, and to an education; for the civic responsibility and decency of every citizen; for prudent foresight in public matters, and for fair play in every relation of our national and economic life. All these efforts are integral parts of the same attempt, the attempt to enthrone justice and righteousness, to secure freedom of opportunity to all of our citizens, now and hereafter, and to set the ultimate interest of all of us above the temporary interest of any individual, class, or group.

The obligations, and not the rights, of citizenship increase in proportion to the increase of a man's wealth or power. The time is coming when a man will be judged, not by what he has succeeded in getting for himself from the common store, but by how well he has done his duty as a citizen, and by what the ordinary citizen has gained in freedom of opportunity because of his service for the common good. The highest value we know is that of the individual citizen and the highest justice is to give him fair play in the effort to realize the best there is in him.

The tasks this Nation has to do are great tasks. They can only be done at all by our citizens acting together, and they can be done best of all by the direct and simple application of homely common sense. The application of common sense to common problems for the common good, under the guidance of the principles upon which this Republic was based, and by virtue of which it exists, spells perpetuity for the Nation, civil and industrial liberty for its citizens, and freedom of opportunity in the pursuit of happiness for the plain American, for whom this Nation was founded, by whom it was preserved, and through whom alone it can be perpetuated. Upon this platform — larger than party differences, higher than class prejudice, broader than any question of profit and loss — there is room for every American who realizes that the common good stands first.[1]

[1] Special message to the two Houses of Congress, January 22, 1909.

V. THE SQUARE DEAL

I

THIS country will not be a good place for any of us to live in if it is not a reasonably good place for all of us to live in.[1]

II

LAWS are enacted for the benefit of the whole people, and can not and must not be construed as permitting discrimination against some of the people. I am President of all the people of the United States, without regard to creed, color, birthplace, occupation, or social condition. My aim is to do equal and exact justice as among them all. In the employment and dismissal of men in the Government service I can no more recognize the fact that a man does or does not belong to a union as being for or against him than I can recognize the fact that he is a Protestant or a Catholic, a Jew or Gentile, as being for or against him.[2]

III

WHEN I say I believe in a square deal I do not mean, and nobody who speaks the truth can mean, that he believes it possible to give every man the best hand. If the cards

[1] Address at Louisville, Kentucky, April 3, 1912. From *Progressive Principles*. Copyright, 1913, by Elmer H. Youngman. Progressive National Service, publishers.

[2] Public statement concerning the case of William A. Miller, September 29, 1903.

do not come to any man, or if they do come, and he has not got the power to play them, that is his affair. All I mean is that there shall not be any crookedness in the dealing. In other words, it is not in the power of any human being to devise legislation or administration by which each man shall achieve success and have happiness; it not only is not in the power of any man to do that, but if any man says that he can do it, distrust him as a quack. If the hand of the Lord is heavy upon any man, if misfortune comes upon him, he may be unable to win; or even if fortune favors him and he lacks the courage, the nerve, the common sense, the ability, to do the best with the chance given him, then he will fail. All any of us can pretend to do is to come as near as our imperfect abilities will allow to securing through governmental agencies an equal opportunity for each man to show the stuff that is in him; and that must be done with no more intention of discrimination against the rich man than the poor man, or against the poor man than the rich man; with the intention of safeguarding each man, rich or poor, poor or rich, in his rights, and giving him as nearly as may be a fair chance to do what his powers permit him to do; always provided he does not wrong his neighbor.[1]

IV

Ours is a government of liberty by, through, and under the law. No man is above it and no man is below it. The crime of cunning, the crime of greed, the crime of violence, are all equally crimes, and against them all alike the law must set its face. This is not and never shall be

[1] Speech at the Banquet at Dallas, Texas, April 5, 1905.

a government either of plutocracy or of a mob. It is, it has been, and it will be a government of the people; including alike the people of great wealth, of moderate wealth, the people who employ others, the people who are employed, the wage-worker, the lawyer, the mechanic, the banker, the farmer; including them all, protecting each and every one if he acts decently and squarely, and discriminating against any one of them, no matter from what class he comes, if he does not act squarely and fairly, if he does not obey the law. While all people are foolish if they violate or rail against the law — wicked as well as foolish, but all foolish — yet the most foolish man in this Republic is the man of wealth who complains because the law is administered with impartial justice against or for him. His folly is greater than the folly of any other man who so complains; for he lives and moves and has his being because the law does in fact protect him and his property.

We have the right to ask every decent American citizen to rally to the support of the law if it is ever broken against the interest of the rich man; and we have the same right to ask that rich man cheerfully and gladly to acquiesce in the enforcement against his seeming interest of the law, if it is the law. Incidentally, whether he acquiesces or not, the law will be enforced; and this whoever he may be, great or small, and at whichever end of the social scale he may be.

I ask that we see to it in our country that the line of division in the deeper matters of our citizenship be drawn, never between section and section, never between creed and creed, never, thrice never, between class and class; but that the line be drawn on the line of conduct, cutting through sections, cutting through creeds, cutting through classes; the line that divides the honest from the dishonest, the line that divides good citizenship from bad citizenship, the line that declares a man a good citizen only if, and always if, he acts in accordance with the immutable law of righteousness, which has been the same from the beginning of history to the present moment and which will be the same from now until the end of recorded time.[1]

V

WE come here to-day to commemorate one of the epoch-making events of the long struggle for the rights of man — the long struggle for the uplift of humanity. Our country — this great republic — means nothing unless it means the triumph of a real democracy, the triumph of popular government, and, in the long run, of an economic system under which each man shall be guaranteed the opportunity to show the best that there is in him. That is why the history of America is now the central feature of the history of the world; for the world has set its face hopefully toward our democracy; and, O my fellow citizens, each one of you carries on your shoulders not only the burden of doing well for the sake of your own country, but the burden of doing well and of seeing that this nation does well for the sake of mankind.

We cannot afford weakly to blind ourselves to the actual conflict which faces us to-day. The issue is joined, and we must fight or fail.

In every wise struggle for human betterment one of

[1] Speech at Spokane, Washington, May 26, 1903.

the main objects, and often the only object, has been to achieve in large measure equality of opportunity. In the struggle for this great end, nations rise from barbarism to civilization, and through it people press forward from one stage of enlightenment to the next. One of the chief factors in progress is the destruction of special privilege. The essence of any struggle for healthy liberty has always been, and must always be, to take from some one man or class of men the right to enjoy power, or wealth, or position, or immunity, which has not been earned by service to his or their fellows. That is what you fought for in the Civil War, and that is what we strive for now.

At many stages in the advance of humanity, this conflict between the men who possess more than they have earned and the men who have earned more than they possess is the central condition of progress. In our day it appears as the struggle of free men to gain and hold the right of self-government as against the special interests, who twist the methods of free government into machinery for defeating the popular will. At every stage, and under all circumstances, the essence of the struggle is to equalize opportunity, destroy privilege, and give to the life and citizenship of every individual the highest possible value both to himself and to the commonwealth. That is nothing new. All I ask in civil life is what you fought for in the Civil War. I ask that civil life be carried on according to the spirit in which the army was carried on. You never get perfect justice, but the effort in handling the army was to bring to the front the men who could do the job. Nobody grudged promotion to Grant, or Sherman, or Thomas, or Sheridan, because they earned it. The only complaint was when a man got promotion which he did not earn.

Practical equality of opportunity for all citizens, when we achieve it, will have two great results. First, every man will have a fair chance to make of himself all that in him lies; to reach the highest point to which his capacities, unassisted by special privilege of his own and unhampered by the special privilege of others, can carry him, and to get for himself and his family substantially what he has earned. Second, equality of opportunity means that the commonwealth will get from every citizen the highest service of which he is capable. No man who carries the burden of the special privileges of another can give to the commonwealth that service to which it is fairly entitled.

I stand for the square deal. But when I say that I am for the square deal, I mean not merely that I stand for fair play under the present rules of the game, but that I stand for having those rules changed so as to work for a more substantial equality of opportunity and of reward for equally good service. One word of warning, which, I think, is hardly necessary in Kansas. When I say I want a square deal for the poor man, I do not mean that I want a square deal for the man who remains poor because he has not got the energy to work for himself. If a man who has had a chance will not make good, then he has got to quit. And you men of the Grand Army, you want justice for the brave man who fought, and punishment for the coward who shirked his work. Is not that so?

Now, this means that our government, national and state, must be freed from the sinister influence or control of special interests. Exactly as the special interests of cotton and slavery threatened our political integrity before the Civil War, so now the great special business interests too often control and corrupt the men and methods of government for their own profit. We must drive the special interests out of politics. That is one of our tasks to-day. Every special interest is entitled to justice — full, fair, and complete, — and, now, mind you, if there were any attempt by mob violence to plunder and work harm to the special interest, whatever it may be, that I most dislike, and the wealthy man, whomsoever he may be, for whom I have the greatest contempt, I would fight for him, and you would if you were worth your salt. He should have justice. For every special interest is entitled to justice, but not one is entitled to a vote in Congress, to a voice on the bench, or to representation in any public office. The Constitution guarantees protection to property, and we must make that promise good. But it does not give the right of suffrage to any corporation.

There can be no effective control of corporations while their political activity remains. To put an end to it will be neither a short nor an easy task, but it can be done.

The absence of effective state, and, especially, national, restraint upon unfair money getting has tended to create a small class of enormously wealthy and economically powerful men, whose chief object is to hold and increase their power. The prime need is to change the conditions which enable these men to accumulate power which it is not for the general welfare that they should hold or exercise. We grudge no man a fortune which represents his own power and sagacity, when exercised with entire regard to the welfare of his fellows. Again, comrades over there, take the lesson from your own experience. Not only did you not grudge, but you gloried in the promotion of the great generals who gained their promotion by leading the army to victory. So it is with us. We grudge no man a fortune in civil life if it is honorably obtained and well used. It is not even enough that it should have been gained without doing damage to the community. We should permit it to be gained only so long as the gaining represents benefit to the community. This, I know, implies a policy of a far more active governmental interference with social and economic conditions in this country than we have yet had, but I think we have got to face the fact that such an increase in governmental control is now necessary.

Nothing is more true than that excess of every kind is followed by reaction; a fact which should be pondered by reformer and reactionary alike. We are face to face with new conceptions of the relations of property to human welfare, chiefly because certain advocates of the rights of property as against the rights of men have been pushing their claims too far. The man who wrongly holds that every human right is secondary to his profit must now give way to the advocate of human welfare, who rightly maintains that every man holds his property subject to the general right of the community to regulate its use to whatever degree the public welfare may require it.

But I think we may go still further. The right to regulate the use of wealth in the public interest is universally admitted. Let us admit also the right to regulate the terms and conditions of labor, which is the chief element of wealth, directly in the interest of the common good. The fundamental thing to do for every man is to give him a chance to reach a place in which he will make the greatest possible contribution to the public welfare. Understand what I say there. Give him a chance, not push him up if he will not be pushed. Help any man who stumbles; if he lies down, it is a poor job to try to carry him; but if he is a worthy man, try your best to see that he gets a chance to show the worth that is in him. No man can be a good citizen unless he has a wage more than sufficient to cover the bare cost of living, and hours of labor short enough so that after his day's work is done he will have time and energy to bear his share in the management of the community, to help in carrying the general load. We keep countless men from being good citizens by the conditions of life with which we surround them. We need comprehensive workmen's compensation acts, both state and national laws to regulate child labor and work for women, and, especially, we need in our common schools not merely education in book learning, but also practical training for daily life and work. We need to enforce better sanitary conditions for our workers and to extend the use of safety appliances for our workers in industry and commerce, both within and between the states. Also, friends, in the interest of the workingman himself we need to set our faces like flint against mob violence just as against corporate greed; against violence and injustice and lawlessness by wage-workers just as much as against lawless cunning and greed and selfish arrogance of employers. If I could ask but one thing of my fellow countrymen, my request would be that, whenever they go in for reform, they remember the two sides, and that they always exact justice from one side as much as from the other.

The American people are right in demanding that New Nationalism, without which we cannot hope to deal with new problems. The New Nationalism puts the national need before sectional or personal advantage. It is impatient of the utter confusion that results from local legislatures attempting to treat national issues as local issues. It is still more impatient of the impotence which springs from overdivision of governmental powers, the impotence which makes it possible for local selfishness or for legal cunning, hired by wealthy special interests, to bring national activities to a deadlock. This New Nationalism regards the executive power as the steward of the public welfare. It demands of the judiciary that it shall be interested primarily in human welfare rather than in property, just as it demands that the representative body shall represent all the people rather than any one class or section of the people.[1]

[1] Speech at Ossawatomie, Kansas, August 31, 1910. From *The New Nationalism*. Copyright, 1910. The Outlook Company, publishers.

VI. THE RIGHT OF THE PEOPLE TO RULE

I

THE great fundamental issue now before the Republican Party and before our people can be stated briefly. It is, Are the American people fit to govern themselves, to rule themselves, to control themselves? I believe they are. My opponents do not. I believe in the right of the people to rule. I believe the majority of the plain people of the United States will, day in and day out, make fewer mistakes in governing themselves than any smaller class or body of men, no matter what their training, will make in trying to govern them. I believe, again, that the American people are, as a whole, capable of self-control and of learning by their mistakes. Our opponents pay lip-loyalty to this doctrine; but they show their real beliefs by the way in which they champion every device to make the nominal rule of the people a sham.

I have scant patience with this talk of the tyranny of the majority. Whenever there is tyranny of the majority, I shall protest against it with all my heart and soul. But we are to-day suffering from the tyranny of minorities. It is a small minority that is grabbing our coal deposits, our water powers, and our harbor fronts. A small minority is battening on the sale of adulterated foods and drugs. It is a small minority that lies behind monopolies and trusts. It is a small minority that stands behind the present law of master and servant, the sweat-shops, and the whole calendar of social and industrial injustice. It is a small minority that is to-day using our convention system to defeat the will of a majority of the people in the choice of delegates to the Chicago Convention.

The only tyrannies from which men, women and children are suffering in real life are the tyrannies of minorities.

Am I overstating the case? Have our political leaders always, or generally, recognized their duty to the people as anything more than a duty to disperse the mob, see that the ashes are taken away, and distribute patronage? Have our leaders always, or generally, worked for the benefit of human beings, to increase the prosperity of all the people, to give to each some opportunity of living decently and bringing up his children well? The questions need no answer.[1]

II

I BELIEVE in a larger opportunity for the people themselves directly to participate in government and to control their governmental agents, because long experience has taught me that without such control many of their agents will represent them badly. By actual experience in office I have found that, as a rule, I could secure the triumph of the causes in which I most believed, not from the politicians and the men who claim an exceptional right to speak in business and government, but by going over their heads and appealing directly to the people themselves.

[1] Address at Carnegie Hall, New York City, March 20, 1912. This and the three succeeding excerpts are from *Progressive Principles*. Copyright, 1913, by Elmer H. Youngman. Progressive National Service, publishers.

I am not under the slightest delusion as to any power that during my political career I have at any time possessed. Whatever of power I at any time had, I obtained from the people. I could exercise it only so long as, and to the extent that, the people not merely believed in me, but heartily backed me up. Whatever I did as President I was able to do only because I had the backing of the people. When on any point I did not have that backing, when on any point I differed from the people, it mattered not whether I was right or whether I was wrong, my power vanished.[1]

III

THE difference between us and our present-day opponents is as old as civilized history.

In every great crisis of the kind we face to-day we find arrayed on one side the men who with fervor and broad sympathy and lofty idealism stand for the forward movement; the men who stand for the uplift and betterment of mankind, and who have faith in the people; and over against them the men of restricted vision and contracted sympathy, whose souls are not stirred by the wrongs of others. Side by side with the latter appear the other men who lack all intensity of conviction, who care only for the pleasure of the day; and also those other men who distrust the people, who if dishonest wish to keep the people helpless so as to exploit them, and who if honest so disbelieve in the power of the people to bring about wholesome reform that every appeal to popular conscience and popular intelligence fills them

[1] Address before the National Convention of the Progressive Party, Chicago, August 6, 1912.

with angry terror. According to their own lights, these men are often very respectable, very worthy; but they live on a plane of low ideals. In the atmosphere they create impostors flourish, and leadership comes to be thought of only as success in making money, and the vision of Heaven becomes a sordid vision, and all that is highest and purest in human nature is laughed at, and honesty is bought and sold in the market-place.

Opposed undyingly to these men are the men of faith and vision, the men in whom love of righteousness burns like a flaming fire, who spurn lives of soft and selfish ease, of slothful self-indulgence, who scorn to think only of pleasure for themselves, who feel for and believe in their fellows, whose high fealty is reserved for all that is good, that is just, that is honorable. By their very nature these men are bound to battle for the truth and the right. They do not address themselves only to the cultured and exclusive few. They prize character even more than intellect. They know well that conscience is not the privilege merely of the men of wealth and cultivation, and they make their appeal to all men alike in the name of the great fundamental qualities, and qualities that every man should have, the qualities of generosity and unselfishness, of fearless honesty and high courage.

We who war against privilege pay heed to no outworn system of philosophy. We demand of our leaders to-day understanding of and sympathy with the living and the vital needs of those in the community whose needs are greatest.

We are against privilege in every form.

We believe in striking down every bulwark of privilege.

Above all we are against the evil alliance of special privilege in business with special business in politics.

We believe in giving the people a free hand to work in efficient fashion for true justice.

To the big man and to the little man, in all the relations of life, we pledge justice and fair dealing.

A period of change is upon us. Our opponents, the men of reaction, ask us to stand still. But we could not stand still if we would; we must either go forward or go backward.

Never was the need more imperative than now for men of vision who are also men of action. Disaster is ahead of us if we trust to the leadership of men whose souls are seared and whose eyes are blinded, men of cold heart and narrow mind, who believe we can find safety in dull timidity and dull inaction.

The unrest cannot be quieted by ingenious trickery of those who profess to advance by merely marking time, or who seek to drown the cry for justice by loud and insincere clamor about issues that are false and issues that are dead.

The trumpets sound the advance, and their peal cannot be drowned by repeating the war-cries of by-gone battles, the victory shouts of vanished hosts.

The principles for which we stand to-day can be set forth in the words which Lincoln used fifty-four years ago, when in speaking of the then phase of the eternal struggle between privilege and justice, between the rights of the many and the special interest of the few, he said:

That is the real issue. That is the issue which will continue in this country when these poor tongues of Judge Douglas and myself shall be silent. It is the eternal struggle between two principles — right and wrong — throughout the world. They are the two principles that have stood face to face from the beginning of time. The one is the common right of humanity, the other the divine right of kings. It is the same principle in whatever shape it develops itself. It is the same spirit that says, "You toil and work and earn bread, and I will eat it." No matter in what shape it comes, whether from the mouth of a king who bestrides the people of his own nation and lives from the fruit of their labor, or from one race of men as an apology for enslaving another race, it is the same tyrannical principle.

IV

WE the people cannot turn back. Our aim must be steady, wise progress. It would be well if our people would study the history of a sister republic. All the woes of France for a century and a quarter have been due to the folly of her people in splitting into the two camps of unreasonable conservatism and unreasonable radicalism. Had pre-Revolutionary France listened to men like Turgot, and backed them up, all would have gone well. But the beneficiaries of privilege, the Bourbon reactionaries, the short-sighted ultra-conservatives, turned down Turgot; and then found that instead of him they had obtained Robespierre. They gained twenty years' freedom from all restraint and reform, at the cost of the whirlwind of the red terror; and in their turn the unbridled extremists of the terror induced a blind reaction; and so, with convulsion and oscillation from one extreme to another, with alternations of violent radicalism and violent Bourbonism, the French people went through misery towards a shattered goal. May we profit by the experience of our brother republicans across the water, and go forward steadily, avoiding

all wild extremes; and may our ultra-conservatives remember that the rule of the Bourbons brought on the
Revolution, and may our would-be revolutionaries remember that no Bourbon was ever such a dangerous
enemy of the people and of freedom as the professed
friend of both, Robespierre. There is no danger of a
revolution in this country; but there is grave discontent
and unrest, and in order to remove them there is need of
all the wisdom and probity and deep-seated faith in and
purpose to uplift humanity, we have at our command.

Friends, our task as Americans is to strive for social
and industrial justice, achieved through the genuine rule
of the people. This is our end, our purpose. The methods for achieving the end are merely expedients, to be
finally accepted or rejected according as actual experience shows that they work well or ill. But in our hearts
we must have this lofty purpose, and we must strive
for it in all earnestness and sincerity, or our work will
come to nothing. In order to succeed we need leaders
of inspired idealism, leaders to whom are granted great
visions, who dream greatly and strive to make their
dreams come true; who can kindle the people with the
fire from their own burning souls. The leader for the
time being, whoever he may be, is but an instrument, to
be used until broken and then to be cast aside; and if he
is worth his salt he will care no more when he is broken
than a soldier cares when he is sent where his life is for-
feit in order that the victory may be won. In the long
fight for righteousness the watchword for all of us is
spend and be spent. It is of little matter whether any
one man fails or succeeds; but the cause shall not fail,
for it is the cause of mankind.

We, here in America, hold in our hands the hope of the world, the fate of the coming years; and shame and disgrace will be ours if in our eyes the light of high resolve is dimmed, if we trail in the dust the golden hopes of men. If on this new continent we merely build another country of great but unjustly divided material prosperity, we shall have done nothing; and we shall do as little if we merely set the greed of envy against the greed of arrogance, and thereby destroy the material well-being of all of us. To turn this Government either into government by a plutocracy or government by a mob would be to repeat on a larger scale the lamentable failures of the world that is dead. We stand against all tyranny, by the few or by the many. We stand for the rule of the many in the interest of all of us, for the rule of the many in a spirit of courage, of common sense, of high purpose, above all in a spirit of kindly justice towards every man and every woman. We not merely admit, but insist, that there must be self-control on the part of the people, that they must keenly perceive their own duties as well as the rights of others; but we also insist that the people can do nothing unless they not merely have, but exercise to the full, their own rights. The worth of our great experiment depends upon its being in good faith an experiment — the first that has ever been tried — in true democracy on the scale of a continent, on a scale as vast as that of the mightiest empires of the Old World. Surely this is a noble ideal, an ideal for which it is worth while to strive, an ideal for which at need it is worth while to sacrifice much; for our ideal is the rule of all the people in a spirit of friendliest brotherhood towards each and every one of the people.[1]

[1] Address at Carnegie Hall, New York City, March 30, 1912.

IV
NATIONAL UNITY — THE BASIS OF NATIONAL STRENGTH

I. CLASS CLEAVAGE

I

DANGER from religious antipathy is dead, and from sectional antipathy dying; but there are at times very ugly manifestations of antipathy between class and class. It seems a pity to have to use the word "class," because there are really no classes in our American life in the sense in which the word "class" is used in Europe. Our social and political systems do not admit of them in theory, and in practice they exist only in a very fluid state. In most European countries classes are separated by rigid boundaries, which can be crossed but rarely, and with the utmost difficulty and peril. Here the boundaries cannot properly be said to exist, and are certainly so fluctuating and evasive, so indistinctly marked, that they cannot be appreciated when seen near by. Any American family which lasts a few generations will be apt to have representatives in all the different classes. The great business men, even the great professional men, and especially the great statesmen and sailors and soldiers, are very apt to spring from among the farmers or wage-workers, and their kinsfolk remain near the old home or at the old trade. If ever there existed in the world a community where the identity of interest, of habit, of principle, and of ideals should be felt as a living force, ours is the one.

Speaking generally, it really is felt to a degree quite unknown in other countries of our size. There are, doubtless, portions of Norway and Switzerland where the social and political ideals, and their nearness to realization, are not materially different from those of the most essentially American portions of our own land; but this is not true of any European country of considerable size. It is only in American communities that we see the farmer, the hired man, the lawyer, and the merchant, and possibly even the officer of the army or the navy, all kinsmen, and all accepting their relations as perfectly natural and simple.

This is eminently healthy. This is just as it should be in our republic. It represents the ideal toward which it would be a good thing to approximate everywhere. In the great industrial centers, with their highly complex, highly specialized conditions, it is of course merely an ideal. There are parts even of our oldest States, as, for example, New York, where this ideal is actually realized; there are other parts, particularly the great cities, where the life is so wholly different that the attempt to live up precisely to the country conditions would be artificial and impossible. Nevertheless, the fact remains that the only true solution of our political and social problems lies in cultivating everywhere the spirit of brotherhood, of fellow-feeling and understanding between man and man, and the willingness to treat a man as a man, which are the essential factors in American democracy as we still see it in the country districts.

The chief factor in producing such sympathy is simply association on a plane of equality, and for a common object. Any healthy-minded American is bound to think well of his fellow-Americans if he only gets to know them. Perhaps I may be pardoned for quoting my own experience as an instance in point. Outside of college boys and politicians my first intimate associates were ranchmen, cow-punchers, and game-hunters, and I speedily became convinced that there were no other men in the country who were their equals. Then I was thrown much with farmers, and I made up my mind that it was the farmer upon whom the foundations of the commonwealth really rested — that the farmer was the archetypical good American. Then I saw a good deal of railroad men, and after quite an intimate acquaintance with them I grew to feel that, especially in their higher ranks, they typified the very qualities of courage, self-reliance, self-command, hardihood, capacity for work, power of initiative, and power of obedience, which we like most to associate with the American name. Then I happened to have dealings with certain carpenters' unions, and grew to have a great respect for the carpenter, for the mechanic type. By this time it dawned upon me that they were all pretty good fellows, and that my championship of each set in succession above all other sets had sprung largely from the fact that I was very familiar with the set I championed, and less familiar with the remainder. In other words, I had grown into sympathy with, into understanding of, group after group, with the effect that I invariably found that they and I had common purposes and a common standpoint. We differed among ourselves, or agreed among ourselves, not because we had different occupations or the same occupation, but because of our ways of looking at life.

The prime lesson to be taught is the lesson of treating each man on his worth as a man, and of remembering that while sometimes it is necessary, from both a legislative and social standpoint, to consider men as a class, yet in the long run our safety lies in recognizing the individual's worth or lack of worth as the chief basis of action, and in shaping our whole conduct, and especially our political conduct, accordingly. It is impossible for a democracy to endure if the political lines are drawn to coincide with class lines. The resulting government, whether of the upper or the lower class, is not a government of the whole people, but a government of part of the people at the expense of the rest. Republics have fallen in the past primarily because the parties that controlled them divided along the lines of class, so that inevitably the triumph of one or the other implied the supremacy of a part over the whole. The result might be an oligarchy, or it might be mob rule; it mattered little which, as regards the ultimate effect, for in both cases tyranny and anarchy were sure to alternate. The failure of the Greek and Italian republics was fundamentally due to this cause. Switzerland has flourished because the divisions upon which her political issues have been fought have not been primarily those of mere caste or social class, and America will flourish and will become greater than any empire because, in the long run, in this country, any party which strives to found itself upon sectional or class jealousy and hostility must go down before the good sense of the people.[1]

[1] From *The Strenuous Life.* Copyright, 1900. The Century Company, publishers.

II

I⊤ behooves our people never to fall under the thralldom of names, and least of all to be misled by designing people who appeal to the reverence for, or antipathy toward, a given name in order to achieve some alien purpose. Of course such misuse of names is as old as the history of what we understand when we speak of civilized mankind. The rule of a mob may be every whit as tyrannical and oppressive as the rule of a single individual, whether or not called a dictator; and the rule of an oligarchy, whether this oligarchy is a plutocracy or a bureaucracy, or any other small set of powerful men, may in its turn be just as sordid and just as bloodthirsty as that of a mob. But the apologists for the mob or oligarchy or dictator, in justifying the tyranny, use different words. The mob leaders usually state that all that they are doing is necessary in order to advance the cause of "liberty," while the dictator and the oligarchy are usually defended upon the ground that the course they follow is absolutely necessary so as to secure "order." Many excellent people are taken in by the use of the word "liberty" at the one time, and the use of the word "order" at the other, and ignore the simple fact that despotism is despotism, tyranny tyranny, oppression oppression, whether committed by one individual or by many individuals, by a state or by a private corporation.

Of course when a great crisis actually comes, no matter how much people may have been misled by names, they promptly awaken to their unimportance. To the individual who suffered under the guillotine at Paris, or in the drownings in the Loire, or to the individual who a century before was expelled from his beloved country, or tortured, or sent to the galleys, it made no difference whatever that one set of acts was performed under Robespierre and Danton and Marat in the name of liberty and reason and the rights of the people, or that the other was performed in the name of order and authority and religion by the direction of the great monarch. Tyranny and cruelty were tyranny and cruelty just as much in one case as in the other, and just as much when those guilty of them used one shibboleth as when they used another. All forms of tyranny and cruelty must alike be condemned by honest men.

We in this country have been very fortunate. Thanks to the teaching and the practice of the men whom we most revere as leaders, of the men like Washington and Lincoln, we have hitherto escaped the twin gulfs of despotism and mob rule, and we have never been in any danger from the worst forms of religious bitterness. But we should therefore be all the more careful, as we deal with our industrial and social problems, not to fall into mistakes similar to those which have brought lasting disaster on less fortunately situated peoples. We have achieved democracy in politics just because we have been able to steer a middle course between the rule of the mob and the rule of the dictator. We shall achieve industrial democracy because we shall steer a similar middle course between the extreme individualist and the Socialist, between the demagogue who attacks all wealth and who can see no wrong done anywhere unless it is perpetrated by a man of wealth, and the apologist for the plutocracy who rails against so much as a restatement of the eighth commandment upon the ground that it will "hurt business." [1]

III

FROM the days when civilized man first began to strive for self-government and democracy, success in this effort has depended primarily upon the ability to steer clear of extremes. For almost its entire length the course lies between Scylla and Charybdis; and the heated extremists who insist upon avoiding only one gulf of destruction invariably land in the other — and then take refuge in the meager consolation afforded by denouncing as "inconsistent" the pilot who strives to avoid both. Throughout past history Liberty has always walked between the twin terrors of Tyranny and Anarchy. They have stalked like wolves beside her, with murder in their red eyes, ever ready to tear each other's throats, but even more ready to rend in sunder Liberty herself. Always in the past there has been a monotonously recurrent cycle in the history of free states; Liberty has supplanted Tyranny, has gradually been supplanted by Anarchy, and has then seen the insupportable Anarchy finally overthrown and Tyranny reëstablished. Anarchy is always and everywhere the handmaiden of Tyranny and Liberty's deadliest foe. No people can permanently remain free unless it possesses the stern self-control and resolution necessary to put down anarchy. Order without liberty and liberty without order are equally destructive; special privilege for the few and special privilege for the many are alike profoundly anti-social; the fact that un-

[1] From *History as Literature*. Copyright, 1913. Charles Scribner's Sons, publishers.

limited individualism is ruinous, in no way alters the fact that absolute state ownership and regimentation spells ruin of a different kind.[1]

IV

I HAVE come from the Atlantic across this continent to the Pacific. I have greeted many audiences. I see a little diversity, but, oh, my fellow citizens, what strikes me most and pleases me most is the fundamental unity, is the fact that wherever I go I speak to an audience of Americans, be they East or be they West. And I make the same appeal with the same confidence, here beside the Golden Gate, that I should make by the Great Lakes or in the upper Mississippi Valley or on the Atlantic Ocean. This is a government of freemen, who have achieved liberty under the law, who have, by force of arms as well as by legislation, established once for all, as the fundamental principle of our government, that there shall not in this country be license; that there shall not be in this country liberty to oppress without the law; that liberty and freedom shall come under and in pursuance of the law, of the law that is no respecter of persons, under a government that is a government neither for the rich man as such nor for the poor man as such, but for every man, rich or poor, if he is a decent man and does his duty to the State.[2]

[1] From *The Great Adventure*. Copyright, 1918. Charles Scribner's Sons, publishers.

[2] Address at Mechanics' Pavilion, San Francisco, California, May 11, 1903. From *California Addresses by President Roosevelt*. The California Promotion Committee, publishers.

II. PARTISANSHIP

I

Parties are good as instruments, and only as instruments. The thing that Americans should recollect is that what matters is not the opinions that divide them one from another so much as it is the great fundamentals upon which they are united. We must have our differences; and it would be a very unhealthy thing if all of us thought alike. We need the friction with people different from ourselves; and my experience with my fellow countrymen is that there will always be plenty of them who will think different ways. We need the intellectual differences that come from such friction, and we must resolutely, but with mutual respect and forbearance among ourselves, battle for our respective opinions. That is good and wholesome; but it is not merely good and wholesome, but vital, to remember that on the really great issues we must all unite.[1]

II

No man is a good American who is not, of course, an American first — an American before he is a member of any section of the American people such as a party or a class. I hold that the only real service which a party man can render his party is to make that party more responsive to the needs of the American people.[2]

[1] Speech at Sioux Falls, South Dakota, September 3, 1910. This and the succeeding excerpt are from *The New Nationalism.* Copyright, 1910. The Outlook Company, publishers.

[2] Speech at Kansas City, Missouri, September 1, 1910.

III. RELIGION AND POLITICS

To discriminate against a thoroughly upright citizen because he belongs to some particular church, or because, like Abraham Lincoln, he has not avowed his allegiance to any church, is an outrage against that liberty of conscience which is one of the foundations of American life. You are entitled to know whether a man seeking your suffrages is a man of clean and upright life, honorable in all of his dealings with his fellows, and fit by qualification and purpose to do well in the great office for which he is a candidate; but you are not entitled to know matters which lie purely between himself and his Maker. If it is proper or legitimate to oppose a man for being a Unitarian, as was John Quincy Adams, for instance, as is the Rev. Edward Everett Hale, at the present moment Chaplain of the Senate, and an American of whose life all good Americans are proud — then it would be equally proper to support or oppose a man because of his views on justification by faith, or the methods of administering the sacrament, or the gospel of salvation by works. If you once enter on such a career there is absolutely no limit at which you can legitimately stop.

So much for your objections to Mr. Taft because he is a Unitarian. Now, for your objections to him because you think his wife and brother to be Roman Catholics. As it happens, they are not; but if they were, or if he were a Roman Catholic himself, it ought not to affect in the slightest degree any man's supporting him for the position of President. You say that "the mass of the voters that are not Catholics will not support a man for any office, especially for President of the United States, who is a Roman Catholic." I believe that when you say this you foully slander your fellow countrymen. I do not for one moment believe that the mass of our fellow citizens, or that any considerable number of our fellow citizens, can be influenced by such narrow bigotry as to refuse to vote for any thoroughly upright and fit man because he happens to have a particular religious creed. Such a consideration should never be treated as a reason for either supporting or opposing a candidate for a political office. Are you aware that there are several States in this Union where the majority of the people are now Catholics? I should reprobate in the severest terms the Catholics who in those States (or in any other States) refused to vote for the most fit man because he happened to be a Protestant; and my condemnation would be exactly as severe for Protestants who, under reversed circumstances, refused to vote for a Catholic. In public life I am happy to say that I have known many men who were elected, and constantly reëlected, to office in districts where the great majority of their constituents were of a different religious belief. I know Catholics who have for many years represented constituencies mainly Protestant, and Protestants who have for many years represented constituencies mainly Catholic; and among the Congressmen whom I knew particularly well was one man of Jewish faith who represented a district in which there were hardly any Jews at all. All of these men by their very existence in political life refute the slander you have uttered against your fellow Americans.

I believe that this Republic will endure for many centuries. If so there will doubtless be among its Presidents Protestants and Catholics, and, very probably at some time, Jews. I have consistently tried while President to act in relation to my fellow Americans of Catholic faith as I hope that any future President who happens to be a Catholic will act towards his fellow Americans of Protestant faith. Had I followed any other course I should have felt that I was unfit to represent the American people.

In my Cabinet at the present moment there sit side by side Catholic and Protestant, Christian and Jew, each man chosen because in my belief he is peculiarly fit to exercise on behalf of all our people the duties of the office to which I have appointed him. In no case does the man's religious belief in any way influence his discharge of his duties, save as it makes him more eager to act justly and uprightly in his relations to all men. The same principles that have obtained in appointing the members of my Cabinet, the highest officials under me, the officials to whom is entrusted the work of carrying out all the important policies of my administration, are the principles upon which all good Americans should act in choosing, whether by election or appointment, the men to fill any office from the highest to the lowest in the land.[1]

[1] Letter to Mr. J. C. Martin, November 6, 1908.

IV. STRAIGHT AMERICANISM

I

THE effort to combine fealty to the flag of an immigrant's natal land with fealty to the flag of his adopted land, in practice means not merely disregard of, but hostility to, the flag of the United States. When two flags are hoisted on the same pole, one is always hoisted undermost. The hyphenated American always hoists the American flag undermost. The American citizen of German birth or descent who is a good American and nothing but a good American, and whose whole loyalty is undividedly given to this country and its flag, stands on an exact level with every other American, and is entitled to precisely the same consideration and treatment as if his ancestors had come over on the Mayflower or had settled on the banks of the James three centuries ago. I am partly of German blood, and I am exactly as proud of this blood as of the blood of other strains that flows in my veins. But — I am an American, and nothing else!

The Americans of German origin have been a peculiarly valuable element in our population. I believe that they are, in overwhelming proportion, thoroughgoing Americans. As I have said, I am partly of German blood. A large number of my closest friends, a large number of the men whom I most respect and honor in American life, are Americans of German parentage or descent or of German birth. One such American, a descendant of one of Blucher's colonels, sat in my Cabinet; and he sat beside another American, a descendant of one of Napoleon's brothers. But each was an American and nothing else! The scientific book of which I was proudest, I wrote in partnership with a close friend, a naturalist who was with me in Africa; he is of German parentage; but he is an American and nothing else. The man who was closest to me politically during the ten years of my service as Governor and President was of German parentage; but he was absolutely straight American. Some of the best men in my regiment, including my orderly and one captain, were of German birth or descent; but they were Americans, pure and simple. Among the clergymen, philanthropists, publicists, good citizens of all kinds, with whom I work in heartiest sympathy, an unusually large proportion are of German descent and some of German birth. I get on with these men and women exactly as well as I do with the men and women of Colonial American descent. But I get on with them because they are Americans and nothing else.

I stand for the American citizen of German birth or descent, precisely as I stand for any other American. But I do not stand at all for the German-American, or any other kind of hyphenated American. When I was President I was brought into close contact with many officers of the army and navy. Col. George Washington Goethals has done the best work done by any American of recent years. He is of Dutch parentage. But he is no more a Dutch-American than I am. He is just plain American. Among my military and naval aides were Lee, Grant, Sheridan and Osterhaus, all descended from generals who fought in the Union or Confederate Armies. Two of them were of old Revolutionary stock,

Scotch or English. The grandfather of the third was born in Ireland, and the grandfather of the fourth in Germany. But they were all Americans and nothing else. General Wood, of Revolutionary stock, started Cuba on the road to self-government; General Barry, of Irish parentage, commanded the army that rescued Cuba from revolution; and one was exactly as good an American as the other. Among the admirals upon whom I leaned were Dewey, Evans, Taylor, and Cameron Winslow, of Revolutionary stock; and O'Neil and Schroeder, one of Irish and the other of German descent; and the last two were exactly as good Americans as the other four. It would have been a crime as well as a calamity to endeavor to divide all these and all the other fine and gallant officers of our army and navy on lines of birth or national origin or creed. It is no less a crime and a calamity to attempt to divide our citizens as a whole along such lines.

There was never a better American than Jacob Riis, who was born in Denmark and whom I always thought about the best American I ever knew. The Americans in whom I believe include Jews and Catholics and Protestants. They include men of old native American descent and other men of recent German, English, French, Irish, Italian, Scandinavian, Magyar and Slavonic descent; but all are Americans entitled to be treated as such, and claiming to be nothing else. I as emphatically condemn opposition to a good American who happens to be of German birth or descent, because of that fact, as I condemn action by such a man designed to serve not the United States, but some foreign power. I speak against the German-American who seeks to use his American citizenship in the interest of a foreign power and who thereby shows himself an unworthy American. I should speak exactly as quickly against the American of English or French or Scandinavian or Irish descent who was guilty of similar conduct. The following letter which I recently wrote explains itself:

"I am very sorry but I cannot sign that appeal. I do not approve of it. You are asking Americans to proclaim themselves Anglo-Americans, and to sympathize with England on the ground that England is the motherland, and in order to make what you call 'hands across the sea' a matter of living policy. I do not believe that this is the right attitude for Americans to take. England is not my mother-land any more than Germany is my father-land. My mother-land and father-land and my own land are all three of them the United States. I am among those Americans whose ancestors include men and women from many different European countries. The proportion of Americans of this type will steadily increase. I do not believe in hyphenated Americans. I do not believe in German-Americans or Irish-Americans; and I believe just as little in English-Americans. I do not approve of American citizens of German descent forming organizations to force the United States into practical alliance with Germany because their ancestors came from Germany. Just as little do I believe in American citizens of English descent forming leagues to force the United States into an alliance with England because their ancestors came from England. We Americans are a separate people. We are separated from, although akin to, many European peoples. The old Revolutionary stock was predominantly English, but by no means exclusively so; for many of the descendants of the Revolutionary New Yorkers, Pennsylvanians and Georgians have, like myself, strains of Dutch, French, Scotch, Irish, Welsh and German blood in their veins. During the century and a quarter that has elapsed since we became a nation, there has been far more immigration from Germany and Ireland and probably from Scandinavia than there has been from England. We have a right to ask all of these immigrants and the sons of these immigrants that they become Americans and nothing else; but we have no right to ask that they become transplanted or second-rate Englishmen. Most emphatically I myself am not an Englishman-once-removed! I am straight United States!

"In international matters we should treat each nation on its conduct and without the slightest reference to the fact that a larger or smaller proportion of its blood flows in the veins of our own citizens. I have publicly and emphatically taken ground for Belgium and I wish that the United States would take ground for Belgium, because I hold that this is our duty, and that Germany's conduct toward Belgium demands that we antagonize her in this matter, and that we emphatically and in practical shape try to see that Belgium's wrongs are redressed. Because of the British attitude toward Belgium I have publicly and emphatically approved of her attitude, that is of Great Britain's conduct in living up to her obligations by defending Belgium, even at the cost of war. But I am not doing this on any ground that there is any 'hands across the sea' alliance, explicit or implicit, with England. I have never used in peace or in war any such expression as 'Hands across the Sea,' and I emphatically disapprove of what it signifies save in so far as it means cordial friendship between us and every other nation that acts in accordance with the standards that we deem just and right. On this ground all Americans, no matter what their race origins, ought to stand together. It is not just that they should be asked to stand with any foreign power on the ground of community of origin between some of them and the citizens of that foreign power. (Signed Theodore Roosevelt.)"

We of America form a new nationality. We are by blood, and we ought to be by feeling, akin to but distinct from every nationality of Europe. If our various constituent strains endeavor to keep themselves separate from the rest of their fellow-countrymen by the use of hyphens, they are doing all in their power to prevent themselves and ourselves from ever becoming a real nationality at all.

An American who is loyal to this great American nation has two duties, and only two, in international matters. In the first place, he is bound to serve the honor and the interest of the United States. In the second place, he is bound to treat all other nations in accordance with their conduct at any given time, and in accordance with the ultimate needs of mankind at large; and not in accordance with the interests of the European nation from which some or all of his ancestors have come. If he does not act along these lines, he is derelict in his duty to his fellow-citizens and he is guilty of betraying the interests of his country.[1]

[1] From *Fear God and Take Your Own Part*. Copyright, 1916. George H. Doran Company, publishers.

II

THE mighty tide of immigration to our shores has brought in its train much of good and much of evil; and whether the good or the evil shall predominate depends mainly on whether these newcomers do or do not throw themselves heartily into our national life, cease to be European, and become Americans like the rest of us. More than a third of the people of the Northern States are of foreign birth or parentage. An immense number of them have become completely Americanized, and these stand on exactly the same plane as the descendants of any Puritan, Cavalier, or Knickerbocker among us, and do their full and honorable share of the nation's work. But where immigrants, or the sons of immigrants, do not heartily and in good faith throw in their lot with us, but cling to the speech, the customs, the ways of life, and the habits of thought of the Old World which they have left, they thereby harm both themselves and us. If they remain alien elements, unassimilated, and with interests separate from ours, they are mere obstructions to the current of our national life, and moreover, can get no good from it themselves.

From his own standpoint, it is beyond all question the wise thing for the immigrant to become thoroughly Americanized. Moreover, from our standpoint, we have a right to demand it. We freely extend the hand of welcome and of good-fellowship to every man, no matter what his creed or birthplace, who comes here honestly intent on becoming a good United States citizen like the rest of us; but we have a right, and it is our duty, to demand that he shall indeed become so, and shall not confuse the issues with which we are struggling by introducing among us Old-World quarrels and prejudices.

There are certain ideas which he must give up. For instance, he must learn that American life is incompatible with the existence of any form of anarchy, or of any secret society having murder for its aim, whether at home or abroad; and he must learn that we exact full religious toleration and the complete separation of Church and State. Moreover, he must not bring in his Old-World religious race and national antipathies, but must merge them into love for our common country, and must take pride in the things which we can all take pride in. He must revere only our flag; not only must it come first, but no other flag should even come second. He must learn to celebrate Washington's birthday rather than that of the Queen or Kaiser, and the Fourth of July instead of St. Patrick's Day. Our political and social questions must be settled on their own merits, and not complicated by quarrels between England and Ireland, or France and Germany, with which we have nothing to do: it is an outrage to fight an American political campaign with reference to questions of European politics. Above all, the immigrant must learn to talk and think and be United States.

Americanism is a question of spirit, conviction, and purpose, not of creed or birthplace. The politician who bids for the Irish or German vote, or the Irishman or German who votes as an Irishman or German, is despicable, for all citizens of this commonwealth should vote solely as Americans; but he is not a whit less despicable than the voter who votes against a good American, merely because that American happens to have been born in Ireland or Germany. Know-nothingism, in any form, is as utterly un-American as foreignism. It is a base outrage to oppose a man because of his religion or birthplace, and all good citizens will hold any such effort in abhorrence. A Scandinavian, a German, or an Irishman who has really become an American has the right to stand on exactly the same footing as any native-born citizens in the land, and is just as much entitled to the friendship and support, social and political, of his neighbors.

We Americans can only do our allotted task well if we face it steadily and bravely, seeing but not fearing the dangers. Above all we must stand shoulder to shoulder, not asking as to the ancestry or creed of our comrades, but only demanding that they be in very truth Americans, and that we all work together, heart, hand, and head, for the honor and the greatness of our common country.[1]

III

THERE are two demands upon the spirit of Americanism, of nationalism. Each must be met. Each is essential. Each is vital, if we are to be a great and proud nation.

The first is that we shall tolerate no kind of divided allegiance in this country. There is no room for the hyphen in our citizenship. There is no place for a 50-50 Americanism in the United States. He who is not with us, absolutely and without reserve of any kind, is against us, and should be treated as an alien enemy, to be interned or sent out of the country. We have room

---

[1] From *American Ideals*. Copyright, 1897. G. P. Putnam's Sons, New York and London, publishers.

in this country for but one flag, the Stars and Stripes, and we should tolerate no allegiance to any other flag, whether a foreign flag or the red flag or black flag. We have room for but one loyalty, loyalty to the United States. We have room for but one language, the language of Washington and Lincoln, the language of the Declaration of Independence and the Gettysburg speech; the English language. English should be the only language used or taught in the primary schools, public or private; in higher schools of learning other modern languages should be taught, on an equality with one another; but the language of use and instruction should be English. We should require by law that within a reasonable length of time, a time long enough to prevent needless hardship, every newspaper should be published in English. The language of the church and the Sunday-school should be English. The government should provide night schools free for every immigrant who comes here, require him to attend them, and return him to his own country unless at the end of five years he has learned to speak and read English. This war has shown us in vivid and startling fashion the danger of allowing our people to separate along lines of racial origin and linguistic cleavage. We shall be guilty of criminal folly if we fail to insist on the complete and thoroughgoing unification of our people. . . .

This is one of the demands to be made in the name of the spirit of American nationalism. The other is equally important. We must treat every good American of German or of any other origin, without regard to his creed, as on a full and exact equality with every other good American, and set our faces like flint against the creatures who seek to discriminate against such an American, or to hold against him the birthplace of himself or his parents.

We must resolutely refuse to permit our great nation, our great America, to be split into a score of little replicas of European nationalities, and to become a Balkan Peninsula on a larger scale. We are a nation, and not a hodgepodge of foreign nationalities. We are a people, and not a polyglot boarding-house. We must insist on a unified nationality, with one flag, one language, one set of national ideals. We must shun as we would shun the plague all efforts to make us separate in groups of separate nationalities. We must all of us be Americans, and nothing but Americans; and all good Americans must stand on an equality of consideration and respect, without regard to their creed or to the land from which their forebears came.

We are the fellow countrymen of Washington and Lincoln, of Lighthorse Harry Lee and his great son, of Grant and Sherman and Farragut, of Marion and Paul Revere and Schuyler, of Washington's General Sullivan and Lincoln's General Sheridan. These men were of diverse ancestry; their forefathers came from England or Ireland or Scotland or Holland or France or Spain. But they were American, and nothing else; and if we are really to be loyal to their spirit, we, in our day, must be Americans, and nothing else. And, above all, we must be Americans, and only Americans, in the face of any and every foreign foe.

We are also, and just as much, the fellow countrymen of Muhlenberg and Custer. There is no more typically American figure in the Revolutionary War than that of

Muhlenberg, the American of pure German blood, the pastor of a Lutheran church at the outbreak of the Revolution. On the Sunday after the call for arms came, he mounted his pulpit; he admonished his flock that there was a time for prayer and a time for battle, and that the time for battle had come. Casting aside his frock, he appeared in the uniform of a colonel of the Continental Army; and on many a stricken field he proved his valor and devotion. Custer, a man of German descent, was one of the most gallant and heroic figures of the Civil War and the Indian Wars; his name and career made up one of the finest traditions of our army. In the Civil War there fought many, many men of German birth; Sigel, Osterhaus, Heintzelman; innumerable others. They proved their Americanism by their deeds. Their grandsons are in our armies and navy to-day. Their undivided loyalty is given to one flag, to our flag. They are incapable of a loyalty different from that of their fellow Americans of different blood. These fellow Americans of theirs who happen to be of different blood must in their turn see to it that any one who discriminates against these men because they are of German blood is himself branded as a traitor.

Above all, we are bound to treat all our fellow Americans with reference solely to their whole-hearted loyalty to American ideals as embodied in the great Americans whose names I have used above. True Americans who are in whole or in part of German blood claim nothing except the right to serve America and to be judged according to their service.[1]

[1] From *The Great Adventure.* Copyright, 1918. Charles Scribner's Sons, publishers.

V

NATIONAL STRENGTH — THE BASIS OF INTERNATIONAL PEACE

Let us speak courteously, deal fairly, and keep ourselves armed and ready.

Theodore Roosevelt

I. NATIONAL PREPAREDNESS

I

There can be no genuine feeling of patriotism of the kind that makes all men willing and eager to die for the land, unless there has been some measure of success in making the land worth living in for all alike, whatever their station, so long as they do their duty; and on the other hand, no man has a right to enjoy any benefits whatever from living in the land in time of peace, unless he is trained physically and spiritually so that if duty calls he can and will do his part to keep the land against all alien aggression.[1]

II

If the people have not vision, they shall surely perish. No man has a right to live who has not in his soul the power to die nobly for a great cause. Let abhorrence be for those who wage wanton or wicked wars, who with ruthless violence oppress the upright and the unoffending. Pay all honor to the preachers of peace who put righteousness above peace. But shame on the creatures

[1] Speech at Cooper Union, New York City, November 3, 1916.

who would teach our people that it is anything but base to be unready and unable to defend right, even at need by the sternest of all tests, the test of righteous war, war waged by a high-couraged people with souls attuned to the demands of a lofty ideal.[1]

III

IF in the future we have war, it will almost certainly come because of some action, or lack of action, on our part in the way of refusing to accept responsibilities at the proper time, or failing to prepare for war when war does not threaten. An ignoble peace is even worse than an unsuccessful war; but an unsuccessful war would leave behind it a legacy of bitter memories which would hurt our national development for a generation to come. It is true that no nation could actually conquer us, owing to our isolated position; but we would be seriously harmed, even materially, by disasters that stopped far short of conquest; and in these matters, which are far more important than things material, we could readily be damaged beyond repair. No material loss can begin to compensate for the loss of national self-respect. The damage to our commercial interests by the destruction of one of our coast cities would be as nothing compared to the humiliation which would be felt by every American worthy of the name if we had to submit to such an injury without amply avenging it. It has been finely said that "a gentleman is one who is willing to lay down his life for little things"; that is, for those things which seem little to the man who cares only whether shares

[1] From *Fear God and Take Your Own Part*. Copyright, 1916. George H. Doran Company, publishers.

rise or fall in value, and to the timid doctrinaire who preaches timid peace from his cloistered study.

Much of that which is best and highest in national character is made up of glorious memories and traditions. The fight well fought, the life honorably lived, the death bravely met — those count for more in building a high and fine type of temper in a nation than any possible success in the stock market, than any possible prosperity in commerce or manufactures. A rich banker may be a valuable and useful citizen, but not a thousand rich bankers can leave to the country such a heritage as Farragut left, when, lashed in the rigging of the Hartford, he forged past the forts and over the unseen death below, to try his wooden stem against the ironclad hull of the great Confederate ram. The people of some given section of our country may be better off because a shrewd and wealthy man has built up therein a great manufacturing business, or has extended a line of railroad past its doors; but the whole nation is better, the whole nation is braver, because Cushing pushed his little torpedo-boat through the darkness to sink beside the sinking Albemarle.

Every feat of heroism makes us forever indebted to the man who performed it. All daring and courage, all iron endurance of misfortune, all devotion to the ideal of honor and the glory of the flag, make for a finer and nobler type of manhood. It is not only those who do and dare and endure that are benefited; but also the countless thousands who are not themselves called upon to face the peril, to show the strength, or to win the reward. All of us lift our heads higher because those of our countrymen whose trade it is to meet danger have met it well

and bravely. All of us are poorer for every base or ignoble deed done by an American, for every instance of
selfishness or weakness or folly on the part of the people
as a whole. We are all worse off when any of us fails at
any point in his duty toward the State in time of peace,
or his duty toward the State in time of war. If ever we
had to meet defeat at the hands of a foreign foe, or had
to submit tamely to wrong or insult, every man among
us worthy of the name of American would feel dishon-
ored and debased. On the other hand, the memory of
every triumph won by Americans, by just so much helps
to make each American nobler and better. Every man
among us is more fit to meet the duties and responsibilities of citizenship because of the perils over which, in
the past, the nation has triumphed; because of the blood
and sweat and tears, the labor and the anguish, through
which, in the days that have gone, our forefathers
moved on to triumph. There are higher things in this
life than the soft and easy enjoyment of material comfort. It is through strife, or the readiness for strife, that
a nation must win greatness.[1]

IV

LET us prepare not merely in military matters, but in
our social and industrial life. There can be no sound
relationship toward other nations unless there is also
sound relationship among our own citizens within our
own ranks. Let us insist on the thorough Americanization of the newcomers to our shores, and let us also

[1] Address before The Naval War College, Annapolis, June, 1897.
From *The Strenuous Life.* Copyright, 1900. The Century Company,
publishers.

insist on the thorough Americanization of ourselves.
Let us encourage the fullest industrial activity, and
give the amplest industrial reward to those whose activities are most important for securing industrial success, and at the same time let us see that justice is
done and wisdom shown in securing the welfare of
every man, woman, and child within our borders. Finally, let us remember that we can do nothing to help
other peoples, and nothing permanently to secure material well-being and social justice within our own borders,
unless we feel with all our hearts devotion to this country, unless we are Americans and nothing else, and unless in time of peace by universal military training, by
insistence upon the obligations of every man and every
woman to serve the commonwealth both in peace and
war, and, above all, by a high and fine preparedness of
soul and spirit, we fit ourselves to hold our own against
all possible aggression from without.

We are the citizens of a mighty Republic consecrated
to the service of God above, through the service of man
on this earth. We are the heirs of a great heritage be-
queathed to us by statesmen who saw with the eyes of
the seer and the prophet. We must not prove false to
the memories of the nation's past. We must not prove
false to the fathers from whose loins we sprang, and to
their fathers, the stern men who dared greatly and
risked all things that freedom should hold aloft an un-
dimmed torch in this wide land. They held their worldly
well-being as dust in the balance when weighed
against their sense of high duty, their fealty to lofty
ideals. Let us show ourselves worthy to be their sons.
Let us care, as is right, for the things of the body; but

let us show that we care even more for the things of the
soul. Stout of heart, and pledged to the valor of righteousness, let us stand four-square to the winds of des-
tiny, from whatever corner of the world they blow. Let
us keep untarnished, unstained, the honor of the flag our
fathers bore aloft in the teeth of the wildest storm, the
flag that shall float above the solid files of a united people, a people sworn to the great cause of liberty and of
justice, for themselves, and for all the sons and daughters of men.[1]

V

FEAR God; and take your own part! Fear God, in the
true sense of the word, means love God, respect God,
honor God; and all of this can only be done by loving our
neighbor, treating him justly and mercifully, and in all
ways endeavoring to protect him from injustice and
cruelty; thus obeying, as far as our human frailty will
permit, the great and immutable law of righteousness.

We fear God when we do justice to and demand justice for the men within our own borders. We are false to
the teachings of righteousness if we do not do such justice and demand such justice. We must do it to the
weak and we must do it to the strong. We do not fear
God if we show mean envy and hatred of those who are
better off than we are; and still less do we fear God if we
show a base arrogance towards and selfish lack of consideration for those who are less well off. We must apply
the same standard of conduct alike to man and to

[1] From *Fear God and Take Your Own Part*. Copyright, 1916.
George H. Doran Company, publishers.

woman, to rich man and to poor man, to employer and employee.

Outside of our own borders we must treat other nations as we would wish to be treated in return, judging each in any given crisis as we ourselves ought to be judged — that is, by our conduct in that crisis. If they do ill, we show that we fear God when we sternly bear testimony against them and oppose them in any way and to whatever extent the needs require. If they do well, we must not wrong them ourselves. Finally, if we are really devoted to a lofty ideal we must in so far as our strength permits aid them if they are wronged by others. When we sit idly by while Belgium is being overwhelmed, and rolling up our eyes prattle with unctuous self-righteousness about "the duty of neutrality," we show that we do not really fear God; on the contrary, we show an odious fear of the devil, and a mean readiness to serve him.

But in addition to fearing God, it is necessary that we should be able and ready to take our own part. The man who cannot take his own part is a nuisance in the community, a source of weakness, an encouragement to wrongdoers and an added burden to the men who wish to do what is right. If he cannot take his own part, then somebody else has to take it for him; and this means that his weakness and cowardice and inefficiency place an added burden on some other man and make that other man's strength by just so much of less avail to the community as a whole. No man can take the part of any one else unless he is able to take his own part. This is just as true of nations as of men. A nation that cannot take its own part is at times almost as fertile a source of mischief in the world at large as is a nation which does wrong to others, for its very existence puts a premium on such wrongdoing. Therefore, a nation must fit itself to defend its honor and interest against outside aggression; and this necessarily means that in a free democracy every man fit for citizenship must be trained so that he can do his full duty to the nation in war no less than in peace.

Unless we are thoroughgoing Americans and unless our patriotism is part of the very fiber of our being, we can neither serve God nor take our own part. Whatever may be the case in an infinitely remote future, at present no people can render any service to humanity unless as a people they feel an intense sense of national cohesion and solidarity. The man who loves other nations as much as he does his own, stands on a par with the man who loves other women as much as he does his own wife. The United States can accomplish little for mankind, save in so far as within its borders it develops an intense spirit of Americanism. A flabby cosmopolitanism, especially if it expresses itself through a flabby pacifism, is not only silly, but degrading. It represents national emasculation. The professors of every form of hyphenated Americanism are as truly the foes of this country as if they dwelled outside its borders and made active war against it. This is not a figure of speech, or a hyperbolic statement.

Patriotism, so far from being incompatible with performance of duty to other nations, is an indispensable prerequisite to doing one's duty toward other nations. Fear God; and take your own part! If this nation had feared God it would have stood up for the Belgians and

Armenians; if it had been able and willing to take its own part there would have been no murderous assault on the Lusitania, no outrages on our men and women in Mexico. True patriotism carries with it not hostility to other nations but a quickened sense of responsible good-will towards other nations, a good-will of acts and not merely of words. I stand for a nationalism of duty, to one's self and to others; and, therefore, for a nationalism which is a means to internationalism. World peace must rest on the willingness of nations with courage, cool fore-sight, and readiness for self-sacrifice to defend the fabric of international law. No nation can help in securing an organized, peaceful and justice-doing world community until it is willing to run risks and make efforts in order to secure and maintain such a community.

The nation that in actual practice fears God is the nation which does not wrong its neighbors, which does so far as possible help its neighbors, and which never promises what it cannot or will not or ought not to per-form.

Peace is not the end. Righteousness is the end. When the Saviour saw the money-changers in the Temple he broke the peace by driving them out. At that moment peace could have been obtained readily enough by the simple process of keeping quiet in the presence of wrong. But instead of preserving peace at the expense of right-eousness, the Saviour armed himself with a scourge of cords and drove the money-changers from the Temple. Righteousness is the end, and peace a means to the end, and sometimes it is not peace, but war which is the proper means to achieve the end. Righteousness should breed valor and strength. When it does breed them, it is triumphant; and when triumphant, it necessarily brings peace. But peace does not necessarily bring righteousness.

As for neutrality, it is well to remember that it is never moral, and may be a particularly mean and hideous form of immorality. It is in itself merely unmoral; that is, neither moral nor immoral; and at times it may be wise and expedient. But it is never anything of which to be proud; and it may be something of which to be heartily ashamed. It is a wicked thing to be neutral between right and wrong. Impartiality does not mean neutrality. Impartial justice consists not in being neutral between right and wrong, but in finding out the right and upholding it, wherever found, against the wrong.

There are schools of pacifists who decline to profit by the exercise of the police power, who decline to protect not merely themselves, but those dearest to them, from any form of outrage and violence. The individuals of this type are at least logical in their horror even of just war. If a man deliberately takes the view that he will not resent having his wife's face slapped, that he will not by force endeavor to save his daughter from outrage, and that he disapproves of the policeman who interferes by force to save a child kidnapped by a black-hander, or a girl run off by a white-slaver, then he is logical in objecting to war. Of course, to my mind, he occupies an unspeakably base and loathsome position, and is not fit to cumber the world — on which, as a matter of fact, he exists at all only because he is protected by the maintenance by others of the very principle which he himself repudiates and declines to share.

Such a position I hold to be as profoundly immoral as it is profoundly unpatriotic.[1]

VI

In Maine there are many seafaring folks. I can illustrate what I mean about the use and abuse of the word safety by the life-saving service. This is a service especially designed to secure greater safety for ships' crews, and generally for persons whose lives are imperiled on the water. It is a service to secure safety. But the safety is secured only because some brave men are willing to risk their own lives in order to save other lives. They do not put "safety first," as far as they themselves are concerned. If they did, no lifeboat would ever be launched from a life-saving station. But the men on a sinking ship who crowd into the lifeboats ahead of the women and children do put "safety first." I will say this for them, however: Whenever they get ashore they do not wear buttons to commemorate the feat — as some of our opponents in the present campaign do.

Life-saving medals are granted every year. Each medal means that a life has been saved; and each means also that in order to save it another life has been put in jeopardy. The "safety first" class does not get such medals. Every life-saving crew is composed of men who are tough, hardy and well-trained. They put safety first as far as self-indulgence, and soft ease, and mere money-getting are concerned; otherwise they would be helpless in a storm. But where duty and safety are concerned, they put duty first and safety last.

[1] From *Fear God and Take Your Own Part.* Copyright, **1916.** George H. Doran Company, publishers.

I wish to see this nation act in similar fashion, both as regards its own safety and as regards the performance of international duty. I wish to see it, by forethought, by effort and hard training, and by the cultivation of a broad and intense feeling of national endeavor and national patriotism, to so develop its courage and its efficient strength as to be able to hold its own against any possible aggression; and then I wish to see it put duty first, not safety first, when any small, well-behaved people is treated as Belgium has been treated. I stand for the safety that is obtained by the performance of duty. I do not stand for the safety that is obtained by the sacrifice of duty.[1]

[1] Speech at Lewiston, Maine, August 31, 1916.

II. NATIONALISM

It is well at this time for sober and resolute men and women to apply that excellent variety of wisdom colloquially known as "horse-sense" to the problems of nationalism and internationalism. These problems will not be solved by rhetoric. Least of all will they be solved by competitive rhetoric. Masters of phrasemaking may win immense, although evanescent, applause by outvying one another in words that glitter, but these glittering words will not have one shred of lasting effect on the outcome except in so far as they may have a very mischievous effect if they persuade good, ignorant people to abandon the possible real good in the fantastic effort to achieve an impossible unreal perfection. Let honest men and women remember that this kind of phrasemongering does not represent idealism. The only idealism worth considering in the workaday business of this world is applied idealism. This is merely another way of saying that permanent good to humanity is most apt to come from actually trying to reduce ideals to practice, and this means that the ideals must be substantially or at least measurably realizable.

The professed internationalist usually sneers at nationalism, at patriotism, and at what we call Americanism. He bids us forswear our love of country in the name of love of the world at large. We nationalists answer that he has begun at the wrong end; we say that, as the world now is, it is only the man who ardently loves his country first who in actual practice can help any other country at all. The internationalist bids us to promise to abandon the idea of keeping America permanently ready to defend her rights by her strength and to trust, instead, to scraps of paper, to written agreements by which all nations form a league, and agree to disarm, and agree each to treat all other nations, big or little, on an exact equality. We nationalists answer that we are ready to join any league to enforce peace or similar organization which offers a likelihood of in some measure lessening the number and the area of future wars, but only on condition that in the first place we do not promise what will not or ought not to be performed, or be guilty of proclaiming a sham, and that in the second place we do not surrender our right and duty to prepare our own strength for our own defense instead of trusting to the above-mentioned scraps of paper.

The horse-sense of the matter is that all agreements to further the cause of sound internationalism must be based on recognition of the fact that, as the world is actually constituted, our present prime need is this sound and intense American nationalism. The first essential of this sound nationalism is that the nation shall trust to its own fully prepared strength for its own defense. So far as possible, its strength must also be used to secure justice for others and must never be used to wrong others. But unless we possess and prepare the strength, we can neither help ourselves nor others. Let us by all means go into any wise league or covenant among nations to abolish neutrality (for of course a league to enforce peace is merely another name for a league to abolish neutrality in every possible war). But let us first understand what we are promising, and count the cost and determine to keep our promises. Above all, let us treat any such agreement or covenant as a mere addition or supplement to and never as a substitute for the preparation in advance of our own armed power.

There is no limit to the greatness of the future before America, before our beloved land. But we can realize it only if we are Americans, if we are nationalists, with all the fervor of our hearts and all the wisdom of our brains. We can serve the world at all only if we serve America first and best. We must work along our own national lines in every field of achievement. We must feel in the very marrow of our being that our loyalty is due only to America, and that it is not diluted by loyalty for any other nation or all other nations on the face of the earth. Only thus shall we fit ourselves really to serve other nations, to refuse ourselves to wrong them, and to refuse to let them do wrong or suffer wrong.[1]

[1] From *The Great Adventure*. Copyright, 1918. Charles Scribner's Sons, publishers.

III. INTERNATIONAL RELATIONS

I

THE MONROE DOCTRINE is not international law, and though I think one day it may become such, this is not necessary as long as it remains a cardinal feature of our foreign policy and as long as we possess both the will and the strength to make it effective. This last point, my fellow citizens, is all-important, and is one which as a people we can never afford to forget. I believe in the Monroe Doctrine with all my heart and soul; I am convinced that the immense majority of our fellow countrymen so believe in it; but I would infinitely prefer to see us abandon it than to see us put it forward and bluster about it, and yet fail to build up the efficient fighting strength which in the last resort can alone make it respected by any strong foreign power whose interest it may ever happen to be to violate it.

Boasting and blustering are as objectionable among nations as among individuals, and the public men of a great nation owe it to their sense of national self-respect to speak courteously of foreign powers, just as a brave and self-respecting man treats all around him courteously. But though to boast is bad, and causelessly to insult another, worse; yet worse than all is it to be guilty of boasting, even without insult, and when called to the proof to be unable to make such boasting good. There is a homely old adage which runs: "Speak softly and carry a big stick; you will go far." If the American Nation will speak softly, and yet build, and keep at a pitch of the highest training, a thoroughly efficient navy, the Monroe Doctrine will go far. I ask you to think over this. If you do, you will come to the conclusion that it is mere plain common sense, so obviously sound that only the blind can fail to see its truth and only the weakest and most irresolute can fail to desire to put it into force.[1]

II

WE want the friendship of mankind. We want to get on well with the other nations of mankind, with the small nations and with the big nations. We want so to carry ourselves that if (which I think most unlikely) any quarrel should arise, it would be evident that it was not a quarrel of our own seeking, but one that was forced on us. If it is forced on us, I know you too well not to know that you will stand up to it if the need comes; but you will stand up to it all the better if you have not blustered or spoken ill of other nations in advance. We want friendship; we want peace. We wish well to the nations of mankind. We look with joy at any prosperity of theirs; we wish them success, not failure. We rejoice as mankind moves forward over the whole earth. Each nation has its own difficulties. We have difficulties enough at home. Let us improve ourselves, lifting what needs to be lifted here, and let others do their own; let us attend to our own, keep our own hearthstone swept and in order. Do not shirk any duty; do not shirk any difficulty that is forced upon us, but do not invite it by foolish language. Do not assume a quarrelsome and unpleasant attitude toward other

[1] Address at Chicago, Illinois, April 2, 1903.

people. Let the friendly expressions of foreign powers be accepted as tokens of their sincere good-will, and reflecting their real sentiments; and let us avoid any language on our part which might tend to turn their good-will into ill-will. All that is mere common sense; the kind of common sense that we apply in our own lives, man to man, neighbor to neighbor; and remember that substantially what is true among nations, is true on a small scale among ourselves. The man who is a weakling, who is a coward, we all despise, and we ought to despise him. If a man cannot do his own work and take his own part, he does not count; and I have no patience with those who would have the United States unable to take its own part, to do its work in the world. But remember that a loose tongue is just as unfortunate an accompaniment for a nation as for an individual. The man who talks ill of his neighbors, the man who invites trouble for himself and them, is a nuisance. The stronger, the more self-confident the nation is, the more carefully it should guard its speech as well as its action, and should make it a point, in the interest of its own self-respect, to see that it does not say what it cannot make good, that it avoids giving needless offense, that it shows genuinely and sincerely its desire for friendship with the rest of mankind, but that it keeps itself in shape to make its weight felt should the need arise.

That is in substance my theory of what our foreign policy should be. Let us not boast, not insult any one, but make up our minds coolly what it is necessary to say, say it, and then stand to it, whatever the consequences may be.[1]

[1] Address at Waukesha, Wisconsin, April 3, 1903.

III

THERE are certain elementary facts to be grasped by this people before we can have any [foreign] policy at all. The first fact is a thorough understanding of that hoary falsehood which declares that it takes two to make a quarrel. It did not take two nations to make the quarrel that resulted in Germany trampling Belgium into the mire. It is no more true that it takes two to make a quarrel in international matters than it is to make the same assertion about a highwayman who holds up a pass-er-by or a black-hander who kidnaps a child. The people who do not make quarrels, who are not offensive, who give no cause for anger, are those who ordinarily furnish the victims of highwaymen, black-handers and white-slavers. Criminals always attack the helpless if possible. In exactly similar fashion aggressive and militarist nations attack weak nations where it is possible. Weakness always invites attack. Preparedness usually, but not always, averts it.[1]

IV

THE policy of milk and water is an even worse policy than the policy of blood and iron.

V

THE advocates of world-wide peace, like all reformers, should bear in mind Josh Billings's astute remark that

[1] This and the following section are from *Fear God and Take Your Own Part*. Copyright, 1916. George H. Doran Company, publishers.

"it is much easier to be a harmless dove than a wise serpent." [1]

VI

I ABHOR war. In common with all other thinking men I am inexpressibly saddened by the dreadful contest now raging in Europe. I put peace very high as an agent for bringing about righteousness. But if I must choose between righteousness and peace, I choose righteousness.

VII

ONE of the main lessons to learn from this war is embodied in the homely proverb: "Speak softly and carry a big stick." Persistently only half of this proverb has been quoted in deriding the men who wish to safeguard our national interest and honor. Persistently the effort has been made to insist that those who advocate keeping our country able to defend its rights are merely adopting "the policy of the big stick." In reality, we lay equal emphasis on the fact that it is necessary to speak softly; in other words, that it is necessary to be respectful toward all people and scrupulously to refrain from wronging them, while at the same time keeping ourselves in condition to prevent wrong being done to us. If a nation does not in this sense speak softly, then sooner or later the policy of the big stick is certain to result in war. But what befell Luxembourg five months ago, what has befallen China again and again during the past quarter of a century, shows that no amount of

[1] This and the two following sections are from *America and the World War*. Copyright, 1915. Charles Scribner's Sons, publishers.

speaking softly will save any people which does not carry a big stick.

America should have a coherent policy of action toward foreign powers, and this should primarily be based on the determination never to give offense when it can be avoided, always to treat other nations justly and courteously, and, as long as present conditions exist, to be prepared to defend our own rights ourselves. No other nation will defend them for us. No paper guarantee or treaty will be worth the paper on which it is written if it becomes to the interest of some other power to violate it, unless we have strength, and courage and ability to use that strength, back of the treaty.

VIII

I HOLD that the laws of morality which should govern individuals in their dealings one with the other are just as binding concerning nations in their dealings one with the other. The application of the moral law must be different in the two cases, because in one case it has, and in the other it has not, the sanction of a civil law with force behind it. The individual can depend for his rights upon the courts, which themselves derive their force from the police power of the State. The nation can depend upon nothing of the kind; and therefore, as things are now, it is the highest duty of the most advanced and freest peoples to keep themselves in such a state of readiness as to forbid to any barbarism or despotism the hope of arresting the progress of the world by striking down the nations that lead in that progress. It would be foolish indeed to pay heed to the unwise persons who desire disarmament to be begun by the very people who, of all

others, should not be left helpless before any possible
foe. But we must reprobate quite as strongly both the
leaders and the peoples who practice, or encourage or
condone, aggression and iniquity by the strong at the
expense of the weak. We should tolerate lawlessness
and wickedness neither by the weak nor by the strong;
and both weak and strong we should in return treat
with scrupulous fairness. The foreign policy of a great
and self-respecting country should be conducted on exactly the same plane of honor, of insistence upon one's
own rights and of respect for the rights of others, as
when a brave and honorable man is dealing with his
fellows. Permit me to support this statement out of
my own experience. For nearly eight years I was the
head of a great nation and charged especially with the
conduct of its foreign policy; and during those years I
took no action with reference to any other people on the
face of the earth that I would not have felt justified in
taking as an individual in dealing with other individuals.[1]

[1] Address delivered at Oxford University, Oxford, England, June 7,
1910. From *African and European Addresses*. Copyright, 1910.
G. P. Putnam's Sons, New York and London, publishers.

IV. INTERNATIONAL ORGANIZATION
FOR PEACE

I

IT was no mere accident that made our three mightiest men, two of them soldiers, and one the great war President. It is only through work and strife that either nation or individual moves on to greatness. The great man is always the man of mighty effort, and usually the man whom grinding need has trained to mighty effort. Rest and peace are good things, are great blessings, but only if they come honorably; and it is those who fearlessly turn away from them, when they have not been earned, who in the long run deserve best of their country. In the sweat of our brows do we eat bread, and though the sweat is bitter at times, yet it is far more bitter to eat the bread that is unearned, unwon, undeserved. America must nerve herself for labor and peril. The men who have made our national greatness are those who faced danger and overcame it, who met difficulties and surmounted them, not those whose lines were cast in such pleasant places that toil and dread were ever far from them.

Neither was it an accident that our three leaders were men who, while they did not shrink from war, were nevertheless heartily men of peace. The man who will not fight to avert or undo wrong is but a poor creature; but, after all, he is less dangerous than the man who fights on the side of wrong. Again and again in a nation's history the time may, and indeed sometimes must, come when the nation's highest duty is war. But peace must be the normal condition, or the nation will come to a bloody doom.

Twice in great crises, in 1776 and 1861, and twice in lesser crises, in 1812 and 1898, the Nation was called to arms in the name of all that makes the words "honor," "freedom," and "justice" other than empty sounds. On each occasion the net result of the war was greatly for the benefit of mankind. But on each occasion this net result was of benefit only because after the war came peace, came justice and order and liberty. If the Revolution had been followed by bloody anarchy, if the Declaration of Independence had not been supplemented by the adoption of the Constitution, if the freedom won by the sword of Washington had not been supplemented by the stable and orderly government which Washington was instrumental in founding, then we should have but added to the chaos of the world, and our victories would have told against and not for the betterment of mankind. So it was with the Civil War. If the four iron years had not been followed by peace, they would not have been justified. If the great silent soldier, the Hammer of the North, had struck the shackles off the slave only, as so many conquerors in civil strife before him had done, to rivet them around the wrists of freemen, then the war would have been fought in vain, and worse than in vain. If the Union, which so many men shed their blood to restore, were not now a union in fact, then the precious blood would have been wasted.

But it was not wasted; for the work of peace has made good the work of war, and North and South, East and West, we are now one people in fact as well as in name;

one in purpose, in fellow-feeling, and in high resolve, as we stand to greet the new century, and, high of heart, to face the mighty tasks which the coming years will surely bring.[1]

II

MOST Western Americans who are past middle age remember young, rapidly growing, and turbulent communities in which there was at first complete anarchy. During the time when there was no central police power to which to appeal, every man worth his salt, in other words every man fit for existence in such a community, had to be prepared to defend himself; and usually, although not always, the fact that he was prepared saved him from all trouble, whereas unpreparedness was absolutely certain to invite disaster.

In such communities before there was a regular and fully organized police force there came an interval during which the preservation of the peace depended upon the action of a single official, a sheriff or marshal, who if the law was defied in arrogant fashion summoned a posse comitatus composed of as many armed, thoroughly efficient, law-abiding citizens as were necessary in order to put a stop to the wrongdoing. Under these conditions each man had to keep himself armed and both able and willing to respond to the call of the peace-officer; and furthermore, if he had a shred of wisdom he kept himself ready in an emergency to act on his own behalf if the peace-officer did not or could not do his duty.

In such towns I have myself more than once seen well-

[1] Address at Galena, Illinois, April 27, 1900. From *The Strenuous Life*. Copyright, 1900. The Century Company, publishers.

meaning but foolish citizens endeavor to meet the exigencies of the case by simply passing resolutions of disarmament without any power back of them. That is, they passed self-denying ordinances, saying that nobody was to carry arms; but they failed to provide methods for carrying such ordinances into effect. In every case the result was the same. Good citizens for the moment abandoned their weapons. The bad men continued to carry them. Things grew worse instead of better; and then the good men came to their senses and clothed some representative of the police with power to employ force, potential or existing, against the wrongdoers.

Affairs in the international world are at this time in analogous condition. There is no central police power, and not the least likelihood of its being created. Well-meaning enthusiasts have tried their hands to an almost unlimited extent in the way of devising all-inclusive arbitration treaties, neutrality treaties, disarmament proposals, and the like, with no force back of them, and the result has been stupendous and discreditable failure. Preparedness for war on the part of individual nations has sometimes but not always averted war. Unpreparedness for war, as in the case of China, Korea, and Luxembourg, has invariably invited smashing disaster, and sometimes complete conquest. Surely these conditions should teach a lesson that any man who runs may read unless his eyes have been blinded by folly or his heart weakened by cowardice.

The immediately vital lesson for each individual nation is that as things are now it must in time of crisis rely on its own stout hearts and ready hands for self-defense. Existing treaties are utterly worthless so far as concerns protecting any free, well-behaved people from one of the great aggressive military monarchies of the world.[1]

III

OUR business is to create the beginnings of international order out of the world of nations as these nations actually exist. We do not have to deal with a world of pacificists and therefore we must proceed on the assumption that treaties will never acquire sanctity until nations are ready to seal them with their blood. We are not striving for peace in heaven. That is not our affair. What we were bidden to strive for is "peace on earth and good-will toward men." To fulfill this injunction it is necessary to treat the earth as it is and men as they are, as an indispensable prerequisite to making the earth a better place in which to live and men better fit to live in it. It is inexcusable moral culpability on our part to pretend to carry out this injunction in such fashion as to nullify it; and this we do if we make believe that the earth is what it is not and if our professions of bringing good-will toward men are in actual practice shown to be empty shams. Peace congresses, peace parades, the appointment and celebration of days of prayer for peace, and the like, which result merely in giving the participants the feeling that they have accomplished something and are therefore to be excused from hard, practical work for righteousness, are empty shams. Treaties such as the recent all-inclusive arbitration treaties are worse than empty shams and convict us as a nation of moral culpability when our representatives sign them at the same

[1] This and the following two sections are from *America and the World War*. Copyright, 1915. Charles Scribner's Sons, publishers.

time that they refuse to risk anything to make good the signatures we have already affixed to the Hague conventions.

Moderate and sensible treaties which mean something and which can and will be enforced mark a real advance for the human race. As has been well said: "It is our business to make no treaties which we are not ready to maintain with all our resources, for every such 'scrap of paper' is like a forged check — an assault on our credit in the world."

IV

THE ultra-pacificists have been fond of prophesying the immediate approach of a universally peaceful condition throughout the world, which will render it unnecessary to prepare against war because there will be no more war. This represents in some cases well-meaning and pathetic folly. In other cases it represents mischievous and inexcusable folly. But it always represents folly. At best, it represents the inability of some well-meaning men of weak mind, and of some men of strong but twisted mind, either to face or to understand facts.

These prophets of the inane are not peculiar to our own day. A little over a century and a quarter ago a noted Italian pacificist and philosopher, Aurelio Bertela, summed up the future of civilized mankind as follows: "The political system of Europe has arrived at perfection. An equilibrium has been attained which henceforth will preserve peoples from subjugation. Few reforms are now needed and these will be accomplished peaceably. Europe has no need to fear revolution."

These sapient statements (which have been paralleled

by hundreds of utterances in the many peace congresses of the last couple of decades) were delivered in 1787, the year in which the French Assembly of Notables ushered in the greatest era of revolution, domestic turmoil, and international war in all history — an era which still continues and which shows not the smallest sign of coming to an end. Never before have there been wars on so great a scale as during this century and a quarter; and the greatest of all these wars is now being waged. Never before, except for the ephemeral conquests of certain Asiatic barbarians, have there been subjugations of civilized peoples on so great a scale.

The effective workers for the peace of righteousness were men like Stein, Cavour, and Lincoln; that is, men who dreamed great dreams, but who were also preëminently men of action, who stood for the right, and who knew that the right would fail unless might was put behind it. The prophets of pacificism have had nothing whatever in common with these great men; and whenever they have preached mere pacificism, whenever they have failed to put righteousness first and to advocate peace as the handmaiden of righteousness, they have done evil and not good.

After the exhaustion of the Napoleonic struggles there came thirty-five years during which there was no great war, while what was called "the long peace" was broken only by minor international wars or short-lived revolutionary contests. Good, but not far-sighted, men in various countries, but especially in England, Germany, and our own country, forthwith began to dream dreams — not of a universal peace that should be founded on justice and righteousness backed by strength, but of a

universal peace to be obtained by the prattle of weaklings and the outpourings of amiable enthusiasts who
lacked the fighting edge. About 1850, for instance, the
first large peace congress was held. There were numbers
of kindly people who felt that this congress, and the con-
temporary international exposition, also the first of its
kind, heralded the beginning of a régime of universal
peace. As a matter of fact, there followed twenty years
during which a number of great and bloody wars took
place — wars far surpassing in extent, in duration, in
loss of life and property, and in importance anything
that had been seen since the close of the Napoleonic contest.

Then there came another period of nearly thirty years
during which there were relatively only a few wars, and
these not of the highest importance. Again upright and
intelligent but uninformed men began to be misled by
foolish men into the belief that world peace was about to
be secured, on a basis of amiable fatuity all around and
under the lead of the preachers of the diluted mush of
make-believe morality. A number of peace congresses,
none of which accomplished anything, were held, and
also certain Hague conferences, which did accomplish a
certain small amount of real good but of a strictly limited kind. It was well worth going into these Hague conferences, but only on condition of clearly understanding
how strictly limited was the good that they accomplished. The hysterical people who treated them as fur-
nishing a patent peace panacea did nothing but harm,
and partially offset the real but limited good the conferences actually accomplished. Indeed, the conferences
undoubtedly did a certain amount of damage because of

the preposterous expectations they excited among well-meaning but ill-informed and unthinking persons. These persons really believed that it was possible to achieve the millennium by means that would not have been every effective in preserving peace among the active boys of a large Sunday-school — let alone grown-up men in the world as it actually is. A pathetic commentary on their attitude is furnished by the fact that the fifteen years that have elapsed since the first Hague conference have seen an immense increase of war, culminating in the present war, waged by armies, and with bloodshed, on a scale far vaster than ever before in the history of mankind.

All these facts furnish no excuse whatever for our failing to work zealously for peace, but they absolutely require us to understand that it is noxious to work for a peace not based on righteousness, and useless to work for a peace based on righteousness unless we put force back of righteousness. At present this means that adequate preparedness against war offers to our Nation its sole guarantee against wrong and aggression.

Emerson has said that in the long run the most uncomfortable truth is a safer traveling companion than the most agreeable falsehood. The advocates of peace will accomplish nothing except mischief until they are willing to look facts squarely in the face.

V

It is with peculiar pleasure that I stand here to-day to express the deep appreciation I feel of the high honor conferred upon me by the presentation of the Nobel Peace Prize. The gold medal which formed part of the prize I shall always keep, and I shall hand it on to my children as a precious heirloom. The sum of money provided as part of the prize by the wise generosity of the illustrious founder of this world-famous prize system, I did not, under the peculiar circumstances of the case, feel at liberty to keep. I think it eminently just and proper that in most cases the recipient of the prize should keep for his own use the prize in its entirety. But in this case, while I did not act officially as President of the United States, it was nevertheless only because I was President that I was enabled to act at all; and I felt that the money must be considered as having been given me in trust for the United States. I therefore used it as a nucleus for a foundation to forward the cause of industrial peace, as being well within the general purpose of your Committee; for in our complex industrial civilization of to-day the peace of righteousness and justice, the only kind of peace worth having, is at least as necessary in the industrial world as it is among nations. There is at least as much need to curb the cruel greed and arrogance of part of the world of capital, to curb the cruel greed and violence of part of the world of labor, as to check a cruel and unhealthy militarism in international relationships.

We must ever bear in mind that the great end in view is righteousness, justice as between man and man, nation and nation, the chance to lead our lives on a somewhat higher level, with a broader spirit of brotherly good will one for another. Peace is generally good in itself, but it is never the highest good unless it comes as the handmaid of righteousness; and it becomes a very evil thing if it serves merely as a mask for cowardice and sloth, or as an instrument to further the ends of despotism or anarchy. We despise and abhor the bully, the brawler, the oppressor, whether in private or public life, but we despise no less the coward and the voluptuary. No man is worth calling a man who will not fight rather than submit to infamy or see those that are dear to him suffer wrong. No nation deserves to exist if it permits itself to lose the stern and virile virtues; and this without regard to whether the loss is due to the growth of a heartless and all-absorbing commercialism, to prolonged indulgence in luxury and soft effortless ease, or to the deification of a warped and twisted sentimentality.

Moreover, and above all, let us remember that words count only when they give expression to deeds or are to be translated into them. The leaders of the Red Terror prattled of peace while they steeped their hands in the blood of the innocent; and many a tyrant has called it peace when he has scourged honest protest into silence. Our words must be judged by our deeds; and in striving for a lofty ideal we must use practical methods; and if we cannot attain all at one leap, we must advance towards it step by step, reasonably content so long as we do actually make some progress in the right direction.

Now, having freely admitted the limitations to our work, and the qualifications to be borne in mind, I feel that I have the right to have my words taken seriously when I point out where, in my judgment, great advance can be made in the cause of international peace. I speak as a practical man, and whatever I now advocate I actually tried to do when I was for the time being the head of a great nation, and keenly jealous of its honor and interest. I ask other nations to do only what I should be glad to see my own nation do.

The advance can be made along several lines. First of all there can be treaties of arbitration. There are, of course, states so backward that a civilized community ought not to enter into an arbitration treaty with them, at least until we have gone much further than at present in securing some kind of international police action. But all really civilized communities should have effective arbitration treaties among themselves. I believe that these treaties can cover almost all questions liable to arise between such nations, if they are drawn with the explicit agreement that each contracting party will respect the other's territory and its absolute sovereignty within that territory, and the equally explicit agreement that (aside from the very rare cases where the nation's honor is vitally concerned) all other possible subjects of controversy will be submitted to arbitration. Such a treaty would insure peace unless one party deliberately violated it. Of course, as yet there is no adequate safeguard against such deliberate violation, but the establishment of a sufficient number of these treaties would go a long way towards creating a world opinion which would finally find expression in the provision of methods to forbid or punish any such violation.

Secondly, there is the further development of the Hague Tribunal, of the work of the conferences and courts at The Hague. It has been well said that the first Hague Conference framed a Magna Charta for the nations; it set before us an ideal which has already to some extent been realized, and towards the full realization of which we can all steadily strive. The second Conference made further progress; the third should do yet more. Meanwhile the American Government has more than once tentatively suggested methods for completing the Court of Arbitral Justice, constituted at the second Hague Conference, and for rendering it effective. It is earnestly to be hoped that the various Governments of Europe, working with those of America and of Asia, shall set themselves seriously to the task of devising some method which shall accomplish this result. If I may venture the suggestion, it would be well for the statesmen of the world, in planning for the erection of this world court, to study what has been done in the United States by the Supreme Court. I cannot help thinking that the Constitution of the United States, notably in the establishment of the Supreme Court and in the methods adopted for securing peace and good relations among and between the different States, offers certain valuable analogies to what should be striven for in order to secure, through the Hague courts and conferences, a species of world federation for international peace and justice.

In the third place, something should be done as soon as possible to check the growth of armaments, especially naval armaments, by international agreement. No one power could or should act by itself; for it is eminently undesirable, from the standpoint of the peace of righteousness, that a power which really does believe in peace should place itself at the mercy of some rival which may at bottom have no such belief and no intention of acting on it. But, granted sincerity of purpose, the great powers of the world should find no insurmountable difficulty in reaching an agreement which would put an end to the present costly and growing extravagance of expenditure on naval armaments. An agreement merely to limit the size of ships would have been very useful a few years ago, and would still be of use; but the agreement should go much further.

Finally, it would be a master stroke if those great powers honestly bent on peace would form a League of Peace, not only to keep the peace among themselves, but to prevent, by force if necessary, its being broken by others. The supreme difficulty in connection with developing the peace work of The Hague arises from the lack of any executive power, of any police power to enforce the decrees of the court. In any community of any size the authority of the courts rests upon actual or potential force; on the existence of a police, or on the knowledge that the able-bodied men of the country are both ready and willing to see that the decrees of judicial and legislative bodies are put into effect. In new and wild communities where there is violence, an honest man must protect himself; and until other means of securing his safety are devised, it is both foolish and wicked to persuade him to surrender his arms while the men who are dangerous to the community retain theirs. He should not renounce the right to protect himself by his own efforts until the community is so organized that it can effectively relieve the individual of the duty of putting down violence. So it is with nations. Each nation must keep well prepared to defend itself until the establishment of some form of international police power, competent and willing to prevent violence as between nations. As things are now, such power to command peace throughout the world could best be assured by some combination between those great nations which sincerely desire peace and have no thought themselves of

committing aggressions. The combination might at first
be only to secure peace within certain definite limits and
certain definite conditions; but the ruler or statesman
who should bring about such a combination would have
earned his place in history for all time and his title to
the gratitude of all mankind.[1]

VI

No man can venture to state the exact details that
should be followed in securing a world league for the
peace of righteousness. But, not to leave the matter neb-
ulous, I submit the following plan. It would prove entirely workable, if nations entered into it with good
faith, and if they treated their obligations under it in the
spirit in which the United States treated its obligations
as regarded the independence of Cuba, giving good government to the Philippines, and building the Panama
Canal; the same spirit in which England acted when the
neutrality of Belgium was violated.

All the civilized powers which are able and willing to
furnish and to use force, when force is required to back
up righteousness — and only the civilized powers who
possess virile manliness of character and the willingness
to accept risk and labor when necessary to the performance of duty, are entitled to be considered in this matter
— should join to create an international tribunal and to
provide rules in accordance with which that tribunal
should act. These rules would have to accept the status
quo at some given period; for the endeavor to redress all

[1] Address before the Nobel Prize Committee at Christiania, Norway, May 5, 1910. From *African and European Addresses*. Copyright, 1910. G. P. Putnam's Sons, New York and London, publishers.

historical wrongs would throw us back into chaos. They would lay down the rule that the territorial integrity of each nation was inviolate; that it was to be guaranteed absolutely its sovereign rights in certain particulars, including, for instance, the right to decide the terms on which immigrants should be admitted to its borders for purposes of residence, citizenship, or business; in short, all its rights in matters affecting its honor and vital interest. Each nation should be guaranteed against having any of these specified rights infringed upon. They would not be made arbitrable, any more than an individual's right to life and limb is made arbitrable; they would be mutually guaranteed. All other matters that could arise between these nations should be settled by the international court. The judges should act not as national representatives, but purely as judges, and in any given case it would probably be well to choose them by lot, excluding, of course, the representatives of the powers whose interests were concerned. Then, and most important, the nations should severally guarantee to use their entire military force, if necessary, against any nation which defied the decrees of the tribunal or which violated any of the rights which in the rules it was expressly stipulated should be reserved to the several nations, the rights to their territorial integrity and the like. Under such conditions — to make matters concrete — Belgium would be safe from any attack such as that made by Germany, and Germany would be relieved from the haunting fear its people now have lest the Russians and the French, backed by other nations, smash the empire and its people.

In addition to the contracting powers, a certain number of outside nations should be named as entitled to the benefits of the court. These nations should be chosen from those which are as civilized and well-behaved as the great contracting nations, but which, for some reason or other, are unwilling or unable to guarantee to help execute the decrees of the court by force. They would have no right to take part in the nomination of judges, for no people are entitled to do anything toward establishing a court unless they are able and willing to face the risk, labor, and self-sacrifice necessary in order to put police power behind the court. But they would be treated with exact justice; and in the event of any one of the great contracting powers having trouble with one of them, they would be entitled to go into court, have a decision rendered, and see the decision supported, precisely as in the case of a dispute between any two of the great contracting powers themselves.

No power should be admitted into the first circle, that of the contracting powers, unless it is civilized, well-behaved, and able to do its part in enforcing the decrees of the court. China, for instance, could not be admitted, nor could Turkey, although for different reasons, whereas such nations as Germany, France, England, Italy, Russia, the United States, Japan, Brazil, the Argentine, Chile, Uruguay, Switzerland, Holland, Sweden, Norway, Denmark, and Belgium would all be entitled to go in.

Of course, grave difficulties would be encountered in devising such a plan and in administering it afterward, and no human being can guarantee that it would absolutely succeed. But I believe that it could be made to work and that it would mark a very great improvement over what obtains now. At this moment there is hell in Belgium and hell in Mexico; and the ultra-pacificists in this country have their full share of the responsibility for this hell. They are not primary factors in producing it. They lack the virile power to be primary factors in producing anything, good or evil, that needs daring and endurance. But they are secondary factors; for the man who tamely acquiesces in wrongdoing is a secondary factor in producing that wrongdoing. Most certainly the proposed plan would be dependent upon reasonable good faith for its successful working, but this is only to say what is also true of every human institution. Under the proposed plan there would be a strong likelihood of bettering world conditions. If it is a Utopia, it is a Utopia of a very practical kind.[1]

[1] From *America and the World War*. Copyright, 1915. Charles Scribner's Sons, publishers.

III
THE MAN IN ACTION

I. MIDWINTER HUNTING

WE struck the head of a long, winding valley with a smooth bottom, and after cantering down it four or five miles, came to the river, just after the cold, pale-red sun had sunk behind the line of hills ahead of us. Our horses were sharp-shod, and crossed the ice without difficulty; and in a grove of leafless cottonwoods, on the opposite side, we found the hut for which we had been making, the cowboy already inside with the fire started. Throughout the night the temperature sank lower and lower, and it was impossible to keep the crazy old hut anywhere near freezing-point; the wind whistled through the chinks and crannies of the logs, and, after a short and by no means elaborate supper, we were glad to cower down, with our great fur coats still on, under the pile of buffalo robes and bearskins. My sleeping-bag came in very handily, and kept me as warm as possible, in spite of the bitter frost.

We were up and had taken breakfast next morning by the time the first streak of dawn had dimmed the brilliancy of the stars, and immediately afterwards strode off on foot, as we had been hampered by the horses on the day before. We walked briskly across the plain until, by the time it was light enough to see to shoot, we came to the foot of a great hill, known as Middle Butte, a huge, isolated mass of rock, several miles in length, and with high sides, very steep toward the nearly level summit; it would be deemed a mountain of no inconsiderable size in the East. We hunted carefully through the outlying foothills and projecting spurs around its base, without result, finding but a few tracks, and those very old ones, and then toiled up to the top, which, though narrow in parts, in others widened out into plateaus half a mile square. Having made a complete circuit of the top, peering over the edge and closely examining the flanks of the butte with the field-glass, without having seen anything, we slid down the other side and took off through a streak of very rugged but low country. This day, though the weather had grown even colder, we did not feel it, for we walked all the while with a quick pace, and the climbing was very hard work. The shoulders and ledges of the cliffs had become round and slippery with the ice, and it was no easy task to move up and along them, clutching the gun in one hand, and grasping each little projection with the other. Climbing through the Bad Lands is just like any other kind of mountaineering, except that the precipices and chasms are much lower; but this really makes very little difference when the ground is frozen as solid as iron, for it would be almost as unpleasant to fall fifty feet as to fall two hundred, and the result to the person who tried it would be very much the same in each case. . . .

We started in the cold gray of the next morning and pricked rapidly off over the frozen plain, columns of white steam rising from the nostrils of the galloping horses. When we reached the foot of the hills where we intended to hunt, and had tethered the horses, the sun had already risen, but it was evident that the clear weather of a fortnight past was over. The air was thick and hazy, and away off in the northwest a towering mass of grayish white clouds looked like a weather-breeder; everything boded a storm at no distant date. The country over which we now hunted was wilder and more mountainous than any we had yet struck. High, sharp peaks and ridges broke off abruptly into narrow gorges and deep ravines; they were bare of all but the scantiest vegetation, save on some of the sheltered sides where grew groves of dark pines, now laden down with feathery snow. The climbing was as hard as ever. At first we went straight up the side of the tallest peak, and then along the knife-like ridge which joined it with the next. The ice made the footing very slippery as we stepped along the ledges or crawled round the jutting shoulders, and we had to look carefully for our footholds; while in the cold, thin air every quick burst we made up a steep hill caused us to pant for breath. We had gone but a little way before we saw fresh signs of the animals we were after, but it was some time before we came upon the quarry itself.

We left the high ground and, descending into a narrow chasm, walked along its bottom, which was but a couple of feet wide, while the sides rose up from it at an acute angle. After following this for a few hundred yards, we turned a sharp corner, and shortly afterward our eyes were caught by some grains of fresh earth lying on the snow in front of our feet. On the sides, some feet above our heads, were marks in the snow which a moment's glance showed us had been made by a couple of mountain sheep that had come down one side of the gorge and had leaped across to the other, their sharp toes going through the thin snow and displacing the earth that had fallen to the bottom. The tracks had evidently been made just before we rounded the corner, and as we had been advancing noiselessly on the snow, with the wind in our favor, we knew that the animals could have no suspicion of our presence. They had gone up the cliff on our right, but as that on our left was much lower, and continued for some distance parallel to the other, we concluded that by running along its top we would be most certain to get a good shot. Clambering instantly up the steep side, digging my hands and feet into the loose snow, and grasping at every little rock or frozen projection, I reached the top; and then ran forward along the ridge a few paces, crouching behind the masses of queerly shaped sand-stone; and saw, about ninety yards off across the ravine, a couple of mountain rams. The one with the largest horns was broadside toward me, his sturdy massive form outlined clearly against the sky, as he stood on the crest of the ridge. I dropped on my knee, raising the rifle as I did so; for a second he did not quite make me out, turning his head half round to look. I held the sight fairly on the point just behind his shoulder and pulled the trigger. At the report he staggered and pitched forward, but recovered himself and crossed over the ridge out of sight. We jumped and slid down into the ravine again, and clambered up the opposite side as fast as our lungs and the slippery ice would let us; then taking the trail of the wounded ram we trotted along it. We had not far to go; for, as I expected, we found him lying on his side a couple of hundred yards beyond the ridge, his eyes already glazed in death. The bullet had gone in behind the shoulder and ranged clean through his body crosswise, going a little forward; no animal less tough than a mountain ram could have gone any distance at all with such a wound.

It was still early in the day, and we made up our minds to push back for the home ranch, as we did not wish to be caught out in a long storm. The lowering sky was already overcast by a mass of leaden-gray clouds; and it was evident that we had no time to lose. In a little over an hour we were back at the log camp, where the ram was shifted from Manitou's back to the buckboard. A very few minutes sufficed to pack up our bedding and provisions, and we started home. Merrifield and I rode on ahead, not sparing the horses; but before we got home the storm had burst, and a furious blizzard blew in our teeth as we galloped along the last mile of the river bottom, before coming to the home ranch-house; and as we warmed our stiffened limbs before the log fire, I congratulated myself upon the successful outcome of what I knew would be the last hunting-trip I should take during that season.[1]

II. NIGHT-HERDING

As soon as the work was over the men rode to the wagons; sinewy fellows, with tattered broad-brimmed hats and clanking spurs, some wearing leather chaps or leggings, others having their trousers tucked into their high-heeled top-boots, all with their flannel shirts and loose neckerchiefs dusty and sweaty. A few were indulging in rough, good-natured horseplay, to an accompaniment of yelling mirth; most were grave and taciturn,

[1] From *Hunting Trips of a Ranchman.* Copyright, 1885. G. P. Putnam's Sons, New York and London, publishers.

greeting me with a silent nod or a "How! friend." A very talkative man, unless the acknowledged wit of the party, according to the somewhat florid frontier notion of wit, is always looked on with disfavor in a cow-camp. After supper, eaten in silent haste, we gathered round the embers of the small fires, and the conversation glanced fitfully over the threadbare subjects common to all such camps; the antics of some particularly vicious bucking bronco, how the different brands of cattle were showing up, the smallness of the calf drop, the respective merits of rawhide lariats and grass ropes, and bits of rather startling and violent news concerning the fates of certain neighbors. Then one by one we began to turn in under our blankets.

Our wagon was to furnish the night guards for the cattle; and each of us had his gentlest horse tied ready to hand. The night guards went on duty two at a time for two-hour watches. By good luck my watch came last. My comrade was a happy-go-lucky young Texan who for some inscrutable reason was known as "Latigo Strap"; he had just come from the south with a big drove of trail cattle.

A few minutes before two, one of the guards wno nad gone on duty at midnight rode into camp and wakened us by shaking our shoulders. Fumbling in the dark I speedily saddled my horse; Latigo had left his saddled, and he started ahead of me. It was a brilliant star-light night and the herd had been bedded down by a sugar-loaf butte which made a good landmark. As we reached the spot we could make out the loom of the cattle lying close together on the level plain; and then the dim figure of a horseman rose vaguely from the darkness and moved by in silence; it was the other of the two midnight guards, on his way back to his broken slumber.

At once we began to ride slowly round the cattle in opposite directions. We were silent, for the night was clear, and the herd quiet; in wild weather, when the cattle are restless, the cowboys never cease calling and singing as they circle them, for the sounds seem to quiet the beasts.

For over an hour we steadily paced the endless round, saying nothing, with our great coats buttoned, for the air is chill towards morning on the northern plains, even in summer. Then faint streaks of gray appeared in the east. Latigo Strap began to call merrily to the cattle. A coyote came sneaking over the butte near by, and halted to yell and wail; afterwards he crossed the coulee and from the hillside opposite again shrieked in dismal crescendo. The dawn brightened rapidly; the little skylarks of the plains began to sing, soaring far overhead, while it was still much too dark to see them.

As it grew lighter the cattle became restless, rising and stretching themselves, while we continued to ride round them.

> " Then the bronc' began to pitch
> And I began to ride;
> He bucked me off a cut bank,
> Hell! I nearly died! "

sang Latigo from the other side of the herd.[1]

[1] From *The Wilderness Hunter.* Copyright, 1893. G. P. Putnam's Sons, New York and London, publishers.

III. THE PRAIRIE

I

NOWHERE, not even at sea, does a man feel more lonely than when riding over the far-reaching, seemingly never-ending plains; and after a man has lived a little while on or near them, their very vastness and loneliness and their melancholy monotony have a strong fascination for him. The landscape seems always the same, and after the traveler has plodded on for miles and miles he gets to feel as if the distance was indeed boundless. As far as the eye can see there is no break; either the prairie stretches out into perfectly level flats, or else there are gentle, rolling slopes, whose crests mark the divides between the drainage systems of the different creeks; and when one of these is ascended, immediately another precisely like it takes its place in the distance, and so roll succeeds roll in a succession as interminable as that of the waves of the ocean. Although he can see so far, yet all objects on the outermost verge of the horizon, even though within the ken of his vision, look unreal and strange. A mile off one can see, through the strange shimmering haze, the shadowy white outlines of something which looms vaguely up till it looks as large as the canvas-top of a prairie wagon; but as the horseman comes nearer it shrinks and dwindles and takes clearer form, until at last it changes into the ghastly staring skull of some mighty buffalo, long dead and gone to join the rest of his vanished race.

When the grassy prairies are left and the traveler enters a region of alkali desert and sage-brush, the look of the country becomes even more grim and forbidding. In places the alkali forms a white frost on the ground that glances in the sunlight like the surface of a frozen lake; the dusty little sage-brush, stunted and dried up, sprawls over the parched ground, from which it can hardly extract the small amount of nourishment necessary for even its weazened life; the spiny cactus alone seems to be really in its true home. Yet even in such places antelope will be found, as alert and as abounding with vivacious life as elsewhere. Owing to the magnifying and distorting power of the clear, dry plains air, every object, no matter what its shape or color or apparent distance, needs the closest examination. A magpie sitting on a white skull, or a couple of ravens, will look, a quarter of a mile off, like some curious beast; and time and again a raw hunter will try to stalk a lump of clay or a burnt stick.[1]

II

I AM writing this on an upturned water-keg, by our canvas-covered wagon, while the men are making tea, and the solemn old ponies are grazing roundabout me. I am going to trust it to the tender mercies of a stray cowboy whom we have just met, and who may or may not post it when he gets to "Powderville," a delectable log hamlet some seventy miles north of us.

We left the Little Missouri a week ago, and have been traveling steadily some twenty or thirty miles a day ever since, through a desolate, barren-looking and yet

[1] From *Hunting Trips of a Ranchman*. Copyright, 1885. G. P. Putnam's Sons, New York and London, publishers.

picturesque country, part of the time rolling prairie and part of the time broken, jagged Bad Lands. We have fared sumptuously, as I have shot a number of prairie chickens, sage hens and ducks, and a couple of fine bucks — besides missing several of the latter that I ought to have killed.

Every morning we get up at dawn, and start off by six o'clock or thereabouts, Merrifield and I riding off among the hills or ravines after game, while the battered "prairie schooner," with the two spare ponies led behind, is driven slowly along by old Lebo, who is a perfect character. He is a weazened, wiry old fellow, very garrulous, brought up on the frontier, and a man who is never put out or disconcerted by any possible combination of accidents. Of course we have had the usual incidents of prairie travel happen to us. One day we rode through a driving rainstorm, at one time developing into a regular hurricane of hail and wind, which nearly upset the wagon, drove the ponies almost frantic, and forced us to huddle into a gully for protection. The rain lasted all night, and we all slept in the wagon, pretty wet and not very comfortable. Another time a sharp gale of wind or rain struck us in the middle of the night, as we were lying out in the open (we have no tent), and we shivered under our wet blankets till morning. We go into camp a little before sunset, tethering two or three of the horses, and letting the others range. One night we camped in a most beautiful natural park; it was a large, grassy hill, studded thickly with small, pine-crowned chalk buttes, with very steep sides, worn into the most outlandish and fantastic shapes. All that night the wolves kept up a weird concert around our camp — they are most harmless beasts.[1]

IV. THE CALL OF THE BULL-ELK

Our tent was pitched in a grove of yellow pine, by a brook in the bottom of a valley. On either hand rose the mountains, covered with spruce forest. It was in September, and the first snow had just fallen.

The day before we had walked long and hard; and during the night I slept the heavy sleep of the weary. Early in the morning, just as the east began to grow gray, I waked; and as I did so, the sounds that smote on my ear, caused me to sit up and throw off the warm blankets. Bull-elk were challenging among the mountains on both sides of the valley, a little way from us, their notes echoing like the calling of silver bugles. Groping about in the dark, I drew on my trousers, an extra pair of thick socks, and my moccasins, donned a warm jacket, found my fur cap and gloves, and stole out of the tent with my rifle.

The air was very cold; the stars were beginning to pale in the dawn; on the ground the snow glimmered white, and lay in feathery masses on the branches of the balsams and young pines. The air rang with the challenges of many wapiti; their incessant calling came pealing down through the still, snow-laden woods. First one bull challenged; then another answered; then another and

[1] Letter to Anna Roosevelt, dated Upper Waters of the Powder River (Montana), August 24, 1884. From *Roosevelt in the Bad Lands*, by Hermann Hagedorn. Copyright, 1921. Houghton Mifflin Company, publishers. By courtesy of Mrs. W. S. Cowles.

another. Two herds were approaching one another from opposite sides of the valley, a short distance above our camp; and the master bulls were roaring defiance as they mustered their harems.

I walked stealthily up the valley, until I felt that I was nearly between the two herds; and then stood motionless under a tall pine. The ground was quite open at this point, the pines, though large, being scattered; the little brook ran with a strangled murmur between its rows of willows and alders, for the ice along its edges nearly skimmed its breadth. The stars paled rapidly, the gray dawn brightened, and in the sky overhead faint rose-colored streaks were turning blood-red. What little wind there was breathed in my face and kept me from discovery.

I made up my mind, from the sound of the challenging, now very near me, that one bull on my right was advancing towards a rival on my left, who was answering every call. Soon the former approached so near that I could hear him crack the branches, and beat the bushes with his horns; and I slipped quietly from tree to tree, so as to meet him when he came out into the more open woodland. Day broke, and crimson gleams played across the snow-clad mountains beyond.

At last, just as the sun flamed red above the hill-tops, I heard the roar of the wapiti's challenge not fifty yards away; and I cocked and half raised my rifle, and stood motionless. In a moment more, the belt of spruces in front of me swayed and opened, and the lordly bull stepped out. He bore his massive antlers aloft; the snow lay thick on his mane; he snuffed the air and stamped on the ground as he walked. As I drew a bead, the motion caught his eye; and instantly his bearing of haughty and warlike self-confidence changed to one of alarm. My bullet smote through his shoulder-blades, and he plunged wildly forward, and fell full length on the blood-stained snow.[1]

V. THE MOCKING–BIRD

ONCE I listened to a mocking-bird singing the livelong spring night, under the full moon, in a magnolia tree; and I do not think I shall ever forget its song.

It was on the plantation of Major Campbell Brown, near Nashville, in the beautiful, fertile mid-Tennessee country. The mocking-birds were prime favorites on the place; and were given full scope for the development, not only of their bold friendliness towards mankind, but also of that marked individuality and originality of character in which they so far surpass every other bird as to become the most interesting of all feathered folk.

On the evening in question the moon was full. My host kindly assigned me a room of which the windows opened on a great magnolia tree, where, I was told, a mocking-bird sang every night and all night long. I went to my room about ten. The moonlight was shining in through the open window, and the mocking-bird was already in the magnolia. The great tree was bathed in a flood of shining silver; I could see each twig, and mark every action of the singer, who was pouring forth such a rapture of ringing melody as I have never listened to before or since. Sometimes he would perch motionless for

[1] From *The Wilderness Hunter*. Copyright, 1893. G. P. Putnam's Sons, New York and London, publishers.

many minutes, his body quivering and thrilling with the outpour of music. Then he would drop softly from twig to twig, until the lowest limb was reached, when he would rise, fluttering and leaping through the branches, his song never ceasing for an instant, until he reached the summit of the tree and launched into the warm, scent-laden air, floating in spirals, with outspread wings, until, as if spent, he sank gently back into the tree and down through the branches, while his song rose into an ecstasy of ardor and passion. His voice rang like a clarionet, in rich, full tones, and his execution covered the widest possible compass; theme followed theme, a torrent of music, a swelling tide of harmony, in which scarcely any two bars were alike. I stayed till midnight listening to him; he was singing when I went to sleep; he was still singing when I woke a couple of hours later; he sang through the livelong night.[1]

VI. 'CROSS COUNTRY

I

THE "pleasant and gentle feat of arms at Ashby-de-la-Zouch" was a trifle compared to the meet here yesterday.

I cannot say how I, and indeed all of us, wished that yourself and spouse were here; I know you would have enjoyed it. The weather was glorious, and everything went off without a hitch; the entire neighborhood turned out in drags, tandems, etc. The field was only about thirty-five in number, mostly in red; but at least

[1] From *The Wilderness Hunter.* Copyright, 1893. G. P. Putnam's Sons, New York and London, publishers.

twenty-five were as hard riding men, mounted on as good hunters, as are to be found on either side the Atlantic; every crack rider of the Meadowbrook and Essex clubs was here, each mounted on his very best horse, and each bound to force the pace from start to finish. The country was too stiff for any timid rider to turn out.

We opened over a necessarily small field with fences by actual measurement from four feet six to five feet; and the fun grew fast and furious very rapidly. The run was for ten miles with one check, over the country you saw. Douglas took my sister's mare out to school her; at the third fence she turned a couple of hand-springs and literally "knocked him silly"; and took half the skin off his face; he rode along the roads the rest of the way. A great many men had falls, and about halfway through I came to grief. Frank is stiff, and the company was altogether too good for him; I had pounded the old fellow along pretty well up with the first rank, but he was nearly done out. Then we came to a five-foot fence, stiffer than iron, that staggered the best; my old horse, completely blown, struck the top rail, did n't make an effort to recover, and rolled over on me among a lot of stones. I cut my face to pieces and broke my left arm (which accounts for my super-ordinarily erratic handwriting). After that I fell behind, as with one hand I could not always make Frank take his fences the first time; however, three or four miles farther on a turn in the line enabled me again to catch up, and I was in at the death, not a hundred yards behind the first half-dozen. I looked pretty gay, with one arm dangling, and my face and clothes like the walls of a slaughter-house. I guess my hunting is over for this season, as my arm will be in splints for a month or six weeks; anyhow, Frank is shut up, gone both before and behind. I have had my money's worth out of him, however, not to mention a healthy variety of experiences on and off his back.[1]

II

It was very good of you and your wife to write even before you heard from me. You need n't feel in the least melancholy about me; I viewed the affair from the first as mainly comic in character. Now I can dress myself all right, and do about everything but ride and row; all I minded was missing the rest of the hunting season — and I question if Frank would carry me much longer at the pace at which I care to go. My face will not be scarred except across the nose — which, however, will not be handsome. The accident did not keep me in five minutes. I rode straight through the rest of the hunt — the arm hurt very little, and indeed I did not know it was actually broken until after going about six fields, when the bones slipped up past each other — went out to dinner that night, and next day took a three hours' walk through the woods with Mrs. Blank (a piece of heroic self-sacrifice I know *you* will appreciate). Douglas nearly had concussion of the brain; he did not intend to follow, but the mare went so beautifully at and over the first fence that he thought she was a natural hunter.

A couple of days ago I walked over the course we

[1] Letter to Henry Cabot Lodge, dated Sagamore Hill, Oyster Bay, October 25, 1885. By courtesy of Mr. Lodge.

went and measured the jumps, having now plenty of time on my hands. We opened over a four-foot six-inch fence, then took a four-foot two, then a double, four-foot seven and four-foot one, where Douglas fell, then a four-foot eleven, which was as high as any we had. Where I fell was only four feet eight; still, that is a big jump in the hunting field, much bigger than in the club after dinner. When riding with one hand I did not have any very big fences, though I went over about twenty; any very big one almost always had the top rail taken off somewhere by one of the men in front; I then had nothing higher than four feet three, and half of them down almost to three feet six. Old Frank was blown or he would n't have fallen. Ralph must be a dandy; but I don't like a horse that gets too hot in the hunting field; Toronto[1] is more my kind.

I would n't mind the broken arm a bit if I was engaged in some work, so that I was occupied; I wish I had got started on the Mexican War; but I am afraid my bolt is shot, in literature as well as politics. At any rate, yours is n't.

I don't grudge the broken arm a bit; I would willingly pay it for the fun I have had on Frank. I have hunted him just eight times; seven times I have been in at the death, and three times took the brush, over a very stiff country and against very hard riders. I am always willing to pay the piper when I have had a good dance; and every now and then I like to drink the wine of life with brandy in it.[2]

[1] "Ralph" and "Toronto" were Mr. Lodge's hunters.

[2] Letter to Henry Cabot Lodge, dated Sagamore Hill, Oyster Bay, October 30, 1885. By courtesy of Mr. Lodge.

VII. THE CIVIC REFORMER

You say that we might possibly suffer at the hands of a mayor who did wrong. That is so, but we would speedily get rid of such a mayor. What we must have is some one man to hold to a definite responsibility. If he does wrong for two years, then it will go hard, indeed, with the citizens of New York if they cannot put him out of office at the expiration of his term. But now we suffer and are helpless. Some exceptionally bad nomination is forced on the mayor by the board of aldermen; there is an outcry against the aldermen collectively; but no one arraigns them individually, for no one knows who they are individually. No one is able at the next election to defeat such-and-such an alderman because of his special vote, for as a matter of fact no one knows how any given alderman voted; they are protected by their own utter insignificance.

With the mayor it is not so. He stands where the full light of the press beats upon him; he stands in the glare of public opinion. Every act he does is criticized; every important step he takes he knows will be remembered; and, knowing that, he shapes his course accordingly. We have seen with the present mayor what a convenient excuse the board of aldermen has afforded for all kinds of appointments. He has sent in some good man first, and the board of aldermen has refused to confirm him; then he says, "Very well, gentlemen, the decent citizens of New York have elected this board of aldermen as your representatives. I have got to conform to their wishes. Now, I will send in some man acceptable to them, and then they will confirm him." Does any man suppose for a moment that the mayor and aldermen really come together and agree upon an officer to be nominated and confirmed, without outside dictation? Do not we all know that where any given appointment is made, it is because two or three men — because very often during the past few months only one man has decided that such-and-such an appointment had to be made? And, mind you, these are men with whose position the public has had nothing to do; they are really, and not nominally, irresponsible autocrats; and certainly I, at least, would rather have a responsible despot than an irresponsible oligarchy; and the latter is what we are now ruled by, an oligarchy composed of the worst, instead of the best, elements.

I do not propose to defend for a moment the people through whose supineness and indifference to the public weal a state of things has been brought about in New York that makes it necessary for us to introduce such a bill. I think that the so-called respectable voters of New York are to be held accountable for many of the greatest sins that are committed in that city, and that they are responsible for the greater part of our bad government. The people that are always clamoring about how bad our government is, but who are not willing to lift their little fingers to make that government better, those people are the real ones who are responsible for our present misgovernment. The decent citizens of New York, more than any other class, are responsible for having let the rogues have full play. It would be difficult for you, gentlemen, who do not reside in the city, to realize how absolutely the majority of our prominent citizens fail in the performance of their public duties; and these citizens should know that, where they fail to perform the common duties of freemen, they have little right to complain of the manner in which they are treated by those who do, whether the treatment be good or bad. But we are always obliged to consider a situation as it is, not as it should be, not as things would be in a perfect state of society. Did every man in New York take the keenest interest in political matters, did every man follow rigidly what his judgment dictated, there might be no necessity to center responsibility in the mayor as I propose to do, but, as a matter of fact, in the hurry and press of New York life, in the sharp and harassing business competition that prevails there, and that must prevail in such a great mercantile center, in the midst of the thousand feverish activities that compose the daily lives of our citizens, it is impossible for them to exercise the strict supervision over their representatives that can be exercised where the population is sparser, and the modes of life simpler. It is all that we can expect if they will, when election day comes around, come out and try to do all they can to insure for the next two years the presence of a man at the head of the government who will devote his energies to administering that government wisely and purely.

And I ask the gentlemen of this House to remember one thing more. It has grown to be a tradition in our system of government that no man should absolutely have the power of making nominations; but that there should be another body to confirm whatever nominations are made. I want for one moment to call your attention to the state of things that formerly existed, and from which arose the present sentiment. In the old days the governor or ruler was appointed by the king, or at least by some power outside of the people, and the only check that, in turn, the people had over his actions, was by the control of the body elected by them, that is, by their control of the legislature, local or state. The governor, nominated by the power without, made the nomination; those elected by the people confirmed or rejected it. But now things are entirely different; the mayor is quite as much the servant of the people, in the true sense of the word he is far more the servant of the people, than are all the aldermen. The mayor has a larger constituency before which to go; the mayor is held to a more strict accountability for his actions. The aldermen are not held to such an accountability; the aldermen are only accountable to their local leaders. The one man is held responsible by the people; the other men only by the bosses who have saddled themselves on the people. It is true we give the mayor power, but we put with that power, accountability. We say, "You will exercise this power unchecked, and for every step that you take we will hold you rigidly responsible. Not a movement will you make that we do not hold you accountable for making. You will no longer be able to shield yourself behind the board of aldermen; you will no longer be able to put them forward as the excuse for your wrongdoing; you will have to stand or fall according to your own actions. You will have undivided power, and you will have an undivided responsibility." Does any man think for a moment that things could be much worse than they are? Even if we grant that they may become no better, do you think that if we have one master in New York we will suffer more than we do with the twenty-four who rule us now, or rather, with the twenty-four who register the decrees of two or three outside rulers? Certainly, it seems to me, this is the must thoroughly democratic bill that could be presented; that it is a bill giving the people power; that it is a bill to break the might of the oligarchy that now rules us.

It is said that here in the new world we have no aristocracy; yet I sometimes think that in our great city we have what might be called, were it not a contradiction in terms, an aristocracy of the bad, or, as an eminent traveler put it, "an aristocracy of blackguards," for those that should be lowest — mind you, I do not mean socially, I mean those who, from their vices, should be lowest — rule over us. It is right, and it is our pride, that the banker and the bricklayer, the merchant and his clerk, the millionaire and the day laborer, should be equal. It is our boast that all positions and degrees in life stand on the same plane before the law, but it is not right that those who, by their pursuits, are most likely to be brought into contact with the criminal classes, and who, indeed, often spring from or sink into these classes, should be men who, above all others, are to be chosen to rule over us. Of the last board of aldermen one half were liquor dealers. Does any man suppose that one half of our mayors would be liquor sellers? — that a man who was a liquor seller could be elected? The board of aldermen has just chosen as its president a man who, I believe, was removed from the board of education on account of grave charges made against him in connection with the misappropriation of money.

Does any man suppose that such a man could be elected mayor of the city of New York? Would it be possible for our people as a whole to elect one such? He is elected easily enough when you get the politicians to dickering and dealing with one another, and no more fruitful field for dickering and dealing exists than in the board of aldermen.

I think that almost without exception the mayor has been a man of far better character than the average member of the board of aldermen; that almost without exception the mayor has been a man who has responded to the will of the people — to the will of the decent people — far more readily than have the board of aldermen. More than that; in times past we have realized that we were electing as mayor a man whose hands were bound. There has been little incentive to exert all our efforts to elect a man when we knew that his endeavors could, and would, be completely nullified by the concerted action of others. Now, I propose in the future to give us a chance to elect a man who shall have the real as well as the nominal power, and I think we shall be far more likely to elect a good mayor than we have been in times past; and if we do not, then we can truly say that we ourselves are to blame — *accountable for his election.*

I have purposely confined my bill purely to taking away the confirming power of the board of aldermen; there are many other changes that it is highly desirable to make, in my opinion, in the city of New York. I think that the mayor should be given absolute power of removal; I think that the departments ought for the most part to be made single-headed; I believe personally

in spring elections; but very many of my friends on this
floor utterly disagree with me upon those points; therefore I have refused to have any amendments put in this
bill, and shall vote against any additional provisions to
be put in, for the reason that I shall regard any attempt
to put other amendments in as efforts to load down the
bill and to prevent its passage, for every such amendment will increase the opposition to the bill. I will
cheerfully vote on the other measures as separate bills;
to give the mayor absolute power of removal; to provide
for spring elections; to provide for single-headed departments. I will vote for each of those measures in turn;
but I propose to have a vote taken in this Legislature
upon this naked proposition, "Are you, or are you not,
willing to give us a responsible government in the city
of New York, unhampered by any other considerations?"
Take that naked question and answer it.[1]

VIII. PREACHING AND PRACTICE

I DO not know that I shall be able to go to Cuba if there
is a war. The army may not be employed at all, and
even if it is employed it will consist chiefly of regular
troops; and as regards the volunteers only a very small
proportion can be taken from among the multitudes
who are even now coming forward. Therefore it may be
that I shall be unable to go, and shall have to stay here.
In that case I shall do my duty here to the best of my
ability, although I shall be eating out my heart. But if I

[1] From Remarks of the Honorable Theodore Roosevelt on the Bill
taking away the confirmatory power from the board of aldermen
of the City of New York, in Assembly February 5, 1884, in Committee
of the Whole House.

am able to go I certainly shall. It is perfectly true that I shall be leaving one duty, but it will only be for the purpose of taking up another. I say quite sincerely that I shall not go for my own pleasure. On the contrary, if I should consult purely my own feelings I should earnestly hope that we would have peace. I like life very much. I have always led a joyous life. I like thought and I like action, and it will be very bitter to me to leave my wife and children; and while I think I could face death with dignity, I have no desire before my time has come to go out into the everlasting darkness. So I shall not go into a war with any undue exhilaration of spirits or in a frame of mind in any way approaching recklessness or levity.

Moreover, a man's usefulness depends upon his living up to his ideals in so far as he can. Now, I have consistently preached what our opponents are pleased to call "Jingo doctrines" for a good many years. One of the commonest taunts directed at men like myself is that we are armchair and parlor Jingoes who wish to see others do what we only advocate doing. I care very little for such a taunt, except as it affects my usefulness, but I cannot afford to disregard the fact that my power for good, whatever it may be, would be gone if I did n't try to live up to the doctrines I have tried to preach. Moreover it seems to me that it would be a good deal more important from the standpoint of the Nation as a whole that men like myself should go to war than that we should stay comfortably in offices at home and let others carry on the war that we have urged.[1]

[1] Letter to Dr. Sturgis Bigelow, March 29, 1898. From *Theodore Roosevelt and His Time*, by Joseph Bucklin Bishop. Copyright, 1920. Charles Scribner's Sons, publishers.

IX. THE BATTLE OF SAN JUAN HILL

WE of the left wing had by degrees become involved in a fight which toward the end became not even a colonel's fight, but a squad leader's fight. The cavalry division was put at the head of the line. We were told to march forward, cross a little river in front, and then, turning to the right, march up alongside the stream until we connected with Lawton. Incidentally, this movement would not have brought us into touch with Lawton in any event. But we speedily had to abandon any thought of carrying it out. The maneuver brought us within fair range of the Spanish intrenchments along the line of hills which we called the San Juan Hills, because on one of them was the San Juan blockhouse. On that day my regiment had the lead of the second brigade, and we marched down the trail following in trace behind the first brigade. Apparently the Spaniards could not make up their minds what to do as the three regular regiments of the first brigade crossed and defiled along the other bank of the stream, but when our regiment was crossing they began to fire at us.

Under this flank fire it soon became impossible to continue the march. The first brigade halted, deployed, and finally began to fire back. Then our brigade was halted. From time to time some of our men would fall, and I sent repeated word to the rear to try to get authority to attack the hills in front. Finally General Sumner, who was fighting the division in fine shape, sent word to advance. The word was brought to me by Mills, who said that my orders were to support the regulars in the assault on the hills, and that my objective would be the

red-tiled ranch house in front, on a hill which we afterwards christened Kettle Hill. I mention Mills saying
this because it was exactly the kind of definite order the
giving of which does so much to insure success in a fight,
as it prevents all obscurity as to what is to be done. The
order to attack did not reach the first brigade until after
we ourselves reached it, so that at first there was doubt
on the part of their officers whether they were at liberty
to join in the advance.

I had not enjoyed the Guasimas fight at all, because I
had been so uncertain as to what I ought to do. But
the San Juan fight was entirely different. The Spaniards
had a hard position to attack, it is true, but we could see
them, and I knew exactly how to proceed. I kept on
horseback, merely because I found it difficult to convey
orders along the line, as the men were lying down; and it
is always hard to get men to start when they cannot see
whether their comrades are also going. So I rode up and
down the lines, keeping them straightened out, and
gradually worked through line after line until I found
myself at the head of the regiment. By the time I had
reached the lines of the regulars of the first brigade I had
come to the conclusion that it was silly to stay in the
valley firing at the hills, because that was really where
we were most exposed, and that the thing to do was to
try to rush the intrenchments. Where I struck the regulars there was no one of superior rank to mine, and after
asking why they did not charge, and being answered
that they had no orders, I said I would give the order.
There was naturally a little reluctance shown by the
elderly officer in command to accept my order, so I said,
"Then let my men through, sir," and I marched through,

followed by my grinning men. The younger officers and the enlisted men of the regulars jumped up and joined us. I waved my hat, and we went up the hill with a rush. Having taken it, we looked across at the Spaniards in the trenches under the San Juan blockhouse to our left, which Hawkin's brigade was assaulting. I ordered our men to open fire on the Spaniards in the trenches.

Memory plays funny tricks in such a fight, where things happen quickly, and all kinds of mental images succeed one another in a detached kind of way, while the work goes on. As I gave the order in question there slipped through my mind Mahan's account of Nelson's orders that each ship as it sailed forward, if it saw another ship engaged with an enemy's ship, should rake the latter as it passed. When Hawkins's soldiers captured the blockhouse, I, very much elated, ordered a charge on my own hook to a line of hills still farther on. Hardly anybody heard this order, however; only four men started with me, three of whom were shot. I gave one of them, who was only wounded, my canteen of water, and ran back, much irritated that I had not been followed — which was quite unjustifiable, because I found that nobody had heard my orders. General Sumner had come up by this time, and I asked his permission to lead the charge. He ordered me to do so, and this time away we went, and stormed the Spanish intrenchments. There was some close fighting, and we took a few prisoners. We also captured the Spanish provisions, and ate them that night with great relish. One of the items was salted flying-fish, by the way. There were also bottles of wine, and jugs of fiery spirit, and as soon as possible I had these broken, although not before one or two of my men had taken too much liquor. Lieutenant Howze, of the regulars, an aide of General Sumner's, brought me an order to halt where I was; he could not make up his mind to return until he had spent an hour or two with us under fire. The Spaniards attempted a counter-attack in the middle of the afternoon, but were driven back without effort, our men laughing and cheering as they rose to fire; because hitherto they had been assaulting breastworks, or lying still under artillery fire, and they were glad to get a chance to shoot at the Spaniards in the open. We lay on our arms that night and as we were drenched with sweat, and had no blankets save a few we took from the dead Spaniards, we found even the tropic night chilly before morning came.[1]

X. THE COAL STRIKE SETTLEMENT

THE crisis came at the last moment. Between the hours of 10 P.M. and 1 A.M., I had Bacon and Perkins on here, on behalf of Morgan, but really representing the operators. Neither Morgan nor any one else had been able to do much with those wooden-headed gentry, and Bacon and Perkins were literally almost crazy. Bacon in particular had become so excited that I was quite concerned over his condition. The operators had limited me down, by a full proviso, to five different types of men, including "an eminent sociologist." This was a ridiculous proviso because I could have appointed bad men in every case and yet be kept to its letter; and they ought to have given me a free hand. The miners, on the other hand,

[1] From *Autobiography of Theodore Roosevelt*. Copyright, 1913. Charles Scribner's Sons, publishers.

wanted me to appoint at least two extra members my-self, or in some fashion to get Bishop Spalding (whom I myself wanted), and the labor union man on the commission. I regarded their contention as perfectly reasonable, and so informed Bacon and Perkins and the operators. The operators refused point-blank to have another man added, and Bacon and Perkins came on nearly wild to say that they had full power to treat on behalf of the operators, but that no extra man should be added. Finally it developed that what they meant was that no extra man should be added if he was a representative of organized labor; and argue as I could, nothing would make them change; although they grew more and more hysterical, and not merely admitted, but insisted, that the failure to agree meant probable violence and possible social war.

It took me about two hours before I at last grasped the fact that the mighty brains of these captains of industry had formulated the theory that they would rather have anarchy than tweedledum, but if I would use the word tweedledee they would hail it as meaning peace. In other words, that they had not the slightest objection to my appointing a labor man as an "eminent sociologist," and adding Bishop Spalding on my own account, but they preferred to see the Red Commune come rather than to have me make Bishop Spalding or any one else "the eminent sociologist" and add the labor man. I instantly told them that I had not the slightest objection whatever to doing an absurd thing when it was necessary to meet the objection of an absurd mind on some vital point, and that I would cheerfully appoint my labor man as the "eminent sociologist." It was almost impossible for me to appreciate the instant and tremendous relief this gave them. They saw nothing offensive in my language and nothing ridiculous in the proposition, and Pierpont Morgan and Baer, when called up by telephone, eagerly ratified the absurdity; and accordingly, at this utterly unimportant price, we bid fair to come out of as dangerous a situation as I ever dealt with.[1]

XI. OREGON LAND FRAUDS

MY DEAR SENATOR, you have written me very frankly. I shall copy your frankness in this closing paragraph. It has been most unfortunate that so many of the friends upon whose behalf you have been active should be among those whose guilt is clearest and deepest. I entirely appreciate loyalty to one's friends, but loyalty to the cause of justice and honor stands above it. I think you are doing yourself an injury by permitting yourself to be made at least to seem to stand as the champion of the men who have been engaged in this widespread conspiracy to defraud the United States Government and therefore the public of your own State. . . . You criticize very captiously what has been done and said by all those whose efforts have resulted in the uncovering of this great wrong, and of the partial punishment of some of the wrongdoers. It is easy to ascribe such motives and to make such criticisms; but what is needed now is not

[1] Letter to Henry Cabot Lodge, October 17, 1902. This and the three succeeding letters by Mr. Roosevelt are from *Theodore Roosevelt and His Time*, by Joseph Bucklin Bishop. Copyright, 1920. Charles Scribner's Sons, publishers.

the picking of holes in those who are engaged in the great work of righteousness, but the sturdy upholding of their hands just so long as they are doing this work.

I am from my position the leader of the entire Republican Party throughout the Union, in Oregon just as much as in New York; and in Oregon and New York alike I shall count it not an attack upon, but a service to, the Republican Party if through my agents I can be instrumental in punishing in the severest possible manner any private citizen, and especially any public servant, who while claiming to be a member of that party has deeply wronged it by wronging the Nation which the party was created to serve. When the party ceases to serve the Nation it will lose its reason for existence; and most emphatically I shall never, under any pressure or for any reason whatever, permit any alleged considerations of partisan expediency to prevent my punishing any wrongdoer, whether he belongs to my party or any other.[1]

XII. EXPEDIENCY AND PRINCIPLE

OF course I should like to be reëlected President, and I shall be disappointed, although not very greatly disappointed, if I am not; and so far as I legitimately can I pay heed to considerations of political expediency — in fact I should be unfit for my position, or for any position of political leadership, if I did not do so. But when questions involve deep and far-reaching principles, then I believe that the real expediency is to be found in straightforward and unflinching adherence to principle, and this without regard to what may be the temporary

[1] Letter to a Senator from Oregon, May 15, 1905.

effect. When the matter is one of elementary justice and decency, then there can be no compromise. Murder is murder, and theft is theft, and there should be no half-way measure with criminality. There are good and bad men of all nationalities, creeds, and colors; and if this world of ours is ever to become what we hope some day it may become, it must be by the general recognition that the man's heart and soul, the man's worth and action, determine his standing. I should be sorry to lose the Presidency, but I should be a hundredfold more sorry to gain it by failing in every way in my power to try to put a stop to lynching and to brutality and wrong of any kind; or by failing on the one hand to make the very wealthiest and most powerful men in the country obey the law and handle their property (so far as it is in my power to make them) in the public interest; or, on the other hand, to fail to make the laboring men in their turn obey the law, and realize that envy is as evil a thing as arrogance, and that crimes of violence and riot shall be as sternly punished as crimes of greed and cunning.[1]

XIII. THE PLAIN PEOPLE

WELL, I have just been inaugurated and begun my second term. Of course, I greatly enjoyed inauguration day, and indeed I have thoroughly enjoyed being President. But I believe I can also say that I am thoroughly alive to the tremendous responsibilities of my position. Life is a long campaign where every victory merely leaves the ground free for another battle, and sooner or later defeat comes to every man, unless death forestalls

[1] Letter to Baron d'Estournelles de Constant, September 1, 1903.

it. But the final defeat does not and should not cancel the triumphs, if the latter have been substantial and for a cause worth championing.

It has been peculiarly pleasant to me to find that my supporters are to be found in the overwhelming majority among those whom Abraham Lincoln called the plain people. As I suppose you know, Lincoln is my hero. He was a man of the people who always felt with and for the people, but who had not the slightest touch of the demagogue in him. It is probably difficult for his countrymen to get him exactly in the right perspective as compared with the great men of other lands. But to me he does seem to be one of the great figures, who will loom ever larger as the centuries go by. His unfaltering resolution, his quiet, unyielding courage, his infinite patience and gentleness, and the heights of disinterestedness which he attained whenever the crisis called for putting aside self, together with his far-sighted, hard-headed common sense, point him out as just the kind of chief who can do most good in a democratic republic like ours.

Having such an admiration for the great rail-splitter, it has been a matter of keen pride to me that I have appealed peculiarly to the very men to whom he most appealed and who gave him their heartiest support. I am a college-bred man, belonging to a well-to-do family, so that, as I was more than contented to live simply, and was fortunate to marry a wife with the same tastes, I have not had to make my own livelihood; though I have always had to add to my private income by work of some kind. But the farmers, lumbermen, mechanics, ranchmen, miners, of the North, East, and West, have felt that I was just as much in sympathy with them, just

as devoted to their interests, and as proud of them and
as representative of them, as if I had sprung from among
their own ranks; and I certainly feel that I do understand them and believe in them and feel for them and
try to represent them just as much as if I had from earliest childhood made each day's toil pay for that day's existence or achievement. How long this feeling toward me
will last I cannot say. It was overwhelming at the time
of the election last November, and I judge by the extraordinary turnout for the Inauguration it is overwhelming
now. Inasmuch as the crest of the wave is invariably
succeeded by the hollow, this means that there will be a
reaction. But meanwhile I shall have accomplished
something worth accomplishing, I hope.[1]

XIV. HOME

I

SAGAMORE HILL takes its name from the old Sagamore
Mohannis, who, as chief of his little tribe, signed away
his rights to the land two centuries and a half ago. The
house stands right on the top of the hill, separated by
fields and belts of woodland from all other houses, and
looks out over the bay and the Sound. We see the sun
go down beyond long reaches of land and of water.
Many birds dwell in the trees round the house or in the
pastures and the woods near by, and of course in winter
gulls, loons, and wild fowl frequent the waters of the
bay and the Sound. We love all the seasons; the snows
and bare woods of winter; the rush of growing things and
the blossom-spray of spring, the yellow grain, the ripen-

[1] Letter to Sir George Otto Trevelyan, March 9, 1905.

ing fruits and tasseled corn, and the deep, leafy shades that are heralded by "the green dance of summer"; and the sharp fall winds that tear the brilliant banners with which the trees greet the dying year.

The Sound is always lovely. In the summer nights we watch it from the piazza, and see the lights of the tall Fall River boats as they steam steadily by. Now and then we spend a day on it, the two of us together in the light rowing skiff, or perhaps with one of the boys to pull an extra pair of oars; we land for lunch at noon under wind-beaten oaks on the edge of a low bluff, or among the wild plum bushes on a spit of white sand, while the sails of the coasting schooners gleam in the sunlight, and the tolling of the bell-buoy comes landward across the waters.

Long Island is not as rich in flowers as the valley of the Hudson. Yet there are many. Early in April there is one hillside near us which glows like a tender flame with the white of the bloodroot. About the same time we find the shy mayflower, the trailing arbutus; and although we rarely pick wild flowers, one member of the household always plucks a little bunch of mayflowers to send to a friend working in Panama, whose soul hungers for the Northern spring. Then there are shadblow and delicate anemones, about the time of the cherry blossoms; the brief glory of the apple orchards follows; and then the thronging dogwoods fill the forests with their radiance; and so flowers follow flowers until the springtime splendor closes with the laurel and the evanescent, honey-sweet locust bloom. The late summer flowers follow, the flaunting lilies, and cardinal flowers, and marshmallows, and pale beach rosemary; and the goldenrod and the asters when the afternoons shorten and we again begin to think of fires in the wide fireplaces.

Our most beautiful singers are the wood thrushes; they sing not only in the early morning but throughout the long hot June afternoons. Sometimes they sing in the trees immediately around the house, and if the air is still we can always hear them from among the tall trees at the foot of the hill. The thrashers sing in the hedgerows beyond the garden, the catbirds everywhere. The catbirds have such an attractive song that it is extremely irritating to know that at any moment they may interrupt it to mew and squeal. The bold, cheery music of the robins always seems typical of the bold, cheery birds themselves. The Baltimore orioles nest in the young elms around the house, and the orchard orioles in the apple trees near the garden and outbuildings. Among the earliest sounds of spring is the cheerful, simple, homely song of the song-sparrow; and in March we also hear the piercing cadence of the meadow-lark — to us one of the most attractive of all bird calls. Of late years now and then we hear the rollicking, bubbling melody of the bobolink in the pastures back of the barn; and when the full chorus of these and of many other of the singers of spring is dying down, there are some true hot-weather songsters, such as the brightly hued indigo buntings and thistlefinches. Among the finches one of the most musical and plaintive songs is that of the bush-sparrow — I do not know why the books call it field-sparrow, for it does not dwell in the open fields like the vesperfinch, the savannah-sparrow, and grasshopper-sparrow, but among the cedars and bayberry bushes and young locusts in the same places where the prairie warbler is found. Nor is it only the true songs that delight us. We love to hear the flickers call, and we readily pardon any one of their number which, as occasionally happens, is bold enough to wake us in the early morning by drumming on the shingles of the roof. In our ears the red-winged blackbirds have a very attractive note. We love the screaming of the red-tailed hawks as they soar high overhead, and even the calls of the night heron that nest in the tall water maples by one of the wood ponds on our place, and the little green herons that nest beside the salt marsh. It is hard to tell just how much of the attraction in any bird-note lies in the music itself and how much in the associations. This is what makes it so useless to try to compare the bird songs of one country with those of another. A man who is worth anything can no more be entirely impartial in speaking of the bird songs with which from his earliest childhood he has been familiar than he can be entirely impartial in speaking of his own family.[1]

II

At Sagamore Hill we like to have the wood-folk and field-folk familiar; but there are necessary bounds to such familiarity where chickens are kept for use and where the dogs are valued family friends. The rabbits and gray squirrels are as plenty as ever. The flying squirrels and chipmunks still hold their own; so do the muskrats in the marshes. The woodchucks, which we used to watch as we sat in rocking-chairs on the broad veranda, have disappeared; but recently one has made

[1] From *Autobiography of Theodore Roosevelt.* Copyright, 1913. Charles Scribner's Sons, publishers.

himself a home under the old barn, where we are doing our best to protect him. A mink which lived by the edge of the bay under a great pile of lumber had to be killed; its lair showed the remains not only of chickens and ducks, but of two muskrats, and, what was rather curious, of two skates or flatfish. A fox which lived in the big wood lot evidently disliked our companionship and abandoned his home. Of recent years I have actually seen but one fox near Sagamore Hill. This was early one morning, when I had spent the night camping on the wooded shores near the mouth of Huntington Harbor. The younger children were with me, this being one of the camping-out trips, in rowboats, on the Sound, taken especially for their benefit. We had camped the previous evening in a glade by the edge of a low sea-bluff, far away from any house; and while the children were intently watching me as I fried strips of beefsteak and thin slices of potatoes in bacon fat, we heard a fox barking in the woods. This gave them a delightfully wild feeling, and with refreshing confidence they discussed the likelihood of seeing it next morning; and to my astonishment see it we did, on the shore, soon after we started to row home.[1]

III

BOOKS are all very well in their way, and we love them at Sagamore Hill; but children are better than books. Sagamore Hill is one of three neighboring houses in which small cousins spent very happy years of childhood. In the three houses there were at one time sixteen of these

[1] From *Outdoor Pastimes of an American Hunter*. Copyright, 1905. Charles Scribner's Sons, publishers.

small cousins, all told, and once we ranged them in order of size and took their photograph. There are many kinds of success in life worth having. It is exceedingly interesting and attractive to be a successful business man, or railroad man, or farmer, or a successful lawyer or doctor; or a writer, or a President, or a ranchman, or the colonel of a fighting regiment, or to kill grizzly bears and lions. But for unflagging interest and enjoyment, a household of children, if things go reasonably well, certainly makes all other forms of success and achievement lose their importance by comparison. It may be true that he travels farthest who travels alone; but the goal thus reached is not worth reaching. And as for a life deliberately devoted to pleasure as an end — why, the greatest happiness is the happiness that comes as a by-product of striving to do what must be done, even though sorrow is met in the doing. There is a bit of homely philosophy, quoted by Squire Bill Widener, of Widener's Valley, Virginia, which sums up one's duty in life: "Do what you can, with what you've got, where you are."

There could be no healthier and pleasanter place in which to bring up children than in that nook of old-time America around Sagamore Hill. Certainly I never knew small people to have a better time or a better training for their work in after life than the three families of cousins at Sagamore Hill. It was real country, and — speaking from the somewhat detached point of view of the masculine parent — I should say there was just the proper mixture of freedom and control in the management of the children. They were never allowed to be disobedient or to shirk lessons or work; and they were encouraged to have all the fun possible. They often went barefoot, especially during the many hours passed in various en-thralling pursuits along and in the waters of the bay. They swam, they tramped, they boated, they coasted and skated in winter, they were intimate friends with the cow, chickens, pigs, and other live stock. They had in succession two ponies, General Grant and, when the General's legs became such that he lay down too often and too unexpectedly in the road, a calico pony named Algonquin, who is still living a life of honorable leisure in the stable and in the pasture — where he has to be picketed, because otherwise he chases the cows. Sedate pony Grant used to draw the cart in which the children went driving when they were very small, the driver be-ing their old nurse Mame, who had held their mother in her arms when she was born, and who was knit to them by a tie as close as any tie of blood. I doubt whether I ever saw Mame really offended with them except once when, out of pure but misunderstood affection, they named a pig after her. They loved pony Grant. Once I saw the then little boy of three hugging pony Grant's forelegs. As he leaned over, his broad straw hat tilted on end, and pony Grant meditatively munched the brim; whereupon the small boy looked up with a wail of anguish, evidently thinking the pony had decided to treat him like a radish.

The children had pets of their own too, of course. Among them guinea pigs were the stand-bys — their highly unemotional nature fits them for companionship with adoring but over-enthusiastic young masters and mistresses. Then there were flying squirrels, and kan-garoo rats, gentle and trustful, and a badger whose tem-per was short but whose nature was fundamentally friendly. The badger's name was Josiah; the particular little boy whose property he was used to carry him about, clasped firmly around what would have been his waist if he had had any. Inasmuch as when on the ground the badger would play energetic games of tag with the little boy and nip his bare legs, I suggested that it would be uncommonly disagreeable if he took advantage of being held in the little boy's arms to bite his face; but this suggestion was repelled with scorn as an unworthy assault on the character of Josiah. "He bites legs sometimes, but he never bites faces," said the little boy. We also had a young black bear whom the children christened Jonathan Edwards, partly out of compliment to their mother, who was descended from that great Puritan divine, and partly because the bear possessed a temper in which gloom and strength were combined in what the children regarded as Calvinistic proportions. As for the dogs, of course there were many, and during their lives they were intimate and valued family friends, and their deaths were household tragedies. One of them, a large yellow animal of several good breeds and valuable rather because of psychical than physical traits, was named "Susan" by his small owners, in commemoration of another retainer, a white cow; the fact that the cow and the dog were not of the same sex being treated with indifference. Much the most individual of the dogs and the one with the strongest character was Sailor Boy, a Chesapeake Bay dog. He had a masterful temper and a strong sense of both dignity and duty. He would never let the other dogs fight, and he himself never fought unless circumstances imperatively demanded it; but he was a murderous animal when he did fight. He

was not only exceedingly fond of the water, as was to
be expected, but passionately devoted to gunpowder in
every form, for he loved firearms and fairly reveled in
the Fourth of July celebrations — the latter being rather
hazardous occasions, as the children strongly objected
to any "safe and sane" element being injected into
them, and had the normal number of close shaves with
rockets, Roman candles, and firecrackers.

As the children grew up, Sagamore Hill remained delightful for them. There were picnics and riding parties,
there were dances in the north room — sometimes fancy
dress dances — and open-air plays on the green tennis
court of one of the cousins' houses. The children are no
longer children now. Most of them are men and women,
working out their own fates in the big world; some in our
own land, others across the great oceans or where the
Southern Cross blazes in the tropic nights. Some of
them have children of their own; some are working at
one thing, some at another; in cable ships, in business
offices, in factories, in newspaper offices, building steel
bridges, bossing gravel trains and steam shovels, or laying tracks and superintending freight traffic. They have
had their share of accidents and escapes; as I write, word
comes from a far-off land that one of them, whom Seth
Bullock used to call "Kim" because he was the friend
of all mankind, while bossing a dangerous but necessary
steel structural job had two ribs and two back teeth
broken, and is back at work. They have known and
they will know joy and sorrow, triumph and temporary
defeat. But I believe they are all the better off because
of their happy and healthy childhood.[1]

[1] From *Autobiography of Theodore Roosevelt*. Copyright, 1913.
Charles Scribner's Sons, publishers.

XV. AFRICA

"I SPEAK of Africa and golden joys"; the joy of wandering through lonely lands; the joy of hunting the mighty and terrible lords of the wilderness, the cunning, the wary, and the grim.

In these greatest of the world's great hunting-grounds there are mountain peaks whose snows are dazzling under the equatorial sun; swamps where the slime oozes and bubbles and festers in the steaming heat; lakes like seas; skies that burn above deserts where the iron desolation is shrouded from view by the wavering mockery of the mirage; vast grassy plains where palms and thorn-trees fringe the dwindling streams; mighty rivers rushing out of the heart of the continent through the sadness of endless marshes; forests of gorgeous beauty, where death broods in the dark and silent depths.

There are regions as healthy as the northland; and other regions, radiant with bright-hued flowers, birds and butterflies, odorous with sweet and heavy scents, but, treacherous in their beauty, and sinister to human life. On the land and in the water there are dread brutes that feed on the flesh of man; and among the lower things that crawl and fly and sting and bite, he finds swarming foes far more evil and deadly than any beast or reptile; foes that kill his crops and his cattle, foes before which he himself perishes in his hundreds of thousands.

The dark-skinned races that live in the land vary widely. Some are warlike, cattle-owning nomads; some till the soil and live in thatched huts shaped like bee-hives; some are fisherfolk; some are ape-like naked savages, who dwell in the woods and prey on creatures not much wilder or lower than themselves.

The land teams with beasts of the chase, infinite in number and incredible in variety. It holds the fiercest beasts of ravin, and the fleetest and most timid of those beings that live in undying fear of talon and fang. It holds the largest and the smallest of hoofed animals. It holds the mightiest creatures that tread the earth or swim in its rivers; it also holds distant kinsfolk of these same creatures, no bigger than woodchucks, which dwell in crannies of the rocks, and in the tree tops. There are antelope smaller than hares, and antelope larger than oxen. There are creatures which are the embodiments of grace; and others whose huge ungainliness is like that of a shape in a nightmare. The plains are alive with droves of strange and beautiful animals whose like is not known elsewhere; and with others even stranger that show both in form and temper something of the fantastic and the grotesque. It is a never-ending pleasure to gaze at the great herds of buck as they move to and fro in their myriads; as they stand for their noontide rest in the quivering heat haze; as the long files come down to drink at the watering-places; as they feed and fight and rest and make love.

The hunter who wanders through these lands sees sights which ever afterward remain fixed in his mind. He sees the monstrous river-horse snorting and plunging beside the boat; the giraffe looking over the tree tops at the nearing horseman; the ostrich fleeing at a speed that none may rival; the snarling leopard and coiled python, with their lethal beauty; the zebras, barking in the moonlight, as the laden caravan passes on its night march through a thirsty land. In after years there shall come to him memories of the lion's charge; of the gray bulk of the elephant, close at hand in the somber woodland; of the buffalo, his sullen eyes lowering from under his helmet of horn; of the rhinoceros, truculent and stupid, standing in the bright sunlight on the empty plain.

These things can be told. But there are no words that can tell the hidden spirit of the wilderness, that can reveal its mystery, its melancholy, and its charm. There is delight in the hardy life of the open, in long rides rifle in hand, in the thrill of the fight with dangerous game. Apart from this, yet mingled with it, is the strong attraction of the silent places, of the large tropic moons, and the splendor of the new stars; where the wanderer sees the awful glory of sunrise and sunset in the wide waste spaces of the earth, unworn of man, and changed only by the slow change of the ages through time everlasting.[1]

XVI. ELEPHANT HUNTING

Hour after hour we worked our way onward through tangled forest and matted jungle. There was little sign of bird or animal life. A troop of long-haired black-and-white monkeys bounded away among the tree tops. Here and there brilliant flowers lightened the gloom. We ducked under vines and climbed over fallen timber. Poisonous nettles stung our hands. We were drenched by the wet boughs which we brushed aside. Mosses and ferns grew rank and close. The trees were of strange

[1] From *African Game Trails.* Copyright, 1910. Charles Scribner's Sons, publishers.

kinds. There were huge trees with little leaves, and small trees with big leaves. There were trees with bare, fleshy limbs, that writhed out through the neighboring branches, bearing sparse clusters of large frondage. In places the forest was low, the trees thirty or forty feet high, the bushes that choked the ground between, fifteen or twenty feet high. In other places mighty monarchs of the wood, straight and tall, towered aloft to an immense height; among them were trees whose smooth, round boles were spotted like sycamores, while far above our heads their gracefully spreading branches were hung with vines like mistletoe and draped with Spanish moss; trees whose surfaces were corrugated and knotted as if they were made of bundles of great creepers; and giants whose buttressed trunks were four times a man's length across.

Twice we got on elephant spoor, once of a single bull, once of a party of three. Then Cuninghame and the 'Ndorobo redoubled their caution. They would minutely examine the fresh dung; and above all they continually tested the wind, scanning the tree tops, and lighting matches to see from the smoke what the eddies were near the ground. Each time after an hour's stealthy stepping and crawling along the twisted trail a slight shift of the wind in the almost still air gave our scent to the game, and away it went before we could catch a glimpse of it; and we resumed our walk. The elephant paths led up hill and down — for the beasts are wonderful climbers — and wound in and out in every direction. They were marked by broken branches and the splintered and shattered trunks of the smaller trees, especially where the elephant had stood and fed, trampling down the bushes for many yards around. Where they had crossed the marshy valleys they had punched big round holes, three feet deep, in the sticky mud.

As evening fell we pitched camp by the side of a little brook at the bottom of a ravine, and dined ravenously on bread, mutton, and tea. The air was keen, and under our blankets we slept in comfort until dawn. Breakfast was soon over and camp struck; and once more we began our cautious progress through the dim, cool archways of the mountain forest.

Two hours after leaving camp we came across the fresh trail of a small herd of perhaps ten or fifteen elephant cows and calves, but including two big herd bulls. At once we took up the trail. Cuninghame and his bush people consulted again and again, scanning every track and mark with minute attention. The sign showed that the elephants had fed in the shambas early in the night, had then returned to the mountain, and stood in one place resting for several hours, and had left this sleeping ground some time before we reached it. After we had followed the trail a short while we made the experiment of trying to force our own way through the jungle, so as to get the wind more favorable; but our progress was too slow and noisy, and we returned to the path the elephants had beaten. Then the 'Ndorobo went ahead, traveling noiselessly and at speed. One of them was clad in a white blanket, and another in a red one, which were conspicuous; but they were too silent and cautious to let the beasts see them, and could tell exactly where they were and what they were doing by the sounds. When these trackers waited for us they would appear before us like ghosts; once one of them dropped down from the branches above, having climbed a tree with monkey-like agility to get a glimpse of the great game.

At last we could hear the elephants, and under Cuninghame's lead we walked more cautiously than ever. The wind was right, and the trail of one elephant led close alongside that of the rest of the herd, and parallel thereto. It was about noon. The elephants moved slowly, and we listened to the boughs crack, and now and then to the curious internal rumblings of the great beasts. Carefully, every sense on the alert, we kept pace with them. My double-barrel was in my hands, and wherever possible, as I followed the trail, I stepped in the huge footprints of the elephant, for where such a weight had pressed there were no sticks left to crack under my feet. It made our veins thrill thus for half an hour to creep stealthily along, but a few rods from the herd, never able to see it, because of the extreme denseness of the cover, but always hearing first one and then another of its members, and always trying to guess what each one might do, and keeping ceaselessly ready for whatever might befall. A flock of hornbills flew up with noisy clamor, but the elephants did not heed them.

At last we came in sight of the mighty game. The trail took a twist to one side, and there, thirty yards in front of us, we made out part of the gray and massive head of an elephant resting his tusks on the branches of a young tree. A couple of minutes passed before, by cautious scrutiny, we were able to tell whether the animal was a cow or a bull, and whether, if a bull, it carried heavy enough tusks. Then we saw that it was a big bull with good ivory. It turned its head in my direction and

I saw its eye; and I fired a little to one side of the eye, at a spot which I thought would lead to the brain. I struck exactly where I aimed, but the head of an elephant is enormous and the brain small, and the bullet missed it. However, the shock momentarily stunned the beast. He stumbled forward, half falling, and as he recovered I fired with the second barrel, again aiming for the brain. This time the bullet sped true, and as I lowered the rifle from my shoulder, I saw the great lord of the forest come crashing to the ground.

But at that very instant, before there was a moment's time in which to reload, the thick bushes parted immediately on my left front, and through them surged the vast bulk of a charging bull elephant, the matted mass of tough creepers snapping like packthread before his rush. He was so close that he could have touched me with his trunk. I leaped to one side and dodged behind a tree trunk, opening the rifle, throwing out the empty shells, and slipping in two cartridges. Meanwhile Cuninghame fired right and left, at the same time throwing himself into the bushes on the other side. Both his bullets went home, and the bull stopped short in his charge, wheeled, and immediately disappeared in the thick cover. We ran forward, but the forest had closed over his wake. We heard him trumpet shrilly, and then all sounds ceased.[1]

XVII. THE PROPHET

My whole concern at this time is practically the same concern that Amos and Micah and Isaiah had for Jeru-

[1] From *African Game Trails*. Copyright, 1910. Charles Scribner's Sons, publishers.

salem nearly three thousand years ago! In those days a prophet was very apt to get himself stoned. Nowadays he merely excites the ire of the persons who would otherwise read the magazines or newspapers in which his prophecies appear. But he has n't any business to damage his magazine or newspaper. I am not dead sure that the prophet business can be combined with keeping up circulation; and moreover I know when a man with strong feelings and intense convictions reaches a certain age he is apt to get cat-a-cornered as regards the surrounding world and therefore his usefulness ceases; and I am quite prepared to feel that now that I am in my sixtieth year it would be to the interest of everybody that I should cease being a prophet and become that far pleasanter and more innocuous person, a sage. But as long as I am in the prophet business I wish to prophesy![1]

[1] Letter to E. A. Van Valkenburg, April 23, 1918. From *Theodore Roosevelt and His Time*, by Joseph Bucklin Bishop. Copyright, 1920. Charles Scribner's Sons, publishers.

EPILOGUE

THERE are questions which we of the great civilized nations are ever tempted to ask of the future. Is our time of growth drawing to an end? Are we as nations soon to come under the rule of that great law of death which is itself but part of the great law of life? None can tell. Forces that we can see and other forces that are hidden or that can but dimly be apprehended are at work all around us, both for good and for evil. The growth in luxury, in love of ease, in taste for vapid and frivolous excitement, is both evident and unhealthy. The most ominous sign is the diminution in the birth-rate, in the rate of natural increase, now to a larger or lesser degree shared by most of the civilized nations of central and western Europe, of America and Australia; a diminution so great that if it continues for the next century at the rate which has obtained for the last twenty-five years, all the more highly civilized peoples will be stationary or else have begun to go backward in population, while many of them will have already gone very far backward.

There is much that should give us concern for the future. But there is much also which should give us hope. No man is more apt to be mistaken, than the prophet of evil. After the French Revolution in 1830, Niebuhr hazarded the guess that all civilization was about to go down with a crash, that we were all about to share the fall of third and fourth century Rome — a respectable but painfully overworked comparison. The fears once expressed by the followers of Malthus as to the future of the world have proved groundless as regards the civilized portion of the world; it is strange indeed to look back at Carlyle's prophecies of some seventy years ago, and then think of the teeming life of achievement, the life of conquest of every kind, and of noble effort crowned by success, which has been ours for the two generations since he complained to high Heaven that all the tales had been told and all the songs sung, and that all the deeds really worth doing had been done. I believe with all my heart that a great future remains for us; but whether it does or does not, our duty is not altered. However the battle may go, the soldier worthy of the name will with utmost vigor do his allotted task, and bear himself as valiantly in defeat as in victory. Come what will, we belong to peoples who have not yielded to the craven fear of being great. In the ages that have gone by, the great nations, the nations that have expanded and that have played a mighty part in the world, have in the end grown old and weakened and vanished; but so have the nations whose only thought was to avoid all danger, all effort, who would risk nothing, and who therefore gained nothing. In the end the same fate may overwhelm all alike; but the memory of the one type perishes with it, while the other leaves its mark deep on the history of all the future of mankind.

A nation that seemingly dies may be born again; and even though in the physical sense it die utterly, it may yet hand down a history of heroic achievement, and for all time to come may profoundly influence the nations that arise in its place by the impress of what it has done. Best of all is it to do our part well, and at the same time to see our blood live young and vital in men and women

fit to take up the task as we lay it down; for so shall our
seed inherit the earth. But if this, which is best, is denied us, then at least it is ours to remember that if we
choose we can be torch-bearers, as our fathers were before us. The torch has been handed on from nation to
nation, from civilization to civilization, throughout all
recorded time, from the dim years before history
dawned, down to the blazing splendor of this teeming
century of ours. It dropped from the hand of the coward and the sluggard, of the man wrapped in luxury or
love of ease, the man whose soul was eaten away by self-
indulgence; it has been kept alight only by those who
were mighty of heart and cunning of hand. What they
worked at, providing it was worth doing at all, was of
less matter than how they worked, whether in the realm
of the mind or the realm of the body. If their work was
good, if what they achieved was of substance, then high
success was really theirs.[1]

[1] Address delivered at Oxford University, Oxford, England, June 7,
1910. From *African and European Addresses*. Copyright, 1910.
G. P. Putnam's Sons, New York and London, publishers.

INDEX

Africa, 296–98.

Alamo, fall of the, 33–36.

Allegiance to nation, undivided, 207–10.

America, sources of danger to, 112–19; corruption in, 116; history of, central feature of history of world, 172; holds the hope of the world, 186; a new nationality formed in, 204.

American, the good, 195; the hyphenated, 190–210, 218; two duties of, 204.

American life, incompatible with anarchy, 206.

American nationalism, 207–10.

Americanism, straight, 199–210; a question of spirit, not of creed or birthplace, 206; two demands upon the spirit of, 207–10; spirit of, necessary for accomplishing good for mankind, 218.

Anarchy, and liberty, and tyranny, 193; American life incompatible with, 206.

Animals, at the time of the backwoodsmen, 12, 19, 21, 24; on Long Island, 290, 291; in Africa, 297, 298.

Antelope, 24, 27–29.

Antelope-goat, white, 31.

"Aristocracy of blackguards," 274.

Armaments, international agreements for reduction of, 245.

Backwoodsmen, their resemblance to each other, 3–6; all American, 4–6; seen at their best in the forests, 6; and the Indians, 7, 13, 14; their weapons, 7; lived in groups of families, 7; their forts, 7, 8; their food, 8;

their cabins, 8, 9; the society and the duties and rights of, 9; early learned lessons of self-help and mutual assistance, 10; their schooling, 11; their domestic utensils, 11; their life, one long struggle, 12; were hunters, 12, 13; their influence in the settlement of the West, 13; their military organization, 13–15; extremes of society among, 15; lawless characters among, 15, 16; forms of punishment among, 16; superstitions of, 16; their religion, 16, 17; summary of their characteristics, 17; no room for coward and weakling among, 45.

Bacon, Robert, 281, 282.

Bad Lands, hunting in the, 253–57; description of life in, 261–63.

Baer, George F., 283.

Barry, General, 201.

Bear, 12, 19, 21, 24, 29.

Belgium, 203, 217.

Bertela, Aurelio, 238.

"Big stick," the, 226, 230, 231.

Billings, Josh, 229.

Birds, on Long Island, 289, 290.

Birth-rate, diminution in, 305.

Blue Licks, battle of the, 22.

Boasting, 226.

Bolshevism, 83, 84.

Boone, Daniel, and the founding of Kentucky, 18–23.

Boonesborough, settlement of, 20; attacked by Indians and others, 22.

"Boss," the, in politics, 105–09.

Bowie, Col. James, 33, 35.

Brown, Major Campbell, 265.